Sonic Literacy

Sonic Literacy

Using Sound to Teach High School Reading and Writing

Danah Hashem
University of Massachusetts Boston

Anne Mooney
Malden High School, Malden, Massachusetts

NCTE
National Council of Teachers of English
340 N. Neil St., Suite #104, Champaign, IL 61820
www.ncte.org

Staff Editor: Cynthia Gomez
Manuscript Editor: Michael Ryan
Interior Design: Jenny Jensen Greenleaf
Cover Design: Adrian Morgan
Cover Image: Shutterstock/-strizh-

ISBN (print): 978-0-8141-0214-5; ISBN (epub): 978-0-8141-0215-2; ISBN (PDF): 978-0-8141-0216-9

It is the policy of NCTE in its journals and other publications to provide a forum for the open discussion of ideas concerning the content and the teaching of English and the language arts. Publicity accorded to any particular point of view does not imply endorsement by the Executive Committee, the Board of Directors, or the membership at large, except in announcements of policy, where such endorsement is clearly specified.

NCTE provides equal employment opportunity to all staff members and applicants for employment without regard to race, color, religion, sex, national origin, age, physical, mental or perceived handicap/disability, sexual orientation including gender identity or expression, ancestry, genetic information, marital status, military status, unfavorable discharge from military service, pregnancy, citizenship status, personal appearance, matriculation or political affiliation, or any other protected status under applicable federal, state, and local laws.

Every effort has been made to provide current URLs and email addresses, but, because of the rapidly changing nature of the web, some sites and addresses may no longer be accessible.

Library of Congress Control Number: 2024945861

To those who refuse to lower their volume, those who are learning to raise their volume, and those who are listening.

CONTENTS

ACKNOWLEDGMENTS

First, always first, we thank our students, who have taught us more about literacy, ourselves, and the world around us than anyone else. We owe a special thanks to Tanya Rodrigue for introducing us to and mentoring us in our dedication to the mode of sound as a tool to empower and to shape literacy in ways that matter. Finally, thanks to our partners and families for their support and patience as we pursued the ways this book captured and enabled our passion for education.

INTRODUCTION

If you're reading this, we're going out on a limb to assume that you have a few things in common with us. We're guessing that, among many other things, you are an educator who cares deeply about your students and your craft. We'd venture to say that, like us, you work hard to create dynamic, relevant, and engaging lessons for your students because you believe in your core that literacy matters, that students who can read and write with their whole selves are what will make all the difference in our ever-changing world.

If you're like us, you're also probably tired; you've been experiencing the harsh reality that is the world of literacy education today. Districts and administrations are asking more of us while often giving us less to work with. However your educational community has been handling the COVID epidemic, we're willing to bet it has put you and your students in impossible situations, losing valuable time and momentum while pushing everyone too far for too long. Reaching students has become increasingly challenging as they face the mounting pressures and emotional toll of social media, the overwhelming weight of the news, and the continued local and global traumas. At the same time, the demands on and the stakes for student literacies are more complex and intense than ever before.

It is not an easy time to be in literacy education. We're not sure it ever has been, but we're feeling confident that this particular moment is an especially challenging and fatiguing one. We've been in this with you for the last ten years; we're in it with you now. And we want to bring you this book because, for us, this material has been what has kept our passion, momentum, and dedication to our teaching alive in the middle of this situational hurricane. Teaching reading and writing with the mode of sound has, for us and for our students, been the thing that's made all the difference, and one of our core beliefs is that it can do the same for you and your students.

In our teaching careers, multimodal literacies—specifically teaching reading and writing using the mode of sound—has made our jobs more interesting, exciting, and meaningful. It has given us a sense of empowerment and control over our curricula, and it has created outlets for us to bring whatever we're most passionate about in that moment into our classrooms. Additionally and far more importantly, reading and writing texts in the mode of sound has, without fail, led to more engaged and more motivated student experiences; it's made for reading and writing assignments that are infinitely more purposeful and relevant to students' lives and the world around them. The mode of sound has so much to offer students—it's got play, experimentation, spaces to do things you never thought you could do. Sound has the ability to transport and transform people like nothing else. It's our belief and experience that reading and writing in the mode of sound is genuinely magical. It has a quality to it that's irresistibly magnetic; you can do things with sound that are completely unique, and students respond to this capability.

Literacy educators have been building on sound's capacity to unlock student potential for years now. Back in 2007, Cynthia Selfe's *Multimodal Composition: Resources for Teachers* opened with its first chapter emphasizing the ways in which multimodal compositions, including sound and "playing and even creating digital music," is just flat-out engaging for students (4). Selfe discusses how these assignments are "refreshing," "meaningful," and "relevant," and how students voluntarily work harder, go the extra mile, "push themselves beyond the boundaries of the assignments," and "demonstrate learning that goes well beyond the teacher's expectations" when working with multimodal compositions, including sound texts like radio ads and audio tracks (4).

This was almost two decades ago. Since then, the pressures, testing, and challenges facing students have only increased, and the burnout and discouragement facing educators has only intensified. At the same time, the mode of sound has become even more relevant and powerful in the world. If Selfe was right in 2007, she's critically and essentially on target now.

If there's ever been a moment in literacy education to try something new with your students, to take a risk and open yourself and your students to something unfamiliar, it's now. And we think bringing the mode of sound into your ELA classrooms is going to be the thing to do it with. We say this because, between the two of us and our shared decade of experience in the classroom, we've seen this in action in a range of scenarios. With Anne's experience teaching in one of the most diverse public schools in Massachusetts alongside Danah's time teaching in a hyper-competitive private college prep school, we've collectively taught students from an expansive diversity of economic, social, cultural, ethnic, and religious backgrounds. We've seen what sound can do for multilingual students, prep school students, students facing challenging remedial work, international students, students with minimal resources, students with every possible resource at their fingertips, students in massive classes with daunting differentiation needs, and students in small and focused accelerated programs. Our list goes on and on. We've taught the assignments and ideas in this book many times and in many different variations.

> If you'd like to get to know us as authors a bit better and get a sense for our scholarly work and classroom experiences, we encourage you to listen to our "About the Authors" conversation.
>
> About the Authors
>
> About the Authors Transcript

And while we value classroom experience above most other qualifications, we haven't just been working on this material in our classrooms with our students. We've been working with organizations like NCTE, Edutopia, and Heinemann to publish content on teaching ELA using the mode of sound. We've been presenting our scholarship at national conferences across the country and organizing panels and workshops for educators looking to infuse life, energy, and relevance into their ELA classrooms. Teaching reading and writing using the mode of sound has been our main game for the last decade, and we're excited to have the opportunity in this book to dig more extensively into some of the content we hope to share with you.

Over the course of this book, our goals are to set you up with everything you need to feel ready to bring the mode of sound into your ELA classroom. We've broken our mission down into the following chapters:

- **Before We Get Started** is where we will lay the basic groundwork to support the discussion in the rest of the book. This chapter is an important place to begin if you're entirely new to reading and writing in the mode of sound, as it explains what we mean when we refer to sound texts, these texts' applications and roles in the world, and the range of genres that exist within this mode.
- **Why Should You Teach Students to Read and Write with Sound Texts?** is dedicated to providing a full, research-supported rationale for the laundry list of benefits and affordances that the mode of sound can bring to an ELA classroom. This chapter is most useful if you're someone who isn't quite sold on the significance of the mode or if you are looking for support in justifying your classroom choices to administrators, parents, or even your own students. Let us convince you, or your admin, of what's in store.
- **The Fundamentals of Studying Sound Texts** is where we get more technical with the terms and theory behind reading and writing in the mode of sound. While some of this content may be familiar to you from your work in other modes, this chapter will apply principles of rhetoric

and genre awareness specifically to the audio mode. The most important part of this chapter includes our discussion of sound composition theory, covering the five sound strategies as tools for understanding and articulating how sound texts are assembled and function.

- In the next two chapters, **The Fundamentals of Reading Sound Texts** and **How to Design Reading Activities Using Sound Texts**, we focus on the practice of reading sound texts with students. The first of these chapters covers the main strategies and reading skills students will need when completing reading assignments with sound texts; we do this while discussing a sample reading assignment of a spoken-word poem. The following chapter offers teachers a classroom-ready set of sound reading activities for a range of reading skills, each complete with worksheets and rubrics for use with students.
- The following two chapters, **The Fundamentals of Writing Sound Texts** and **How to Design Writing Activities Using Sound Texts**, specifically address the process of asking students to compose their own original sound texts. The first of these chapters uses a corresponding list of skills from the audio reading chapters, but it applies this skill list to necessary writing practices, all while discussing a writing assignment that asks students to compose a research podcast. In the following chapter, we share a set of classroom-ready activities that ask students to write sound texts in a variety of genres, each complete with process documents including prewriting and reflection materials as well as rubrics to help teachers assess student work.

As you read this book, you'll notice that the introductions and conclusions to each chapter are QR codes that will take you to audio files with associated transcripts. We've tried to use this opportunity to give you a few different examples and ideas of how sound can integrate into scholarship in ways that are relevant and engaging. Throughout the book, you'll also find links to a variety of supplemental materials. These include classroom-ready materials, additional resources for teachers, and other helpful tools.

We also want to take a moment to directly address educators reading this book who are already working with the mode of sound in their ELA classrooms. You're our people; we're really glad you're here. While much of our content, particularly in the chapters on fundamentals, is addressed to educators who are new to using this mode in their classrooms, we're sure there's material in these chapters to take your use of sound to the next level. Whether you use one of our sample assignments, explore a sound text genre you've never tried before, or just get some different ideas on how to talk about this material with your students, we encourage you to use our chapter summaries to jump around this text and find the content that's most useful for you.

We're not here to create more work for you; we're actually angling to do the opposite. The last thing we want is to be another item on another overworked educator's to-do list. We *are* here to offer teachers who are beside us in the trenches a superpowered tool, a beacon that has the potential to shed some light on the shadowy corners of our ELA classrooms: the mode of sound. We hope that if you're skeptical, you'll give us a chance to convince you, and, if you're already convinced, you'll give us a chance to share some of our experiences and resources with you. We're here to do everything we can to make your job more rewarding, less taxing, and more exciting for you and your students, and we're going to use the mode of sound to get there.

BEFORE WE GET STARTED

INTRODUCTION

Before We Get Started Introduction Audio

Before We Get Started Introduction Transcript

WHAT IS A SOUND TEXT?

Throughout this discussion, you'll hear us refer regularly to the idea of both reading and writing sound texts, so we want to start out with a clear explanation of what we mean by that. We think it's important here to bring your already-established knowledge as ELA teachers to your understanding of this definition. As teachers, we know that texts are works or pieces of literature that have been intentionally written by authors to achieve a particular purpose, perhaps to make an argument, to capture an image, or to re-create a memory. A sound text is, quite simply, a text that has been written using the mode of sound.

While many different texts, including films or plays, can use the mode of sound in different ways, when we talk about sound texts, we're referring to texts that rely primarily on the mode of sound, without significant reliance on visual modes, to communicate the meaning of the text. That means that it is a text made up of recorded audio instead of printed words or images. These recorded sounds can be the human voice speaking particular words, as in a spoken-word poem or a speech, or they can be sounds other than words, things like musical instruments, sound effects, or even a well-placed, poignant silence. In a sound text, the important thing is that these recorded audio sounds come together as an intentional work that the author has assembled for a particular purpose.

Where Do Sound Texts Live in the World?

One of the best things about sound texts is that they are active and living in our own and our students' daily lives, even if we or they aren't entirely aware of them. We're surrounded by sound texts! The podcast we flip on as we sit in our cars on our daily commutes? That's a sound text. The hit song our students cluster around a single set of headphones to gently nod their heads to before class begins? That's a sound text. The thirty-second advertisement that subsequently interrupts their focused Spotify listening? That's one, too.

Most sound texts live in one of three places: online, on live public radio, or in live performances. The majority of sound texts live online and are most readily and commonly available to download or to stream on a personal listening device, so they go where we go and live where we live. They are active and influential in the realms that our students are the most tuned in to. From politics to entertainment to technology to our local businesses to anything you can imagine, sound texts are on the scene, and important people and groups of people are spending time and money to write them.

What Do Sound Texts Do in the World?

For this question, we'll again ask you as ELA teachers to bring your own experience to the table. When we ask what role sound texts play in the world around us, the answer reflects the larger question of what role writing plays in the world around us because sound texts are a form of a written text; they have just been written using tools that aren't always the ones we use in the traditional high school classroom. So, just like when we explain to our students how writing is a means of thinking, persuading, sharing, and connecting, we use these same rationales and explanations in understanding the function sound texts fill in the world around us.

The songs students listen to may be making arguments or asking important questions. The speech a politician makes after being elected is establishing authority, celebrating, and reassuring voters. The advertisement that interrupts your playlist is persuading you to try a new product. Sound texts do a lot of heavy lifting in the world.

Who Do Sound Texts Impact in the World?

This question unveils some of the richness and wide applicability of sound texts because it asks us to consider who sound texts are intended for. Who is the target audience for sound texts? At first, we may be tempted to consider the audience to be the tech-savvy high schooler whose smartphone is constantly streaming music or the latest celebrity podcasts, but sound texts reach so much further. Classic sports radio shows, avant-garde audio dramas, performance spoken-word poems, or archival interview recordings are all sound texts with audiences in very different spheres of life. Different sound texts influence listeners of all backgrounds and ages in all disciplines and interest areas.

SOUND TEXT GENRES

You may have noticed the answers to some of the previously listed questions considering the context, purpose, and audience for different sound texts largely come down to the issue of genre, or the category or type of sound text. Just like texts you're already using in your classroom, sound texts can take the forms of a wide variety of genres. We've mentioned a few of these so far in this section, including poetry, advertisement, speeches, dramas, etc., but the list is vast. To give you an idea of some of the major genre categories for sound texts, including the ones we'll be discussing most often throughout this book, we've included Table 1. It's important to emphasize that this list is incomplete; it has to be. Genres evolve, emerge, and disappear constantly as society and the rhetorical situations in which we live shift and change.

We've created this list to capture *some* of the major categories that we are seeing in our current moment, but we excitedly anticipate new additions to and subcategories within this list.

To get an idea of what some of these genres look like in real life, check out our sound text library. It's organized by genre, so you can listen to samples in the genres that interest you most.

Sound Text Library

TABLE 1. Overview of Audio Genres

Audio Genres	Description	Where Does This Sound Text Live?	What Does This Sound Text Do?	Who Does This Sound Text Impact?	Traditional Texts That Pair Well
Podcast	Podcasts are episodic audio programs that cover particular topics. They can vary in length, style, and regularity of publication but are often recurring.	Most podcasts have a dedicated website with a brief overview, a list of episodes with summaries, and sometimes some cover art. Different platforms have created libraries of podcasts that listeners can scan to find and review episodes; the most commonly used one is Apple's iTunes podcast library, but others include Spotify and Podchaser.	Podcasts are usually informative or persuasive. A host or organization generally assembles speakers and sound clips on a certain topic with the intent of teaching their audience something new about the topic or of constructing a particular argument.	While research suggests that younger audiences under the age of 35 are more likely to listen to podcasts, the ease of making and distributing podcasts has caused the topics of podcasts to diversify. With available podcasts on anything from knitting to cooking to home repair, podcast audiences are expanding.	Podcasts are particularly useful in helping students develop skill in research writing or argumentative essays. All these texts focus on a central idea supported by a variety of pieces of information woven together to inform or persuade on the central topic in ways that hold the reader/listener's interest.
Speech	A speech is a monologue written and delivered by an individual (or sometimes individuals) in real time to a target audience, usually with the intent to persuade on a current, real-world issue.	Speeches are most often thought of as being consumed in real time; however, many speeches have been recorded and can be revisited via YouTube, Spotify, or historical archives. Many universities and historical organizations maintain libraries of recorded speeches that can be downloaded.	Speeches are most often intended to persuade or argue. They are very often given in response to particular situations in order to direct how listeners respond to that situation.	The audiences of speeches often have a specific political or social identity. Speeches are usually the product of political or social movements, and so they are intended to target people in groups involved in those movements. However, recorded speeches hold particular value for historians, scholars, and students looking to study these particular movements.	Speeches pair well with persuasive essays and works of journalism, as all of these genres blend information and argumentation in ways that are both factually accurate and, at the same time, emotionally engaging and effective.

TABLE 1. (continued)

Audio Genres	Description	Where Does This Sound Text Live?	What Does This Sound Text Do?	Who Does This Sound Text Impact?	Traditional Texts That Pair Well
Audio Drama	Audio dramas construct narratives, fictional or not, using a blend of dialogue between characters, music, sound effects, and sometimes narration.	Audio dramas can be found on podcast library platforms like Apple iTunes or Spotify, but they are also often played on live FM radio. Many universities or radio theaters maintain websites and digital archives where students or artists can share audio dramas for listeners to stream or download. Some organizations like the BBC Radio Drama Collection record audio dramatizations of literary works, and these are available to purchase and download as audiobooks to personal listening devices.	Audio dramas usually follow a typical plot structure and convey a particular theme. Like traditional plays, audio genres are created to immerse the audience in the universe of the story and characters.	Audio dramas cover a wide array of subgenres including texts like the traditional radio drama programs popular in the early 1900s, more recent episodic dramas that live alongside podcasts, all the way to more experimental, avant-garde work created by university students looking to push the boundaries of theater and composition. Because of this diversity of subgenres and contexts, the audience for audio dramas will depend heavily on the individual audio drama and the situation in which it is operating.	Audio dramas work well when working with plays or novels because these texts ask students to consider characterization, creation of tone and themes in a plot, dramatization, and narrative structure.

TABLE 1. (continued)

Audio Genres	Description	Where Does This Sound Text Live?	What Does This Sound Text Do?	Who Does This Sound Text Impact?	Traditional Texts That Pair Well
Interview	Interviews involve a recorded set of questions between at least one interviewer and their subject(s). They are usually informational and factual, with the majority of the interest in the content coming from the identity and/or background of the interviewee(s).	Interviews can be found in various locations, including within other genres, preserved archivally, as well as in live performances. Podcasts, for example, can include episodes that consist solely of interviews. Many universities and historical organizations maintain archives of interviews that can be downloaded. Live radio shows also often invite guests for real time interviews.	Interviews usually serve the purpose of discovering and preserving answers to questions through recorded firsthand accounts and personal opinions and experiences. The focus of these questions is vast and largely dependent on the person(s) being interviewed. While some interviews may serve to gather information about the interviewee(s), other interviews can serve to gain insight on a particular topic from an expert in the field.	Interviews are consumed by a vast audience. Because interviews can be found on various platforms and within several genres, the audience for interviews is expansive and will depend on the situation in which the interview functions. While archival interviews are generally intended for historians and academia, interviews with pop culture figures or artists may be geared toward a broader, younger audience of fans.	Interviews pair well with units on informational or research texts such as biographies or archival news articles, as they prompt students to consider what is most relevant and interesting about factual situations and individuals and how to best organize and present that information.

TABLE 1. (continued)

Audio Genres	Description	Where Does This Sound Text Live?	What Does This Sound Text Do?	Who Does This Sound Text Impact?	Traditional Texts That Pair Well
Audio Memoir	Audio memoirs involve an individual or group of individuals recounting a narrative of their experiences during a particular event or period of time in an effort to re-create that memory as closely as possible to their experience. Sometimes authors of traditional printed memoirs create audiobook versions of their texts, adding layers of meaning through their reading. This can include the author singing portions of a song, speaking in various languages and/or accents, or emoting heavily with their voice; we consider these texts to be audio memoirs as well.	Audio memoirs can be found on podcast library platforms like Apple iTunes or Spotify, but they can also be found on university and historical organizations' archives for download.	Audio memoirs serve to recount the life or a particular moment in the life of the author, preserving memory and experience. They are often deeply personal and share especially profound moments from the author's life.	The content, depth, and length of audio memoirs varies dramatically. Accordingly, the audience also varies. While longer, more historical or sociopolitical memoirs target academic audiences, NPR's *Moth Radio Hour* is intended for a casual radio listener.	Pairing audio memoirs with traditional written memoirs is particularly powerful, as students will be able to use these texts to consider what is most important when re-creating and preserving a memory, particularly in a personal, subjective account.

TABLE 1. (continued)

Audio Genres	Description	Where Does This Sound Text Live?	What Does This Sound Text Do?	Who Does This Sound Text Impact?	Traditional Texts That Pair Well
Spoken-Word/ Slam Poetry	Spoken-word poetry is a performance art in which the author recites their poem live, focusing on the aesthetics of their delivery in ways that rely on rhyme, repetition, rhythm, intonation, voice inflection, and improvisation.	Spoken-word poetry can be found on platforms like YouTube and SoundCloud. Some radio broadcast organizations, podcasts, and branches of TED Talks also host and archive performances of spoken-word poetry. Major cities, college campuses, and occasionally cafes also often host live poetry slams where poets perform their work.	Spoken-word poetry, like traditional poetry, covers a wide range of subgenres and content, all with different goals. Because spoken-word poetry developed out of movements centered on social justice, spoken-word performances are often political in nature and oriented toward raising awareness for social justice issues. They can also narrate personal experiences and emotions, or spoken-word poetry can have a goal of simply creating beauty and art.	Spoken-word poetry largely originates in the 1960s, making it a relatively recent genre; it has been adopted by a younger audience and often appears closely linked to pop culture and social trends. As a result, most audiences of spoken-word poetry are younger. Due to spoken-word poetry's close ties to social justice, the audiences are often unified and/ or motivated by political or social causes.	Working with spoken-word poetry while reading and writing traditional printed poetry deepens a student's understanding of poetic devices such as repetition, meter, alliteration, imagery, rhyme, and many others. Exploring the aesthetics and layered meanings of poetry in both the printed and audio modes will challenge the way students approach poetry as a genre.

TABLE 1. (continued)

Audio Genres	Description	Where Does This Sound Text Live?	What Does This Sound Text Do?	Who Does This Sound Text Impact?	Traditional Texts That Pair Well
Song/Music	Whether with or without lyrics, a piece of music is a short, aesthetic text intended to evoke emotion through narrative, poetic devices, or the use of sound devices such as rhythm, harmony, and tone.	Perhaps the most common places to find music are on personal listening devices through streaming platforms like Spotify, YouTube, and Apple Music. This is closely followed by radio broadcasting and live performance.	Songs and music, perhaps more than any other genre of sound text we will discuss in this book, cover a complicated and diverse network of subgenres and contexts. For this reason, attempting to isolate the goals for music in general is an impossible task; however, depending on topic, culture, subgenre, and a host of other factors, music can be used to evoke emotion, share narratives, promote political change, subvert societal expectations, etc.	Given the complicated and diverse network of subgenres and contexts, it is not possible to determine the audience of music as a whole. By further defining some of the factors that shape music, such as cultural background, goals, etc., it is possible to narrow audiences more specifically, but this requires knowledge of the specific piece of music.	Music supports the exploration of a variety of texts in that it can create tone, theme, motif, and emotional appeals. When teaching poetry, novels, or short stories, asking your students to consider how composers reach their audiences through music can prompt innovative approaches to the traditional genres.

TABLE 1. (continued)

Audio Genres	Description	Where Does This Sound Text Live?	What Does This Sound Text Do?	Who Does This Sound Text Impact?	Traditional Texts That Pair Well
Advertisement	Audio advertisements are brief, scripted recordings intended to market and sell a branded product or service. These are usually carefully edited to maximize content and impact on their intended audience.	Advertisements are often consumed through platforms that host other sound genres. Advertisements can be found on radio shows, podcasts, and music streaming services, for example.	The purpose of an advertisement is to persuade the audience to consume a particular product.	The audience for advertisements is vast but is also dependent on the particular product being discussed as well as the platform hosting the ad.	The persuasive goals of advertisements make them powerful tools to use when working with students on the traditional persuasive essay. Understanding the audience awareness required to make effective rhetorical appeals in audio advertising challenges students to think critically about how to write persuasively.
Audio Journalism and Newscasting	This genre most commonly consists of a summary of current events spoken or read by a newscaster or journalist. These segments rarely include stylistic edits like sound effects or background music, and they can range anywhere from a brief one-minute summary to an hour-long radio broadcast. Some broadcasts may include interviews or recorded sound clips.	Audio journalism most frequently appears on radio news stations like NBC, the BBC, or NPR. While you can access these on an AM/FM radio, most radio news stations also have companion websites that stream radio programs as well as organize and archive their radio broadcasts for future listeners.	Sound texts in this genre give clear, concise, ideally unbiased reports of current events to a wide audience of listeners. The goal is to inform listeners of important information and happenings.	It's difficult to say exactly who consumes radio news; however, in 2022, the Pew Research Center reported that 8 out of 10 Americans aged 12 and up listened to AM/FM radio in a given week, and that nearly half of US adults report either "sometimes" or "often" getting their news from the radio. One out of every 5 US adults reported that they "often get local news from radio stations" (Forman-Katz). The suggestion here is that the reach of radio news is broad and accessible to a wide range of demographics.	Integrating print and sound journalism is an incredibly powerful way to consider how rhetoric appears to function in different modes when communicating information clearly and concisely to audiences. It can also make for an extremely interesting evaluation of bias and perspective to pair news articles with audio newscasts on the same topic.

WHAT DOES IT MEAN TO READ AND WRITE USING SOUND?

Now that we've established a common understanding of what exactly a sound text is, we'll need to explore the idea of what it means to read and write these sound texts. While the concepts of reading and writing are, of course, familiar to us, how they apply in the mode of sound will look different than in traditional printed writing. There will also certainly be many similarities, but sound is a unique mode that brings new ideas and options to the table for teachers and their students.

What Does It Mean to Read Using Sound?

Reading using sound is something we explain by going back to the traditional, dictionary definition of reading. Merriam-Webster quite simply defines reading as an effort "to interpret the meaning or significance of" something. When we say we're going to teach students reading skills using sound texts, we mean that we're going to ask our students to interpret the meaning of complicated sound texts, including genres like podcasts and audio dramas, the same way we'd ask them to interpret the meaning of a printed essay or novel.

Some of this process will be familiar to students, and we view this as a positive. A close reading of a sound text still offers opportunities for students to consider traditional literary tools. Students will still need to analyze elements such as diction, tone, genre, organizational structure, and literary devices when listening to a political speech, spoken-word poem, or radio advertisement. However, the way students discuss these elements in a sound text will be slightly different from traditional printed texts. As students listen, they will also be paying attention to the author's use of sound effects, music, silence, and vocal tones. As students analyze tone in a sound text, they will need to consider both the diction as well as the music and sound effects. They will need to pay attention to how the speaker articulates the words in addition to what words the speaker actually uses.

So, while reading sound texts with students, we are indeed asking them "to interpret the meaning and significance" of the author's work, and students will find many opportunities to exercise the skills they are developing in working with traditional printed texts. But reading sound texts also invites students to stretch their interpretive skills in new ways that are only available when using the mode of sound.

What Does It Mean to Write Using Sound?

Writing using sound in the classroom involves students creating meaning in the same ways they would when composing a traditional essay or a short story; instead of using printed words on a page, however, you and your students will be using recorded sounds. These sounds can, just like words or images, be arranged, assembled, presented, and layered in different ways to achieve a wide variety of communicative effects.

Much like when reading using sound, elements of writing using sound texts will already be familiar to you and your students. Students will still need to go through the writer's process of brainstorming, outlining, drafting, and revising; much of this can still be done using pen and paper, which students will probably have more confidence with. Peer feedback will remain a powerful writing tool as well. This process will still involve student writers considering how to use diction, tone, genre, organizational structure, and literary devices in their work. However, when writing using sound, some of this process will be unique to the mode. In addition to considering how to use traditional elements in their drafting, student writers will now be planning how to use sound effects, music, voices, and silence to accomplish their goals for their work, all of which will create added opportunities for complexity, play, and audience awareness. When writing using sound, students will need guidance on how to gather, record, and edit the sounds they plan to use; factors like layering sounds, smoothing transitions, and balancing volume come into play. This will require some technical support, but we have resources to support you in that later in the book.

When you ask your students to write and create their own sound texts, you truly are asking them to build on their already existing writing skills and identities in ways that expand and challenge them.

CONCLUSION

Before We Get Started Conclusion Audio

Before We Get Started Conclusion Transcript

1

Why Should You Teach Students to Read and Write with Sound Texts?

Introduction

Chapter 1 Introduction Audio

Chapter 1 Introduction Transcript

Expanding Multimodality

Multimodality has been a buzzword in ELA pedagogy studies for quite some time now. Current accepted wisdom within the world of teaching reading and writing has enthusiastically embraced the importance of multimodal texts. For the past few decades, research, publications, conferences, and teacher resources have excitedly mined the idea of reading and writing across multiple modes as one of the most significant ways to empower our students to read and write effectively for diverse purposes, contexts, and audiences. Standardized tests including the SAT and the AP exam, major textbook publishers, and educational institutions at all levels are excitedly working multimodality into their materials. There is also a critically important and ever-expanding body of research exploring the ways in which many students of color engage multimodal literacies as a way to create their "counterstor[ies] against dominant narratives" (Player 434). The enthusiasm for multimodal reading and writing in a high school classroom is high, and so we aren't here to build a case for it; we feel that this case has been made thoroughly and effectively already.

In the middle of all this enthusiasm for multimodality, we're here to assert that sound is getting the short end of the stick. We aren't the first ones to notice this. Jon Wargo refers to the mode of sound as a "blind spot" in our explorations of multimodal composing, calling it "the lesser-known modal resource" ("Rhythmic Rituals" 395). We agree wholeheartedly. As far as we can tell, sound isn't always included in the conversation and practice taking place around multimodal reading and writing in many classrooms and institutions, and we think that's an oversight worth fixing.

Of all the communicative modes that we practically interact with in our daily lives, sound is right up there with visual and tactile. But, in practice, when we hear the phrase "multimodal reading or writing" in a high school context, it most often refers to some kind of visual text: paintings, graphic novels, infographics, film, etc. Despite the common acceptance of the idea that reading and writing in multiple media and modes is necessary, oftentimes the only way we see this appear in the classroom, in teaching resources, or on assessments is through visuals; sound, a mode all of our students interact with on a daily basis, almost never makes the cut. Basically, it's pretty rare that we see sound being used to teach reading and writing in the classroom, and we think that both we and our students are missing out on some of what multimodality has to offer because of that.

In a world where podcasts, radio broadcasts, and the music industry command massive influence socially, culturally, politically, and financially, we feel that reading and writing classrooms are seriously lacking when they overlook the mode of sound. And we aren't the only ones:

- The National Council of Teachers of English's (NCTE's) 2005 position statement on *Multimodal Literacies* lists several sound texts, including music and speech, as critical ways of making meaning that the literate student should have exposure to.
- In a 2006 article, Heidi McKee identifies sound as a necessary aspect of effectively and competently writing complicated multimodal texts ("Sound Matters: Notes Toward the Analysis and Design of Sound in Multimodal Webtexts").
- In a 2007 book by Cynthia Selfe called *Multimodal Composition: Resources for Teachers*, the first chapter of the book defines multimodal texts as those that include "images, animations, color, words, music and sound" (1).
- Selfe returned more explicitly to stress the importance of sound in her 2009 article "The Movement of Air, the Breath of Meaning: Aurality

and Multimodal Composing" in which she argues that the lack of information and pedagogy available on sound writing "has limited our understanding of composing as a multimodal rhetorical activity and has thus deprived students of valuable semiotic resources for making meaning" (617).

- Citing the WIDE Research Project, the National Writing Project et al., in their 2010 book *Because Digital Writing Matters*, argue that "students need to understand how these media [text with images, audio, hyperlinks] work for different audiences and in various contexts and how to layer and juxtapose media to create sophisticated messages" (40).
- Jon Wargo has published several articles beginning in 2017 that explore using the mode of sound to write with elementary and high school students, exploring the capabilities that sound or sonic composition has to promote creative energies, shape writerly identities, foster twenty-first-century literacies, and challenge problematic power structures that govern how we write in academic settings.
- Courtney Danforth, Kyle Stedman, and Michael Farris released their book *Soundwriting Pedagogies* in August of 2018, coining the term "soundwriting" and exploring the exceptional potential inherent in using sound in the reading and writing classroom.
- Most recently in 2022, Tanya Rodrigue and Kyle D. Stedman published their book *Soundwriting: A Guide to Making Audio Projects*, a textbook entirely dedicated to writing in the mode of sound, one of the first texts we have come across that emphasizes some of the less familiar audio genres like audio essays, audio documentaries, and personal narratives.

The idea isn't original to us, and it isn't exactly new, but we are here to add our voices to this chorus and to write this book to offer some ideas and resources that make this idea more readily available to high school ELA classrooms looking to expand their use of multimodality.

You might be wondering why, of all the modes, we've chosen to single out sound. If we're vocal supporters of multimodal reading and writing, why limit ourselves to a single mode? Does sound have something to offer that other modes don't? In short, the answer to that last question is YES! Each mode brings something unique to the table, and that is why multimodality is so important. It allows students to access the concept of making and sharing meaning in diverse, authentic, and relevant ways. We echo Jon Wargo's challenge for all educators to ask themselves, "What . . . [is] amplified through composing with sound that other modes may silence?" ("Rhythmic Rituals" 405).

> **Examples from the Classroom**
>
> Anne has challenged herself with Wargo's question in her classroom when she and her seniors create a multimodal narrative in preparation for a traditional printed narrative essay. She offers students the option to create a visual graphic novel or an audio drama. By providing this choice, Anne has found that each student is able to access and demonstrate their narrative skills in unique and important ways, and, often, students who choose the audio option remark that working with this mode in the classroom made them think about their writing in a new and deeper way. When students are faced with choosing from an array of modes to accomplish their writing goals, it invites them "to reconsider what counts as language in the ELA classroom" (de los Ríos et al. 6). Offering an option for students to demonstrate their abilities using the modes of both sound and visuals allows the idea of multimodality to function to its fullest extent, creating diverse and varied access points to accommodate and engage each student uniquely.

As you can see in the example from Anne's classroom, we are huge fans of visual modes in the reading and writing classroom. Our intent is in no way to downplay the significance of the visual, but if we are only teaching visual and traditional printed modes, we aren't preparing our students to truly develop multimodal reading and writing skills, especially when a mode with as much influence and potential as sound is available to us.

In addition to all of this, the mode of sound's relevance and applicability in recent years has skyrocketed. As Rodrigue and Stedman put it, "this is an exciting moment for sound" (9). Compositions like podcasts, audio clips on social media, and voice-overs on videos are increasingly positioning themselves as critical players in the social, cultural, and political landscapes of our daily lives. Rodrigue and Stedman report that "students from every major are making powerful audio projects like podcasts, audio essays, personal narratives, and documentaries that they're proud of and want to share with the world" (9). Overlooking the mode of sound in our multimodal ELA classrooms is not only shortchanging the full breadth and benefits of a multimodal classroom; it's also neglecting the mode's significant influence and relevance in our current rhetorical moment.

We also acknowledge that using sound to teach multimodal reading and writing in the high school classroom hasn't been entirely overlooked, particularly with regards to podcasting. There are some resources and ongoing dialogues (see "A Non-Exhaustive List of Available Resources for Podcasting in the Classroom" sidebar for a few examples) available to high school teachers who are passionate about podcasting with their students, and we love this! But it's important that we not limit ourselves or our students to the podcasting genre when exploring reading and writing using sound. Sound as a tool is much too broad, diverse, and full of potential, as we've already seen in "Before We Get Started," to be entirely captured within a single genre, especially when that particular genre only represents a fraction of the sound texts our students organically interact with on a daily basis. So, while the mode of sound may appear in some high school reading and writing classrooms, our intent is to expand on that in order to access everything multimodality has to offer.

As a community of educators, we largely agree that multimodal reading and writing is a powerful way to help our students develop strong, flexible, and relevant skills for their daily lives. If we're going to practice what we preach, then the mode of sound has been waiting in the wings to offer our students some great opportunities.

A Non-Exhaustive List of Available Resources for Podcasting in the Classroom

Digital

- NPR's guide for student podcasting as part of their Student Podcast Challenge
- Princeton University's The McGraw Center's "Podcasting assignments" and associated materials
- Penn State's set of "Podcasting Tutorials"
- *National Geographic*'s "Strategy Share: Creating Podcasts in the Classroom" by Jenny Bolch

Books

- *Digital Voices: Podcasting in the Creative Writing Classroom* by Saul Lemerond and Leigh Camacho Rourks
- *Podcasting for Teachers: Using a New Technology to Revolutionize Teaching and Learning* by Kathleen P. King and Mark Gura
- *Student-Powered Podcasting: Teaching for 21st Century Literacy* by Christopher Shamburg
- *Kidcast: Podcasting in the Classroom, 2nd Edition* by Dan Schmit

Fostering Student Interest, Engagement, and Confidence

There's a reason our students, when left to their own devices, are rarely seen without small, white earbuds tucked into one if not both ears. Sound as a mode just happens to be supremely relevant in the moment in which we find ourselves as educators. Some of the texts that our students will most naturally find themselves drawn to outside of our class are going to be sound texts—podcasts, music, advertisements, celebrity interviews. Sound is an integral and vibrant part of the pop culture, media, and trends that drive our students' attention and days. And according to the *Framework for Success in Postsecondary Writing*, which was developed collaboratively by the Council of Writing Program Administrators, NCTE, and the National Writing Project, engagement is a critical component to the habits of mind that students need in order to succeed after high school.

Examples from the Classroom

There's no doubt that many of these same benefits that we're discussing here come with the use of visual modes as well, but teaching reading and writing using sound allows students to engage with a whole range of relevant and exciting texts that visuals alone don't cover. Danah's AP Language students have mixed feelings about poetry analysis, but when she tells them that they'll be listening to and analyzing Beyoncé's "Freedom" featuring Kendrick Lamar, she'll tell you firsthand that she is never met with groans. They even get excited about writing a traditional analysis essay on the song because their Beyoncé fandom knows no bounds. The current social and cultural relevance of sound texts in our society and students' lives make it easy to ask students to exercise classic reading and writing skills on sound texts that they are organically excited about and invested in.

The reality is that a lot of very cool texts, texts that even our students will agree are cool, are written using sound. And if there's one thing guaranteed to engage student interest, it's whatever is cool. We absolutely see the beauty and skill in helping students see the "cool" in classic, canonical texts, but we also see huge value in engaging students rigorously with their current passions and interests as well.

Because of how engaged and connected students are to different kinds of sound texts, bringing these texts into our classrooms also creates scenarios where we'll find that our students feel and actually are more equipped to act as relative experts in our work together; they will be more able to take some ownership of their learning. Whether we're referring to the newest hit single or to the string of audio advertisements that students had to listen through to access that new single on their streaming service, so many students are going to enter our lessons already in possession of some serious confidence, background, and emotional connection to sound. This means that we as educators are able to take a step back in our reading and writing classroom, decentralizing ourselves and letting our students take the wheel in their own learning experiences.

Student expertise with sound texts can take many different forms. On the most basic level, almost all of our students will be familiar with the experience of emotionally and personally connecting with a particular song; significantly fewer of our students will walk through our doors immediately able to name a traditional printed text that they have a deep emotional connection with, revisit regularly, and love deeply. This means that they bring personal connection to and experience with interpreting, analyzing, and responding to sound texts; they have instinct and preestablished skills on which we as educators can build. Students will also bring some real-life genre familiarity to our work together that may help them navigate concepts like audience awareness and writer choices like tone and structural organization. Last but not least, most of our students are going to be pretty familiar with the digital tools we use to consume sound texts. Some may even have some experience with the tools needed to produce sound texts. Whether it be the wide range of personal listening devices or online streaming services, the odds will be high that our students are going to bring a lot of technical knowledge to the table, enabling them to approach their classwork with confidence.

Despite this familiarity with sound texts from their extracurricular lives, for most students, approaching sound texts as scholarly work will be new. Podcasts and radio advertisements as academic genres will feel unexpected to most high school ELA students. This invites play and experimentation, qualities that can often be somewhat elusive in high school reading and writing classes. Our students are part of a system that is hyper-focused on grades, standardized exams, and competition; it's hard, but deeply necessary, to make room for intellectual play in that environment. Sound texts often lack the established, rigid, and standardized genre rules and expectations that students may be used to in more traditional texts. However, as we mentioned earlier, most students will have enough practical experience and confidence with sound texts from their lives outside the classrooms to allow them to engage with this potential for flexibility without resorting to a nervous reliance on explicit teacher direction.

Whether because their favorite musician released a new single, a famous YouTuber is featured on a particular podcast, or a new streaming site allows you to share custom playlists in a new way, students love sound texts. They are navigating them constantly outside of our classes. We'd be missing a pretty big opportunity if we didn't take advantage of this already existing passion and interest, channeling it toward the goals of developing our students into relevant, flexible, and thoughtful readers and writers.

Examples from the Classroom

In an effort to achieve the highest grades possible, Danah's student Emily was anxiously dedicated to the five-paragraph essay format, and Danah struggled to encourage her to try something new and break out of that traditional, institutionalized genre. However, when asked to organize her argument into an investigative, interview-driven podcast, Emily thrived, naturally moving away from preestablished argumentation structures and inventing new organization strategies to present her points. She had heard something similar in a true crime podcast she listened to with her family and felt comfortable enough to try it out on her own. The ability to demonstrate her writing skills through a sound text accessed Emily's prior knowledge and personal interest in podcasts in a way that invited confidence and engagement with the writing process, qualities that traditional writing assignments had caused Emily to struggle with.

Meeting the Same Standards in New Ways

Whether we like it or not, the Common Core is a major part of our curricula; the fact is that most states have adopted the ELA Common Core Standards. While standardizing our learning goals increases consistency and the ease with which we assess student work, it can also increase the potential for formulaic assignments and activities. It's important to persist in approaching these standards with creativity and innovation, insisting that the skills the Common Core outlines be addressed with relevance and enthusiasm. We believe that the mode of sound is an exciting and untapped resource for energizing Common Core use in the classroom.

We are, of course, aware that the Common Core has Speaking and Listening Standards; however, we believe that sound allows us to practice reading and writing skills in new and relevant ways as well. Students are able to interact with sound texts in the same ways they would traditional printed texts, which makes sound texts powerful resources with which to address the Common Core reading and writing skills. According to recent studies, brain mapping appears the same when the brain listens as when the brain reads information (Deniz et al.). In other words, the processes occurring within the brain are the same whether a person is reading the words on a page or listening to them out loud. This means that, when reading and analyzing sound texts, we are still asking students to identify central ideas and their development, cite textual evidence to back their analyses, and analyze authorial choices surrounding diction, syntax, and tone. Those skills will easily transfer to all the classic printed literature that we may wish to apply it to, but we're willing to bet that students will be able to access and explore the skills much more authentically and organically by using sound. It also follows that, when writing using sound, we are still looking for students to construct arguments supported by evidence, reasoning, and analysis, create narratives with intentional details and structures, and consider elements of development, organization, and style in their work. Because of our brains' ability to process the mode of sound in this way, sound is an ideal mode for students to exercise Common Core Reading and Writing Standards in relevant and exciting ways.

Beyond the Reading and Writing Standards, the Common Core also calls for us, as educators, to ensure that our students are developing college and career readiness in the twenty-first-century world. Our students will use digital tools in their future jobs in ways that we can't even imagine yet, so we need to teach students not just how to use specific digital tools but instead the skills involved in learning to use new digital tools more generally. By teaching these skills, we are not only teaching students digital literacy, but we are also helping them learn flexibility and adaptability, skills not only critical in our ever-evolving world but also skills highlighted as necessary for current literacy by the National Council of Teachers of English's 2019 "Definition of Literacy in a Digital Age."

Because sound is so current and relevant as a mode of expression, it often relies on equally current and relevant technological tools for its production and consumption. Recording, editing, streaming, and sharing sound texts asks students to thoughtfully and competently navigate software, hardware, communities, and networks that are extremely powerful for sharing and receiving new ideas. Confidence and experience with these tools and resources are going to go a long way in preparing students for college and future careers.

Whether helping students access traditional reading and writing skills or enabling them to strengthen and develop career-ready adaptability with digital tools and technology, reading and writing with sound helps our students meet necessary requirements in the Common Core as well as many other high school level standards. While there are many ways to meet these standards, some of which we're sure many of you are already implementing, we've seen in our classrooms just how empowering sound can be in preparing our students for what comes next.

Examples from the Classroom

Anne has seen firsthand how exploring the mode of sound in class gives students a leg up once they've graduated. After having been assigned a podcast research assignment in his twelfth-grade English class with Anne, Daniel, a new college first-year student, excitedly emailed her the link to his podcast hosted on his university's radio program. Daniel said his experience with creating a podcast in Anne's class had given him the confidence to explore this new opportunity when he entered college, and he shared his excitement at being able to include his podcast on his CV.

Danah's student Jayna was passionate about journalism, which prompted her to choose the research podcast project option for one of her assignments in Danah's class. Following the genre model of an investigative journalist podcast, Jayna created an engrossing exposé on an alleged school scandal. She used this same piece to apply for and earn a full-ride scholarship for the journalism program at the university of her choice; the admissions committee expressed specifically that her work on this podcast set her apart from the other applicants in a world where multimedia journalism is critical.

Promoting Racial and Cultural Equity

Defining Terms: Inclusivity and Equity

Before we go further, we want to clarify what we mean when we talk about cultural inclusivity and equity. While these two terms are related and oftentimes confused with one another, we define cultural inclusivity as a means to pursuing genuine cultural equity. Cultural inclusivity is not only about including people and voices from various cultures, races, ethnicities, religions, and so forth into curricula and academic communities, but it is also about clearly and purposefully valuing those voices. A culturally inclusive classroom decentralizes the white narrative and instead shares and supports voices of all cultural backgrounds. While we understand these principles of cultural inclusivity are not exclusive to the mode of sound, we feel it is important to explain where we are coming from when we say that sound is a powerful tool for upholding it.

Cultural equity in education, however, is about consistently evaluating the systems and practices in our classrooms and curricula to create spaces that are equally accessible for students of all cultural and ethnic backgrounds. Dr. Darnisa Amante-Jackson explains it as the process of asking, "who are the communities that have been historically marginalized, communities that have had to face institutional and structural barriers that prevent them from getting what they need and what they deserve?" (qtd. in Wilkerson, "Building Equity from the Ground Up" 17:03). She goes on to discuss how wrestling ideas of equity may prompt us to "even redefine what education is, since it was often not defined with the voices of the marginalized communities and peoples that we're trying to support the most" (17:35). Equity and equality are often conflated;

however, there are key differences between them. Referring to Walter Secada's work, Felix Maringe and Nevensha Sing distinguish between the two terms by explaining, "equality speaks to creating the same opportunities for all, while equity interrogates the justice and fairness associated with creating those equal opportunities" (766). When reading and writing multimodally, particularly in the mode of sound, educators and students will be revisiting traditional assumptions about literacy education and creating new avenues for students of all backgrounds to interact authentically and fully in our ELA classrooms.

Sound, like any mode, is not inherently inclusive or equitable; however, the mode is uniquely able to support culturally inclusive learning in the reading and writing classroom so long as we as educators are intentional about selecting and assigning sound texts that allow students to experience these affordances. In the next few paragraphs, we'll identify and briefly discuss some of the possibilities to keep in mind when deciding how to approach reading and writing using sound to help achieve your goal of fostering cultural inclusivity and equity in your students and your curricula.

Promoting Empathy

One of the key ways in which sound uniquely promotes empathy, cultural inclusivity, and human connection relies on the fact that most sound texts teachers will work with feature, in some way or another, the human voice. Erin Anderson identifies the human voice as a unique and powerful sound because it is "produced by and emitted from the human body. Inevitably, when we hear a voice, we hear a body." This makes it harder for students to disengage with the human being on the other side of the words, making sound a deeply humanizing mode and supporting Cati V. de los Ríos et al.'s dreams of a world where educators work together to leverage our ELA classrooms "to disrupt and stop the systemic dehumanization of bodies of color" (2). Sound's capacity to evoke a sense of a fellow human being's physical body makes it a unique mode for supporting this dream. While the emergence of artificial intelligence and automated voices may impact this sometime in the future, we find that our

> **Examples from the Classroom**
>
> Danah has seen the phenomenon of embodied voice play out with her own students regularly. When Danah's students record and share podcasts with one another, she is always surprised by the level of intimacy and community the process creates. One year, after hearing a Chinese student share in her podcast how frustrating it is for her to hear people mispronounce her Chinese name, several American students apologized and sat in a circle after class learning the correct pronunciation. There are several Chinese students in Danah's school, and the frequent mispronunciation of their names often leads them to take on Americanized names. Danah's classes are all aware of this; however, this student's ability to use voice in her writing to share how this impacted her, the agency of correctly pronouncing her name for her class in her podcast, connected Danah's students in new ways.

current students are well positioned to connect deeply with the personhood inherent in the sound of a human voice.

Additionally, expanding our classroom texts and genres to include texts in the audio mode will further "push on the ways that strict adherence to the idea of a canon is contrary to the spirit of empathy" (Mirra 20). Nicole Mirra argues that engaging with diverse modes and genres of literature can "become a mutually humanizing experience that can spur social action" (20). When we open ourselves and our classrooms up to everything that the mode of sound has to offer, we create an explosion of new opportunities for new perspectives, ideas, and human connection.

Undermining Harmful Language Practices

Reading and writing sound texts such as poems, interviews, or podcasts can also provide unique opportunities to invite cultural inclusivity into our classrooms by teaching students that the English language can be used effectively in a variety of ways by a diversity of cultures and people groups. Particularly when it comes to the rigid and limiting assumptions writing classrooms so often promote around what Laura Greenfield refers to as "standardized" English, students with diverse linguistic backgrounds lose out.

While the majority of classroom novels or poems generally reflect the Western academic tradition of "standardized" English, sound genres such as interviews, podcasts, music, and poetry are often organically more effective when they feature many different variations of the English language, code-switching, and Vershawn Ashanti Young's concept of code-meshing. As Cati V. de los Ríos et al. assert, "it is no longer acceptable to relegate students of color for not . . . sounding like their white, middle-class counterparts" (2). April Baker-Bell reinforces how the linguistic liberation of students of color, particularly Black students, relies on educators valuing all language equitably and interrogating our assumptions around "standardized" English being *correct* or *academic*. Our students need ELA classrooms that meaningfully integrate the full range of the English language. Sound texts offer this in many unique ways; not only do sound genres invite this linguistic diversity, but they also have the capacity to preserve and respect it by asking students to seriously and thoughtfully study and write texts spoken in all varieties of English, affirming the scholarly importance of culturally diverse texts and all forms of English.

Creating Equity for Bi/Multilingual Students

The ELA classroom can be an intimidating space for bi/multilingual students, and there are many theories on how best to invite bi/multilingual students into full participation in our classwork. Many of these commonly known and used practices rely on what appears to be a deficit-based mindset; we believe that sound texts offer an inroad for students of all language backgrounds to develop their literacy skills in ways that leverage their current knowledge and celebrate linguistic differences. Eunjeong Lee identifies multimodal writing in general as "a window through which to understand multilingual students' critical knowledge of and relationships with different names, languages, modalities, and literacies that constitute their [meaning-making] repertoire" (60). Sound in particular has a lot to offer in this regard.

One of the primary ways sound texts effectively and compellingly promote equity for students of all linguistic backgrounds is by providing natural translanguaging opportunities for bi/multilingual students. Carla España and Luz Yadira Herrera define translanguaging as "when a multilingual person's full linguistic repertoire is used and honored, instead of trying to keep narrowly focused on a single language" ("Se Hace Camino" 20). Translanguaging centers the literacy practices of multilingual students "without regard for the watchful adherence to the . . . defined boundaries of named . . . languages" (qtd. in Grosjean 171). Sound texts provide a particularly generative platform for translanguaging in that many sound genres integrate multilingual voices, relying not just on words in other languages but also accents that reflect diverse language backgrounds.

Examples from the Classroom

When Anne reads a printed short story by Julia Alvarez aloud to her class, she attempts to say the Spanish words as best she can, though she does not speak Spanish fluently; however, to value Julia Alvarez's story, Anne disrupts the flow of the reading, slowing her pace in order to prioritize correct pronunciation of words in a language in which she is not fluent, which often prompts her Spanish-speaking students to assist her. Additionally, when reading this printed text, the Spanish words are italicized in the print, which Epsaña and Herrera identify as a literary practice that can "otherize" Spanish words (*En Comunidad*). Alternatively, when her students listen to a spoken word poem by Denice Frohman, they can fully appreciate Frohman's fluency with the Spanish words. Anne doesn't need to worry about mispronouncing the critically important words in the text, nor do her Spanish-speaking students need to feel any pressure to assist her; instead, everyone is able to listen to and appreciate the beauty of the flawless blending of English and Spanish within one text, decentralizing the English language as a language of power and scholarly superiority and equalizing all languages in the classroom.

Studying texts by a voice speaking words from languages other than English or with varying accents demonstrates to students that these qualities in no way impact the value of a person's words; in fact, studying texts in this mode can validate and elevate the voices of students and their families who speak using multiple languages and accents. Because of sound's ability to integrate these multilingual voices in ways that are effective, anticipated, and respectful, reading and writing in the mode of sound invites students to bring their full selves to the ELA classroom in a way that is unique when compared to other modes.

Sound is also beneficial for helping multilingual students develop oral language proficiency in a new language (Echevarría et al.), which is necessary in order for multilingual students to improve their reading and writing skills in that language. However, Echevarría and Graves make the distinction that not just any oral language practice is beneficial; having students speak conversationally with peers, for example, doesn't benefit their reading and writing skills. Rather, multilingual students must be given the opportunity to engage with deeper levels of oral language. One way in which multilingual students can be exposed to these deeper-level conversations is through reading and writing intentionally selected sound texts.

Inviting Inclusivity through Music

Additionally, when working with sound to promote cultural inclusivity, music functions as a rich and effective tool for reflecting a wide range of cultures. In addition to any language diversity in the lyrics, music also makes use of different cultural instruments, tonal scales, and traditions. In their study of "cross-cultural perspectives on music and musicality," Sandra E. Trehub, Judith Becker, and Iain Morley assert that "music-making is necessarily a cultural performance because conventions about the structure of music, its instrumentation, context of performance and meaning are all learned" (1). Integrating music from a student's culture into their reading or writing for our classes meaningfully includes their identity in their classroom community, and exposing students to music from different cultures promotes respect and understanding for communities and identities different from their own.

> **Examples from the Classroom**
>
> During a podcasting assignment in Danah's classroom, her student Elianny was writing a series of episodes on her own personal journey of embracing her natural hair. Elianny's father was from Ghana, and her mother was Dominican, and Elianny had only recently begun to educate herself on how to style, care for, and celebrate her naturally textured hair. Elianny expressed that this had been a process of both self-acceptance as well as cultural self-reflection for her, and she wanted her podcast episodes to reflect this. To accomplish this, Elianny selected clips from a variety of Ghanian and Dominican songs to mark transitions in her episodes, infusing the episodic discussion of her personal hair journey with the sounds of the two cultures that played such instrumental roles in that journey and her own identity.

Honoring Diverse Oral Traditions

In general, the mode of sound has a culturally and ethnically diverse legacy that unlocks a host of opportunities and access points for our students of color; oral traditions are heavily valued in a wide range of cultures, many of which are non-Western, non-White, and independent of economic class. From the African American call-and-response tradition to the Indonesian religious practice of Maca Syekh to the lyric songs and myths of Chinese ethnic minorities to the Cuban *Misa* spiritual performances and to so many more (Sale, Sukirno, Bamo, Vété-Congolo), many of our students will enter our classrooms with a high degree of comfort and cultural identity in audio forms of communication. Despite this, our academic systems have traditionally favored "colonial practices that have previously disparaged the language practices of students of color" (de los Ríos et al. 6). Printed alphabetic texts, while certainly able to challenge and subvert these practices, have been part of a legacy that has more often reinforced them. We believe that integrating the mode of sound into our classrooms has the potential to create learning opportunities that honor a wide range of cultural traditions and literacy practices.

> **Examples from the Classroom**
>
> One of Danah's favorite assignments is when she asks her ELA class to compose something in any mode other than alphabetic to express their position on a larger social or political issue that matters to them personally. Some students create posters, pamphlets, informational websites, paintings, dances, podcasts, songs, etc. Students become very inventive with their exploration of how various modes can accomplish their social and/or political goals regarding their chosen issues. One of Danah's Chinese students, Chun, adapted a lullaby her grandmother used to sing, rewriting the lyrics to reflect the isolation and fear that civilians in her hometown were experiencing in the face of extreme COVID isolation practices and regulations at the time. Chun shared how her song, explores her own feelings and beliefs about the COVID restrictions keeping her away from that same grandmother. The option to compose in a mode reflecting her home cultural practices empowered Chun to create a sophisticated, nuanced, and meaningful audio text that she was able to share with her multicultural learning community.

Robert Lake (Medicine Grizzlybear) composed a letter to his young son's (Wind-Wolf's) teacher "about the abilities his son possesses and how judging his achievement through Western society's standards works to construct his child as deficient" (qtd. in Coles et al. 165). Our traditional literacy practices have left many of our students of color on the outside, omitting the literacy practices and identities that support the ways they make meaning in the world. Integrating sound texts into our students' regular academic lives presents an opportunity to decolonize our literacy practices, inviting all students to bring their composing knowledge and home literacy practices to the academic table.

Equity for Disabled Students

Just like racial and cultural inclusivity and equity are critical for our students, it's important to also consider how the mode of sound can contribute to inclusivity and equity specifically for our disabled students. Reading and writing using sound allows disabled students to gain necessary skills and standards but with a mode that may better serve and support their disabilities. For example, students with dyslexia—"the most common learning disability in the United States" (Emanuel)—will benefit from practicing their reading and writing skills using sound texts; with the barrier of printed text removed, students will be able to demonstrate their mastery of the skills rather than demonstrating a manifestation of their disability. Similarly, for some students with ADHD who find it difficult to remain seated and still, reading printed texts may be challenging; however, with sound texts, students can feel free to move around without missing critical content because their devices and headphones can move with them. Rodrigue and Stedman point out how the mode of sound "invites listening in contexts where print books don't fit: in earbuds, while walking across campus, or in the car during a commute" (21). This can be a game changer for students who learn better while in motion.

Of course, for students who are deaf or significantly hard of hearing, sound won't be an effective meaning-making mode; however, here is where transcripts can be a powerful classroom tool. Although they are still traditional printed, alphabetic texts, transcripts allow hard-of-hearing students to engage with sound texts while also inviting all students into an interesting comparison of the capabilities and limitations of different modes. Reading and writing transcripts also exposes students to a real-world genre that promotes accessibility and inclusivity for all.

Examples from the Classroom

Having worked with many students who are impacted by ADHD, Anne has seen firsthand how helpful sound texts can be. Many of her students can be found bouncing or rolling on exercise balls and other flexible seating choices while tackling a challenging text. When reading printed texts, she's found that students with ADHD often take longer breaks during the reading to move around, as they are unable to carry their books and effectively read while doing so. When Anne assigns sound texts, however, students don't need to pause their work in order to partake of the perks their flexible seating or movement breaks provide because their headphones and portable listening devices move with them. Students are able to engage with and focus on the texts for a more extended time, which allows them to more seamlessly follow the text.

And while it may seem that sound would disadvantage some students who are hard of hearing, we have found in our experience that this is not always the case. Danah's student Tiffany participates in class with the support of her hearing aids, and she expressed enjoying when Danah assigned listening to QCODE's audio drama *Carrier*, as she was able to adjust the volume and pause or replay portions of the sound text as she needed.

Ultimately, sound, like all modes, cannot empower all learners equally. This is why pursuing a truly multimodal classroom is so important for our students and for their learning.

Conclusion

Chapter 1 Conclusion Audio

Chapter 1 Conclusion Transcript

2

The Fundamentals of Studying Sound Texts

Introduction

Chapter 2 Introduction Audio

Chapter 2 Introduction Transcript

Terminology and Theory for Studying Sound Texts

General Terminology and Theory

Before we move into terminology and theory that is exclusive to sound texts, we'd like to start with some ideas and principles that apply to reading and writing in any mode so that we can take a look at how we can use those concepts when reading and writing sound texts in particular.

Rhetoric

Whether you're looking at the College Board AP language exam, the SAT essay, or the Common Core Standards, principles of rhetoric are appearing more and more in reading and writing classrooms. Fortunately, sound and rhetorical awareness are natural partners, and an intentional use of rhetoric when studying sound texts in the high school ELA classroom can enrich our students' experience and benefit them in powerful ways. We define **rhetoric** generally as the study of how to use writing effectively, intentionally, and persuasively to accomplish specific purposes. This can include our reading of others' writing or our own writing. For the purposes of the average high school classroom and the discussions in this book, the two most important elements of rhetoric in the classroom are the rhetorical situation and rhetorical appeals.

The first of these elements, the **rhetorical situation**, is one of the central concepts within rhetoric because it is a tool students can use to both make meaning out of complicated texts as well as to make intentional choices in their own texts as writers.

This concept asks students to consider and analyze the context and surroundings that give rise to a particular text. Considering the rhetorical situation encourages students to ask questions like: Why was this text written? What is it responding to? How might the society, culture, or time period in which the text was or is being created impact the text itself along with its meaning? It asks students to investigate the situation in which the text functions.

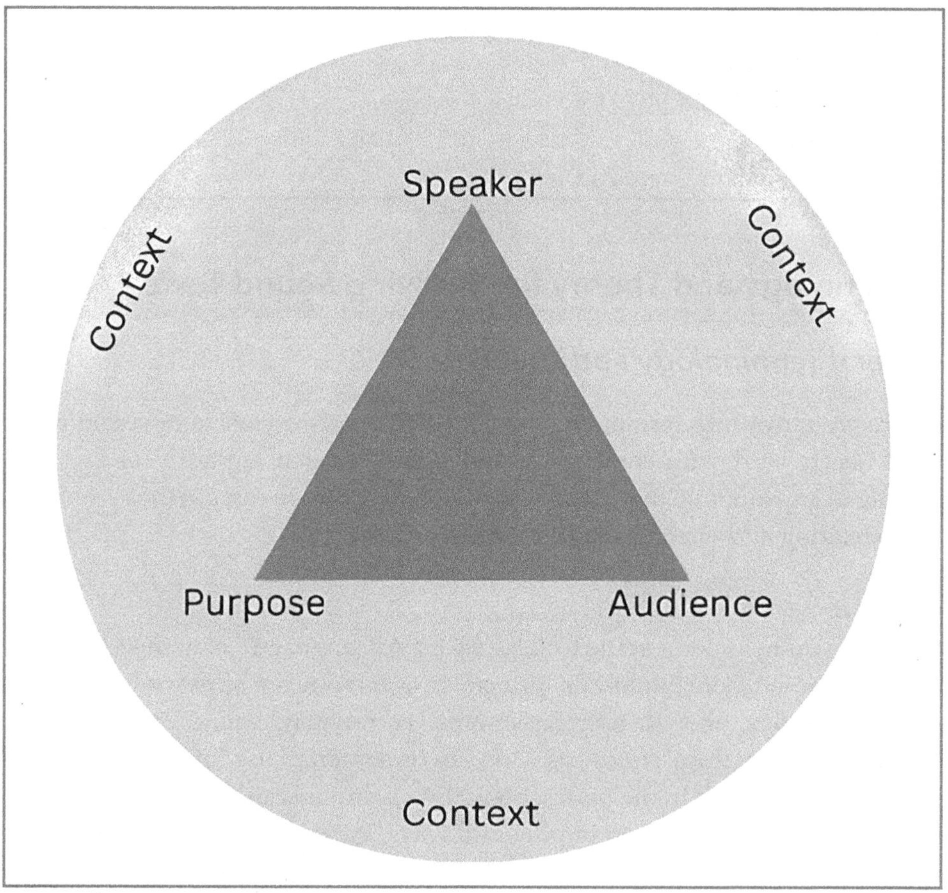

FIGURE 2.1: Rhetorical Situation

While the rhetorical situation for any text is a complicated idea with many moving parts to keep in mind, we like to approach it simply by asking students to identify three primary elements: the author, the audience or reader, and the purposes the author wants the text to achieve. (In a classroom setting, while we explain both purpose and argument, we generally find that we spend the most time on argument. To differentiate the two for students, we define purpose as the overall reason or goal of the text whereas the argument is the central claim of the text itself.) When considering these primary elements of the rhetorical situation (sometimes referred to as the rhetorical triangle), we offer students a foothold from which to begin when approaching their work with sound texts. Sound texts, like any mode that feels new or unfamiliar, can appear intimidating; it can be hard to know how and where to begin. However, framing our work through the use of the rhetorical situation, particularly focusing on these three primary elements, not only gives students a clear starting point, but it also equips them to meet some of the important academic standards in their lives as students.

The second important element in helping our students apply rhetoric to their reading and writing in any mode, not only the mode of sound, is the use of the three **rhetorical appeals**: ethos, pathos, and logos. Whether you ask students to use these Greek terms or simply be aware of the ideas behind them, these terms are important tools for understanding how an author goes about accomplishing their purposes with and constructing their arguments for their audience.

When reading, whether the author is asserting their credibility and personal trustworthiness in an **ethos** appeal, targeting their audience's emotions in a **pathos** appeal, or applying clear logic in a **logos** appeal, the three rhetorical appeals provide students with the clear language and ideas they need to discuss how and why an author makes the choices they make in their texts and for what purpose or argument. When writing, particularly in unfamiliar modes like sound, these appeals help students plan out how to approach the writing task with their audience, argument, and purpose in mind.

The rhetorical appeals will be particularly helpful when working with sound texts because they will help students understand the use of some of the elements of reading and writing that are unique to sound. Music is very often applied as a pathos device to generate particular emotions in a listener; however, particularly in the genre of hip-hop music, the ethos of the author or artist is often central to the genre, as the "authenticity" of the "rap artist persona" becomes one of the major draws of the music (Hess 297). In audio genres like news segments, podcasts, or radio advertisements, the voices of particular celebrities or experts in a field can lend credibility to a text. When writing sound texts, if students use their rhetorical skills to attempt to create a pathos appeal in order to generate a feeling of tension in their listeners, they'll need to think about how sound effects and particular tones of voice can be used to generate that appeal. The awareness of rhetorical appeals' uses, particularly in partnership with an understanding of the rhetorical situation, is an important part of reading and writing in any mode, but we hope that, as you continue reading, you'll see how it can pack a major punch when you pair it with sound texts.

TABLE 2.1: Overview of Rhetorical Appeals

Ethos *How credible is the author?*	**Pathos** *What feelings is the author hoping to create in the audience?*	**Logos** *What logical arguments or claims is the author making?*
• Author's Background/ Profession • Author's Experience • Author's Position or Role in the Situation • Example in a Radio Ad: The Law Offices of John M. Phillips	• Emotionally Loaded Language or Music • Personal Examples • Figurative Language • Examples in a Radio Ad: Pet Rescue.com Political Ad for the American Tea Party	• Facts • Statistics • Data • Information • Example in a Radio Ad: Town Fair Tire

Genre Awareness

From the Common Core to several NCTE position statements, most ELA institutions promote the importance of giving students intentional experience with a wide variety of genres for diverse rhetorical situations. Within the topic of teaching high school reading and writing, we explain a **genre** as a series of expectations for a particular text that is typically produced in response to a particular rhetorical situation or purpose. Generally, as Amy Devitt points out, "genres develop . . . because they respond appropriately to situations that writers encounter repeatedly" (576). For example, the genre of an argumentative essay is made up of norms or standards that have developed over time as we as a society have streamlined what is most effective for creating a thesis-driven, evidence-based argument. An argument needs to be made (that's the rhetorical purpose), and society has expectations for how this will be done (thus, the genre). As this rhetorical situation, and the responding essay, recur, these expectations formalize into conventions, or **genre norms**. Many creative, experimental essays deviate from these expected genre norms, but we have generally established this genre through our collective experience and expectations. For an example that falls within the mode of sound, the genre of a radio advertisement includes expectations for length and content based on what has successfully marketed products to listeners, setting the genre apart from other genres.

While an understanding of individual genres is important, our ultimate goal as educators is to support students in developing **genre awareness**. This involves asking them to be conscious of what genre norms exist in certain texts in different rhetorical situations and when authors will be more or less effective in deviating from those expected norms. When someone wants to share their personal narrative, how do they usually do it? When someone wants to advertise a new product, what patterns do they usually follow? What kind of texts do they usually create and why? What happens when a particular expectation is subverted or omitted? Does the text become more or less effective, and why? Kerry Dirk explains that genre awareness "is more important than mastering one particular genre" because it "helps us to recognize and determine appropriate responses to different situations" (259). This awareness allows students to notice genre patterns, including when genres blend, bend, and/or break, creating new ones altogether.

The mode of sound and genre awareness work closely with one another, and asking students to study sound texts in the classroom without some integration of genre awareness will put them at a disadvantage. Reading and writing using sound in particular is very closely tied to technology and media due to the nature of the mode and how we use and share it. Technology and media are constantly evolving, which means that sound texts themselves are also constantly evolving. This means that new sound genres are cropping up every day while many of the old, familiar ones are developing and changing. The genre of the podcast, which is one of the most significant and influential genres of sound text in our society today, wasn't even developed or named until the early 2000s ("What is Podcasting?"). If we're going to ask our students to read and write using sound, they'll need to have some kind of comfort level working with the idea of genre and how and why genres are created and then potentially subverted.

Conversely, if we're looking to help our students strengthen their ability to detect genre norms and to understand how different genres respond to situations in the world, the mode of sound has a lot to offer. Fortunately, because our students will almost definitely have some practical experience with sound texts like music, podcasts, and advertisements from their daily lives, most students will bring some genre awareness of sound texts into the classroom; this is hugely valuable and can be used to build more complex genre awareness skills. No matter how you slice it, genre awareness and reading and writing using sound are important to one another.

We've found in our own work that these two areas of theory, rhetoric and genre awareness, are not only deeply meaningful to students as they study sound, but they also pair together extremely well, supporting and informing one another in ways that make our classwork applicable and relevant to our students' academic and extracurricular lives. While it is of course possible to approach sound without explicitly addressing either of these areas of theory, we strongly recommend you use both together, not just because of what they can do for your students' work with sound texts but also because of what your students' work with sound texts can do for their skills in the areas of rhetoric and genre awareness.

Sound Specific Terminology and Theory

Rhetoric and genre awareness—being, in our opinion, critically important to reading and writing sound texts in the classroom—are not necessarily specific to the mode of sound. In this next section, we'd like to cover some theory and terminology that apply exclusively to sound texts.

Clarifying the Idea of the Author

With traditional texts, we most commonly refer to the writer or author of that text, and students are very familiar with what we mean by that. While those terms of writer and author still apply to both reading and writing sound texts, when we discuss the author of a sound text in particular, the wording we use may vary. While the most common way we refer to the author of a sound text, as you may have noticed, is using the word "speaker," we may also use a variety of other words depending on the particular genre of sound text we are discussing. For example, we generally refer to the author of a song as the "singer," the author of a podcast as the "host," or the author of an interview series as the "interviewer." These words all accurately reflect the role of the author in these respective sound texts.

To further complicate matters, just like in printed texts, there are some genres of sound texts in which the author and the speaker are not the same person. For example, in an audio drama or short conversation in a radio advertisement, the characters speaking are most likely not the authors who wrote that text. While these ideas may seem obvious, we recommend explicitly discussing these with your students when working with sound texts. This will help them and you keep track of who and what you are analyzing as you discuss the authors and speakers in complicated sound texts. In this book, we will also try to be as clear as possible in our language as we discuss these roles, occasionally calling attention to how and why we have chosen the terminology we did.

Sound Strategies

When having our students read and write using sound, one of the most important things to begin with is making sure they have the language and framework to meaningfully discuss and analyze the particular elements present in a sound text. While many traditional literary and textual elements can be found in sound texts (more on this later), there are certain elements that are unique to the mode of sound. In their 2016 webtext, "Navigating the Soundscape, Composing with Audio," Tanya Rodrigue et al. defined and named these elements as the **sound strategies** (see Table 2.2). The sound strategies are a set of five sound-specific elements or devices that are used to create sound texts; while not every sound strategy will be found in every sound text, understanding each individually will enable students to better interact with the sound texts we use.

"Navigating the Soundscape, Composing with Audio" by Rodrigue et al.

TABLE 2.2: The Five Sound Strategies (Rodrigue et al.)

Sound Effects	**Sound effects** are recorded sounds that are typically not vocal or musical but are instead isolated sounds that are usually environmental. Examples include the sound of tapping computer keys, a blaring car horn, or a door slamming shut. The main purpose of **sound effects** is to provide a sense of context or place against which a story or narration can unfold. For example, in an audio drama that takes place at a mall, **sound effects** including the busy chatter of shoppers, checkout register dings, or footsteps on tiled floors might create a sense of setting and environment. **Sound effects** can also trigger particular memories or associations. For example, in a podcast about the stress of academic life, the editors may use the **sound effect** of a stereotypical school's class-change bell to mark transitions in the podcast; if the podcast's listeners are likely to be current or past high school students, that sound can potentially trigger memories of rushing to a new class. In a podcast reflecting on school anxiety and pressure, this is a powerful association to create. **Sound effects** can also function to create mood or tone in a sound text. In an audio memoir of someone recounting a time they were walking alone in an alleyway at night, the **sound effect** of a single, echoing set of footsteps or a slow, steady drip of water might create an eerie, abandoned feel that contributes to the intensity of the memoir's narrative.
Music	**Music** is a powerful tool for creating "tone, atmosphere, setting, and/or transitions" (Rodrigue et al.). It can also "give us the ability to express things that are hard or impossible to say otherwise" (Rodrigue and Stedman 100). The emotive nature of **music** carries the ability to evoke strong emotional responses in listeners in ways that add meaning and depth. In some cases, **music** can also be used to transition between different sections in a sound text, as when podcasts use **music** to transition from the introduction and title into the main body of the podcast episode. Much like **sound effects**, **music** also has a strong ability to "make and create associations" in a listener's experience, quickly connecting a reader to a particular idea, mood, or place (Rodrigue and Stedman 103). Whether a central feature in a sound text, like a song, or a background element in a sound text, like a spoken word poem or audio drama, **music** has the ability to shape and direct an audience's response to the text as a whole.

Continued on next page

TABLE 2.2: Continued

Voice or Vocal Tones	**Voice** or **vocal tones** is one of the most accessible and influential strategies available to writers using sound. Not all vocalization in sound texts communicates words; for example, shouts, laughter, crying, or humming are vocalizations without words. However, **voice** and **vocal tones** is the only strategy through which words can play a role in sound texts, and so it is hugely significant. In this sound strategy, it is not just about what words are being said but who is saying them and how they are being said. When analyzing how voices function in sound texts, **vocal tones** are a way of considering how the **voice** is expressing itself. In an audio memoir, if the **voice** recounting a memory trembles slightly, it has a very different impact than if the **voice** were to speak the same words in an angry shout. The tone of a **voice** in a sound text can create emotional responses in listeners—intimacy, anxiety, fear, or joy.
Silence	**Silence** is one of the easiest sound strategies to overlook in a sound text, but the absence of noise can have a huge impact. It has the power to "create or break tension, establish structure, signal change, pose questions, and invite answers" (Rodrigue et al.). Consider the poignant **silence** of an unanswered question between lovers in an audio drama or of the long pause after an awkward comment in an interview. Rodrigue and Stedman observe that **silence** "can carry words, meaning, and emotions in the absence of sound" (115). These **silences** are anything but neutral, acting as devices that shape the meaning of the sound text. Additionally, **silence** as a sound strategy is particularly unique in its ability to "invite co-creation" from your listeners (Rodrigue and Stedman 119). By inserting a gap in the noise of a sound text, you offer "the listener the chance to create their *own* experience" (Rodrigue and Stedman 119). This invites the listener into the sound text in ways that shape their individual experiences with and interpretations of the text; it allows the listener to fill in the gaps, so to speak, with ideas, implications, and emotions that represent their experiences and identities. **Silence** can be a bit complex in that it is not always created by a complete absence of sound; for example, in an audio drama, a break in conversation between two characters may still include various **sound effects** in the background, perhaps to create setting, but the break in their words to one another could still be examined as a **silence**. What is most important about **silence** as a sound strategy is simply to remember its presence and to pay attention to what it creates in its listeners.
Layering	We list the sound strategy of **layering** last because it is a strategy that comes into play in a sound text when two or more of the above strategies in this list occur at the same time, interacting with one another. For example, if an emotionally strained male **voice** tells the story of the loss of his beloved while soft orchestral **music** plays in the background, this sound text is using the strategies of **voice** and **vocal tones** along with **music**, but the two strategies are also impacting one another, acting at the same time through the sound strategy of **layering**. The actor's **voice** is influenced by the instrumental **music** and vice versa; something is created by the interplay of the two strategies. This strategy allows authors of sound texts to creatively balance multiple elements at the same time: Conversation while environmental **sound effects** play or dramatic **silence** in conversation marked by the opening measures of a musical number. Sound texts can get complicated as their authors engage **layering** to intensify and deepen the meaning and impact of their texts.

We predict that, of all the theory and terminology in this chapter, you'll use these sound strategies the most when reading and writing using sound in your classrooms. Awareness of these strategies allows students to observe the choices authors of sound texts make and to consider these important choices in their own writing.

Sound Text Vocabulary

As you and your students discuss the sound strategies from the section above or the different qualities in the sound texts you read and write, it can be helpful to have a shared vocabulary to draw from. This not only promotes clear communication; it also empowers students to make more specific, insightful, and poignant observations and choices in their work with the mode of sound. In Table 2.3, we've identified and defined some key vocabulary terms that you may want to familiarize yourself and your students with so that you're able to competently and clearly discuss sound texts.

TABLE 2.3: Key Vocabulary When Working in the Mode of Sound

Balance	We use this word primarily to refer to volume, particularly when multiple sounds are **layered** over one another. This means that the listener should be able to hear and discern all the sounds **layered** in a single section; however, the primary sound or sounds are dominant because they are louder, communicating to the listener that they are the most significant. If background **music** plays beneath dialogue between two characters in an audio drama, we consider the volume balanced if we can hear the background **music** playing, but the words of the **voice** actors are prominent, louder, and easy to understand.
Clipping	This refers to when the audio that has been recorded is too loud and exceeds the capabilities of your equipment. This can cause distortion at the loudest points in the recording, or it can cause the audio to cut out entirely.
Fade In	This is when a recording or particular sound within a recording begins with **silence**, but the volume gradually increases to the intended volume. Most sound texts employ fade ins to ease listeners into new sounds or recordings and to avoid choppy editing.
Fade Out	Similar to a fade in, a fade out is when the volume of the sound text or particular sound within a sound text gradually decreases to **silence**. This generally marks the end of something.
Pitch	This has to do with the frequency of the sound wave that carries a particular noise. It determines how high or low a **voice** or **sound effect** or note sounds to a listener. A child's piercing scream has a high pitch while the rumbling notes of a bass guitar have a low pitch.
Reverb	This is the name for the phenomenon that occurs when sounds are made in an open space and sound waves travel out in all directions, slowly dying off as they travel and bounce off surrounding surfaces. Reverb can sound like a very short echo, and writers in the mode of sound often add reverb to their recordings to create a sense of depth or space. Unless an audio recording is completed in an effectively soundproofed room, most spaces will create some degree of reverb.
Tempo	This refers to the speed or pace at which a sound recording unfolds. This can refer to **music**, someone's speech, the rate at which a text transitions between different parts or sounds, or a wide range of elements.
Transition	These are about moving from one element to another. This can refer on a smaller scale to moving between multiple speakers or different sound strategies. On a larger scale, it can refer to the way a sound text moves between sections or parts. Transitions can be created in a myriad of ways, but the main idea is to communicate a change in setting, speaker, topic, rhetorical purpose, or anything else to the listener.

We don't include this sound-specific terminology and theory to overcomplicate studying and creating texts in the mode of sound. You may not rely heavily on these; working in the mode of sound is often more intuitive than people expect. However, we have found that having some basic framework and shared vocabulary to work with deepens and enriches our work in the mode of sound. Sometimes both we and our students find ourselves listening to a sound text or reading a sound text writing assignment and thinking, "What am I supposed to say about this?" or "Where am I supposed to start with this?" This chapter is about giving you and your students some starting points to draw from.

Conclusion

Chapter 2 Conclusion Audio

Chapter 2 Conclusion Transcript

3

The Fundamentals of Reading Sound Texts

Introduction

Chapter 3 Introduction Audio

Chapter 3 Introduction Transcript

Close Reading

When teaching reading, whether with traditional printed texts, images, or sound texts, one of the central tasks we ask students to engage in is close reading. We consider close reading to be the process of carefully reading and rereading a text in order to interpret its overall meaning through a deep and thorough analysis of its various components as well as how those components are assembled. Teaching students to perform a close reading on a text involves teaching them to identify and understand how the various elements of a text (diction, tone, literary devices, etc.) work together to create the overall meaning.

In order to successfully perform a close reading of a text, students require a variety of reading skills. An insightful close reading will require that students are aware of the genre in which they are reading, interpret literary devices, determine a theme, and other such skills. In the next section, we will discuss some of the core reading skills we believe are necessary to perform rigorous and engaging close readings in any mode.

Core Close Reading Skills

Although the Common Core Standards compile a list of nationally recognized reading skills that all students should practice, we have created our own list based on some broader categories and our own experiences with reading in the mode of sound with students (see Table 3.1).

In summary, we believe students need the first three skills (awareness of author's persona, awareness of audience, and identification of an argument) in order to be fully successful in the following three skills (awareness of genre, interpretation of literary devices, and awareness of organization and structure). We also believe that the identification of mood, tone, theme, and rhetorical appeals are most meaningful and thorough when students have some degree of mastery of the previous six skills.

TABLE 3.1: Core Close Reading Skills

1	Awareness of Author's Persona	The first three skills ask student readers to identify and interpret foundational rhetorical information about a text. These three components get at the main components of the rhetorical situation, which is why we begin with them.
2	Awareness of Audience	
3	Identification of an Argument	
4	Awareness of Genre	Once students have developed the skills that enable them to identify these primary rhetorical elements in a text, the next three skills will become much more accessible. Students will be able to see how authors make choices about which genre and literary devices to use or how to organize and structure their arguments based on their particular rhetorical situations. Certain genres, literary devices, or organization strategies are better suited to certain audiences, authorial roles, or arguments.
5	Interpretation of Literary Devices	
6	Awareness of Organization and Structure	
7	Identification of Mood	The final four skills are higher-level, big-picture skills that will require students to have some comfort with the six previous skills. In order to make the necessary inferences to interpret the overall mood and tone of a text, students will rely on an understanding of the genre, literary devices, and overall structure of the text. In order to identify a theme and analyze its development in a text, students will need to synthesize factors like tone, structural organization, and literary devices. Finally, identifying rhetorical appeals (ethos, pathos, and logos) will be possible for students when they are able to reflect on the elements of the rhetorical situation, the genre, any literary devices, and the overall organization of a text.
8	Identification of Tone	
9	Identification of Theme	
10	Identification of Rhetorical Appeals	

The analysis portion of all of these skills comes into play when you synthesize the skills and use them to build on one another. Students are able to identify tone by analyzing an author's persona, their use of literary devices, and the argument their text makes. Students will be able to develop an awareness of how an argument is organized and structured by analyzing the individual pieces that make up that argument, the author's target audience, and the way the author has chosen to deploy a particular genre of writing. So, although none of our skill categories begin with the word "analysis," we assure you that students will need to engage their analytical skills to the max if they are going to be able to use these skills in completing the reading activities we suggest.

We acknowledge that these skills are not specific to the mode of sound. This is intentional on our part; these are skills student readers need when reading in any mode. Our goal in the next section is to demonstrate how the mode of sound can uniquely develop these reading skills in ways students can apply across all of their reading practices. We will also consider how these skills function in sound texts in particular, noting where those functions are different and/or the same when compared to how they appear in traditional printed texts.

Let's Try It Out: A Close Reading of Jamila Lyiscott's "3 Ways to Speak English"

To help practically demonstrate how our ten reading skills apply when performing a close reading of a sound text, we're going to walk you through a close reading and analysis of the spoken word poem, "3 Ways to Speak English" by Jamila Lyiscott, emphasizing some of the approaches we use with our own students. This discussion is not formatted as a series of activities for use with students, so it is not directly ready for classroom use. (We have some ready-made activities coming up in the next chapter.) Before we dig into that, we want to demonstrate some of the ideas that will support the upcoming activities.

"3 Ways to Speak English" by Jamila Lyiscott

Our hope is that our discussion of Lyiscott's poem will demonstrate how reading sound texts integrates both traditional, literary reading practices and elements as well as sound-specific reading practices and elements, both of which work together to offer students new and engaging opportunities to develop their skills as dynamic and intuitive twenty-first-century readers. Additionally, you may notice that we've linked to a video of Lyiscott's performance of the poem; although her TED Talk includes the visual elements of her embodied performance, we recommend playing only the audio for students to prompt them to focus entirely on her use of sound in the piece.

You will notice that, when applying several of these close reading skills to Lyiscott's text, we have demonstrated how students will use many of the same strategies that we use in alphabetic texts, and also how students will be able to use sound-specific strategies to take full advantage of the mode's capabilities. Whenever applicable, we have created separate tables for traditional and sound-specific applications of these skills to emphasize some of the differences.

Skill 1: Awareness of Author's Persona

The importance of understanding the position and role of the author of a particular text is critical; it is a foundational understanding that readers use to make meaning of a text through close reading. We know that "authorial identity" might be a more common term for this idea, but identity is complicated and consists of elements that we can't often fully glean from a single text or even from several texts. Identity can integrate gender, racial background, cultural identifications, and a wide range of nuanced elements; we believe students should practice refraining from making assumptions about these things. Persona, on the other hand, is a term we feel more comfortable asking students to make inferences with. We consider an author's persona to be the role or **voice** they intentionally choose and project throughout a text. This may include elements of their identity, but it is the author's choice to emphasize elements of that identity when projecting their persona in a text. A skilled reader knows how and where to look for indications of an author's persona to help them understand the text more fully, and the mode of sound offers students unique ways to explore this skill.

When listening to Lyiscott's "3 Ways to Speak English," it may be tempting for students to make assumptions about her authorial identity based on some of the things she shares and the ways in which she shares them. A student may make an observation or statement about Lyiscott's gender, culture, or race. This can provide an opportunity for an educator to challenge whether or not we have the information we need to draw those conclusions. We encourage educators to direct student reflections regarding authorial persona by always asking, "Has the author given us what we need to assume that?"

As demonstrated in Table 3.2, students can use very traditional reading skills around supporting claims with evidence to practice this skill. However, we encourage students to use how the author speaks just as much as what the author says when choosing evidence to support their claims about authorial persona. Table 3.3 explores some of the options for reading Lyiscott's poem closely with an emphasis on the features of the text that are specific to the mode of sound.

With these observations around Lyiscott's position as an author of this text, students will be able to gain a deeper sense of her overall goals for and messages in this text. Lyiscott's role as a multicultural academic who has been penalized by Western, racially biased language practices gives her credibility and emotional sway as she proudly claims her linguistically diverse language skills and denounces the injustice of a system that would judge her for them.

TABLE 3.2: Examples of Close Reading for Persona in Lyiscott's "3 Ways to Speak English" Emphasizing Traditional Analysis

Evidence	**Discussion**
She references her professors and teaching (00:29, 2:20).	*This suggests that she's an academic, both a student at the college level as well as a professor herself.*
She describes some of her own dialects as "tainted with the connotation of urbanized suggestion" (00:29).	*This also identifies her as an individual who makes regular use of a dialect of the English language, indicating that her linguistic background will tell us something important about her persona and socio-cultural identity.*
She recounts a conversation with her father where he asks her, "Wha' kinda ting is dis?" (00:34).	*Lyiscott's use of Jamaican patois is a meaningful element of the text to discuss. However, both to avoid the practice of making assumptions about a speaker's identity based on their language usage as well as to support respectful and informed interpretations of Lyiscott's persona in the text, we encourage teachers to provide students with prereading materials both about the history of Jamaican patois as well as Lyiscott's own Jamaican heritage.*
She identifies herself as traditionally "intellectual" according to "Eurocentric ideals" (02:51) and uses words like "multifaceted" (1:51). She chooses an elevated and academic diction, and she also demonstrates her understanding of the grammatical rules around present participles.	*This further establishes her as a member of the academic community according to the Western standards she is questioning.*

TABLE 3.3: Examples of Close Reading for Persona in Lyiscott's "3 Ways to Speak English" Emphasizing Sound-Specific Analysis

Evidence	**Discussion**
When listening to the poem, students have the benefit of hearing Lyiscott shift seamlessly between her three dialects.	*Hearing her speak allows students to experience her linguistic fluidity and skill in ways that printed words could never achieve.*
Lyiscott's tone of ***voice*** *escalates in intensity throughout the poem, arguably culminating in her account of how her cultural language "was raped away, along with [her] history" (02:59). Her volume increases, her pitch lowers into a gravelly rumble, and she punctuates her enunciation.*	*This communicates generational rage and trauma, emphasizing the ways in which her lived experiences with linguistic and institutional racism have impacted her personally.*

Skill 2: Awareness of Audience

Understanding who a text is intended for or aimed at is another foundational close reading skill. Meghan Sweeney explains that, for students "to effectively read with audience awareness, [they] must consider how [and if] they are being written to and how their contexts and worldviews affect the uptake of the message" so that they can "adjust their reading processes based on their awareness of themselves as the intended or unintended audience" (66, 76). While some texts outright state their intended audience, it is much more common for students to have to deduce or infer the targeted recipient. Once readers have an idea of who a text is for, they will be able to read the author's choices with an understanding of the context, and this will guide them to interpret things like an author's tone, content, language, and various other considerations.

Lyiscott's text offers several opportunities for students to make inferences about her intended audience. While this is not an explicit element of the text itself, we know she performed this poem at a TED conference, which immediately gives us insight into her audience as being largely Western, somewhat educated, and having sufficient disposable income to attend a conference. If students were to consider the text outside of its rhetorical context, they could still glean information about her audience by considering her use of the pronoun "you." She refers to the audience as "you" on several occasions, positioning them as part of the Western academic system that has judged her. She includes lines like "You may think that it is ignorant to speak broken English" (1:16) and "Now, you may think that's too hood, that's not cool, but I'm here to tell you that even our language has rules" (01:35). By saying this, she places herself in opposition to the audience, demonstrating that, as an intellectual audience at a United States conference, she presumes that they are participants in a system that linguistically and racially discriminates against her.

Understanding that Lyiscott is sharing these anecdotes and this perspective with an audience that she perceives to be participants in the judgment and bias that has impacted her so significantly will help student listeners to interpret her tone and message. Additionally, Lyiscott's use of "you" provides students an opportunity to demonstrate an understanding of when the pronoun "you" refers to them as a reader and when it refers to an audience different from themselves; this distinction can drastically change how a student reads and engages with a text.

Skill 3: Identification of an Argument

While we understand that many philosophies separate argumentative, informational, and literary texts into different categories, we believe that all texts in all modes make arguments. While the traditional persuasive essay may explicitly state an author's argument or thesis, we believe that all the choices and messages authors infuse into their texts contribute to their underlying arguments and positions. Andrea A. Lunsford et al. express this in their aptly titled book *Everything Is an Argument* when they explain that "all language is *inherently* a form of argument" (viii). They posit that "language is a human activity and because humans exist in a complex world of goals, purposes, and activities, language cannot be anything *but* motivated" (viii). Novels like *The Great Gatsby* make important arguments about race, class, and gender. Songs like "This Is America" by Childish Gambino argue essential positions on political and social issues that Black Americans have faced and continue to face. Accordingly, we consider the skill of identifying the arguments in texts to be foundational to performing a successful and rigorous close reading of any text in any mode.

Lyiscott's poem, while it may not present a consolidated thesis statement that exists fully in a single line, makes a very clear argument for the value and ethical implications of diverse English dialects in the face of Western academia's long-standing tradition of racial, cultural, and economic bias. Lyiscott supports this central argument with anecdotes from her personal life, a comparison between British and American dialects of English, and a brief summary of historical and political forces that led to the way the English language is used in our present day. In identifying the argument of this poem, students should be able to essentially outline the core claims supporting Lyiscott's central argument, inventorying the different pieces of evidence she uses.

We should add that while we do differentiate between an author's purpose and their argument, acknowledging that they may be different in some cases, we don't always require students to do a full analysis of this difference. However, an extension activity that teachers may consider is to challenge students to take their assessment of a text's central argument and expand it into a claim regarding the author's purpose. This activity may require a student to refer to the prior skills (author's persona and audience awareness) as well.

If Lyiscott's argument centers on the idea that linguistic injustice in our country, particularly academia, continues a tradition of disadvantaging and abusing people of color, and if Lyiscott is addressing a largely Western intellectual audience whom she assumes adheres to traditional, problematic beliefs about the English language, and if Lyiscott is speaking as a linguistically diverse academic who has been limited by Western academia's racial and cultural biases, what do we think she hopes this poem achieves? What is her purpose for the poem? We would argue that Lyiscott is hoping to change mentalities and perspectives in the minds of her audience in ways that might impact the way they use and understand diverse English dialects in their daily lives, continuing a necessary movement pushing for linguistic justice and equity.

Skill 4: Awareness of Genre

When performing a close reading on any text, having a firm grasp of the genre in which you are reading is necessary for understanding an author's choices and an audience's expectations. Fostering real and practical understanding of the concept of genre in students can be extremely challenging. We want to avoid teaching students that genre is a list of static and arbitrary rules that a particular kind of writing follows, or a "a classification system . . . that names types of texts according to their forms" (Devitt 574). Instead, we want to help students understand genre as a dynamic pattern that emerges as a response to social behavior and rhetorical situations. Certain groups of people develop expectations around how they communicate with one another in certain contexts, and these expectations are repeated often enough to generate genres. This is why we place this skill after the previous three; once students learn to assess these foundational elements of the rhetorical situation (an author's role, their intended audience, and the argument they hope to make and/or the purpose they hope to achieve), they may be able to evaluate genre more meaningfully.

Reading in the mode of sound is particularly powerful for helping students grasp the concept of genre for a few reasons:

- There are many sound genres that have parallel genres in traditional alphabetic modes. This allows students to experience the core elements of a genre in different ways. Students can explore poetry through sound poems, novels through audio dramas or audiobooks, memoirs through audio memoirs, and many more. Developing a sense for what elements of the genre are essential in any mode and how those elements shift in different modes fosters a more complex and genuine understanding of that genre.
- There are several genres that exist only in the mode of sound. Things like songs, radio advertisements, and banter-based talk-show podcasts offer fairly unique genre expectations that don't often appear in other modes. Experiencing, reading, and analyzing genres that are isolated to a particular mode will offer students the unique experience of understanding how genres develop in different modes.
- Finally, because of the particularly relevant nature of sound texts, students are more likely to have already existing knowledge surrounding the context of a sound text. Genres evolve out of certain social and cultural contexts. Rhetorical information surrounding the events, cultural references, individuals, and movements that give rise to a particular

sound text are most likely going to be more accessible and interesting to students. For example, analyzing a podcast by a student's favorite athlete discussing a sport they love and a major game they recently watched is going to help students understand particular genre choices in this podcast. Students are less likely to have that high of a degree of contextual knowledge around some traditional print genres like poetry, essays, or novels.

When analyzing Lyiscott's spoken word poem, there are two different elements of genre awareness that are relevant for students to consider (see Table 3.4).

TABLE 3.4: Examples of Close Reading for Genre Norms in Lyiscott's "3 Ways to Speak English" Emphasizing Traditional Analysis

<table>
<tr><th colspan="2">Meeting Genre Norms</th><th colspan="2">Subverting Genre Norms</th></tr>
<tr><th>Evidence</th><th>Discussion</th><th>Evidence</th><th>Discussion</th></tr>
<tr><td>Lyiscott uses a Biblical allusion to the God of Genesis (02:03).</td><td rowspan="6">Lyiscott's poem integrates many of the traditional genre norms of poetry. She often speaks rhythmically, repeats certain words and motifs, uses figurative language, and intermittently relies on rhyme. Many of the genre expectations that students will be exploring regarding the genre of poetry will be strengthened by reading this poem.</td><td rowspan="5">Lysicott is performing her poem at a TED Talk conference.</td><td rowspan="5">TED Talks are traditionally expected to be lectures or speeches. However, just as the message of her poem challenges our expectations of what is considered academic or culturally valuable, her choice to share her message through a poem as opposed to the expected and more traditionally academic genre of a lecture also challenges those same expectations. Understanding her unexpected choice of genre in this particular context may lead to a deeper and more nuanced understanding of her argument and purpose.</td></tr>
<tr><td>She uses simile to compare accidentally choosing an unintentional dialect in her code-switching to "cooking in the bathroom" (02:33).</td></tr>
<tr><td>The word "raped" takes on a metaphorical meaning (3:03, 3:30).</td></tr>
<tr><td>The word "articulate" is repeated eight times throughout the piece.</td></tr>
<tr><td rowspan="2">Several of Lyiscott's rhyme schemes are most noticeable in the audio mode, as she emphasizes them with her rhythm and intonation.</td></tr>
<tr><td>In her poem, Lysicott moves between three diverse dialects of English.</td><td>Generally, poems have one language or dialect, sometimes two; it's not the norm for poems to include more than that and to do so as frequently as Lysicott does. Analyzing this unexpected, frequent change of dialects will allow students to gain a deeper meaning from her poem.</td></tr>
</table>

Asking students to consider these aspects of genre in Lyiscott's poem will strengthen and challenge their concept of genre as well as their ability to interpret the meaning and message behind her text.

Skill 5: Interpretation of Literary Devices

The term *literary devices* covers a dauntingly large span of literary techniques, elements, strategies, and constructions. When working with students, instead of getting into the weeds with categories and terminology, we try to emphasize literary devices conceptually as intentional choices or what Lindsay Illich and Melissa Alter Smith refer to as "moves" that an author makes with their words, meaning, or form that deepen, complicate, or nuance the interpretation(s) of their text. We believe that noticing when an author makes an interesting, powerful, or unexpected choice or "move" and being able to deduce meaning from that choice is more important to the quality and depth of a close reading than knowing the names of different terms. So, while we may mention certain terms as we discuss how the mode of sound can teach students to recognize and interpret literary devices in new and creative ways, we won't be getting too technical in that area; however, we wholeheartedly support teachers who do.

There are a number of literary devices in Lyiscott's poem that students would benefit from analyzing when performing a close reading as shown in Tables 3.5 and 3.6.

Discussing these choices, where they appear, what they mean, and why Lyiscott made them is an essential practice in close reading. We believe it is deeply important students understand that devices can be used as strategies in a variety of ways in differing modes and genres, and experiencing and discussing them across modes and genres can give students new perspectives on how to interpret them.

TABLE 3.5: Examples of Close Reading for Literary Devices in Lyiscott's "3 Ways to Speak English" Emphasizing Traditional Analysis

Evidence	***Discussion and Analysis***
Lyiscott uses a Biblical allusion to the God of **Genesis** *(02:03).*	*This contributes to her depiction of a Western Eurocentric center of power as a source of authority and influence for both her and her audience.*
She uses simile to compare accidentally choosing an unintentional dialect in her code-switching to "cooking in the bathroom" (02:33).	*This captures her sense of disorientation and confusion when she makes a mistake navigating her multiple dialects in different contexts and situations.*
The word "raped" takes on a metaphorical meaning (3:03, 3:30).	*Through this metaphorical use of the word, Lyiscott conveys a sense of intimate personal violence inherent in Western discrimination around language and culture, at least as she is expressing it.*
The word "articulate" is repeated eight times throughout the piece.	*The repetition returns the listeners to this culturally and socially charged word, challenging them to consider what it truly means as her message unfolds.*

TABLE 3.6: Examples of Close Reading for Literary Devices in Lyiscott's "3 Ways to Speak English" Emphasizing Sound-Specific Analysis

Evidence	***Discussion and Analysis***
Several of Lyiscott's rhyme schemes are most noticeable in the audio mode, as she emphasizes them with her rhythm and intonation.	*There is not a consistent rhyme scheme throughout the poem, so when a rhyme does appear, there is value in debating why Lyiscott chose to place it where and when she did, something that is much easier to recognize and dissect when listening to the piece.*
As mentioned earlier, her repetition of the words "articulate" and "raped" is important to understanding the poem's overall meaning. She most commonly accentuates the word "articulate" with a brief pause, a silence, before and after. These pauses are repeated alongside each use of the word. When pronouncing the word "raped," she increases volume and lowers pitch.	*It would be difficult for students to fully understand Lyiscott's intent for the words without considering how she pronounces them; students may miss the connotations of violence and pain that her* ***voice*** *and vocal qualities bring to the words. These sound qualities are an essential component of the device in her poetry.*
Lyiscott's use of pacing and speed in her speech is also an important device. She accelerates her language and enunciation to speak rapidly during the most emotionally and conceptually intense portions of her poem, pausing and shifting tone abruptly at the line, "That's why I put trilingual on my last job application" (03:47). She juxtaposes the intense, emotive tone of the prior lines with her casual, comedic delivery of this line, indicating a sudden tone shift.	*This juxtaposition in tone is predominantly emphasized by the audio mode and would be much less noticeable if the poem were to be printed in alphabetic form. The shift breaks the building tension in the poem and begins the conclusion of her message and text.*

If you and your students are up for a challenge in your close reading of the literary devices in sound texts, it can be an interesting exercise to explore the idea of how the sound strategy of **sound effects** and occasionally **music** can function as symbols. We define the literary device of a symbol as something that stands for or represents something else. Most often, the symbol is less abstract than the idea or thing that it represents. When a **sound effect** or piece of **music** functions as a symbol in a sound text, it can stand for or represent a more complicated memory, object, or idea. For example, in a podcast discussing the topic of high school dating, a loud kissing **sound effect** played dramatically in the background can act as a symbol for the sometimes comically complicated world of high school romance. It is not literally capturing a kiss taking place as the narrator speaks; it represents the larger idea of dating. In an audio memoir recounting an elected official's time serving their country, playing the **music** of the national anthem acts as a symbol representing the complicated ideals of patriotism and honor that often accompany political service. It carries additional, more complicated meaning for listeners who recognize the symbolic nature of the song. Analyzing particular sounds as symbols in a sound text is a high-order reading task, and we expect students to need a good amount of support to understand this concept should you decide to integrate it; however, it is definitely an aspect of close reading that is entirely unique to sound texts.

In Lyiscott's poem, we could argue that her use of the word "articulate" functions as a symbol. While she is using the literal meaning of the word, she is also vocally accentuating it and employing it to stand in for the long history of Western culture holding racially biased standards for diverse dialects of the English language. She is alluding to and representing the socially, culturally, and racially charged significance behind that word that has been the source of significant pain, misrepresentation, and discrimination for people of color in the United States. Her enunciated and intentional pronunciation of the word itself is a less complicated sign standing in for an extremely complicated concept and legacy, making it a sound symbol.

Skill 6: Awareness of Organization and Structure

The goal of this skill is to prompt students to "perceive the meaningful relations between information units . . . in a text" in order to identify and assess how a text is "organized on a global level" (Bogaerds-Hazenberg et al. 434). Is the thesis in the beginning, middle, or end of the piece? Is the thesis explicitly stated or implied throughout? In what order are the supporting claims arranged, and why? What strategies or devices does the author use to introduce the argument, to transition between different parts, or to conclude the text, and why? If students have taken the time to evaluate the purpose of a text, how does this arrangement serve the author's overall purpose? Student readers who are able to use questions like these to mentally organize the information in a particular text are going to have more coherent and complex understandings of those texts (Bogaerds-Hazenberg et al. 434). Questions like these are also related closely to genre, as certain genres in all modes have expected standards for organization and structure. It is worthwhile for a student to note when a text follows along with or innovates those standards, perhaps employing unusual chronology or an unexpected thesis placement.

This aspect of close reading remains similar for sound texts as it does for traditional printed texts. The central task is still to understand the shape and structure of the text, what the individual components are, and how those components are arranged. What may differ is that, in addition to considering the content of the words and their locations and arrangements in the text, students will also need to consider the sound strategies. If **music**, **sound effects**, or pointed **silence** appear in the sound text, where are they located? What sounds and words surround them? How do they contribute to the organization of ideas? Are they being used to transition between ideas or conclude the text as a whole?

The goal is still to consider and understand the organization of the text, but the tools at students' disposal as they do so include the sound strategies in addition to any words in the text.

In analyzing the structural organization of Lyiscott's poem, we would direct students to observe how she opens with a series of personal anecdotes exploring different elements of her identity, all circling around the concept of being "articulate." This escalates in the second half of the poem into a more direct and explicit argument about the results of colonialism and Eurocentrism on Lyiscott's personal life and the broader culture. Her argument climaxes near the end of the poem, after which Lyiscott resolves her poem with a demonstration of her "trilingual" ability and a return to the word "articulate." Her organization of her content intensifies and presents her main message in progressively accusatory and frank tones, speeding toward a somewhat abrupt resolution that returns to the idea with which she opened, ending with a notable shift in tone, returning to the casual and conversational mood from the beginning.

Considering this arrangement will allow students to meaningfully interpret a variety of textual elements, like the development of a central argument or theme, her intent or purpose for the piece, and how she would like to position herself as an author relative to her audience.

Skill 7: Awareness of Mood

Mood refers to the feelings the author's choices in the text create in the reader or "the atmosphere that the author creates [for the reader] through their word choices, style, and use of imagery" along with other literary devices (Öhman and Rossi 1). In sound texts, while visual elements like punctuation and syntax are not available the way they are in alphabetic texts, many of these traditional elements will still be present to support analysis of mood. Analysis of elements like diction, point of view, style, and literary devices is still available to students.

However, in addition to these traditional elements, mood in sound texts will also include the particular sounds in the text itself. This can involve all five of the sound strategies. **Sound effects, music, voice and vocal tones, silence,** and **layering** can each play an important role in creating the mood of a sound text. For example, in an audio drama horror story, the **sound effect** of a howling wolf can create a spooky, haunted mood. In a radio advertisement, the use of mournful instrumental **music** may create an emotional, sympathetic mood in the listener in order to prime them for an emotionally charged appeal. In a speech, the way the speaker uses their **voice** to project and rally listeners can create a feeling of inspiration and hopefulness in their audience. The **silence** on the other end of a phone call in an audio drama can create an ominous or anxious feeling in the listener. All of these sound strategies can work together to create an overall mood for the audience; students will gain a richer understanding of mood when analyzing traditional elements and sound strategies together.

Students will be able to analyze both traditional and sound-specific choices in Lyiscott's "3 Ways to Speak English" in order to decipher and construct a claim about the mood of the piece.

TABLE 3.7: Examples of Close Reading for Mood in Lyiscott's "3 Ways to Speak English" Emphasizing Traditional Analysis

Evidence	Discussion and Analysis
The pronoun "you" is used to address the audience.	*This makes the audience feel separate from her.*
The diction choice of repeating the word "raped."	*This, coupled with the separation from her audience, creates a shameful and guilt-ridden mood.*
Lysicott implores her audience to "pay attention" (0:30).	*This creates a sense of urgency and responsibility within the audience.*

When analyzing the sound strategies in Lysicott's poem in order to determine mood, students will focus primarily on her **voice** *and vocal qualities as well as her use of* **silence***, demonstrated in Table 3.8.*

TABLE 3.8: Examples of Close Reading for Mood in Lyiscott's "3 Ways to Speak English" Emphasizing Sound-Specific Analysis

Evidence	Discussion and Analysis
Lyiscott spits out the word "raped," allowing a moment of brief ***silence*** *before and then directly after the line, "as has been raped away from our people" (3:27) Her softer, slower pace of speech as she delivers this line invites the audience to join her in a literal moment of* ***silence****.*	*While the diction choices can be analyzed traditionally, they cannot be fully understood without considering the tone of* ***voice*** *in which she says them. The way in which she says "raped" here accentuates the painful and arguably guilty mood of the text. The pacing of this section also creates a mood of mourning for what she and others have lost.*
Lyiscott shares her anecdotes about correcting her professor for using the wrong dialect when he "comes on the block" (1:25), and her mother when "Mommy mocks [her]" with an English dialect that reflects their culturally diverse home life, she corrects both respectively by saying "No" with a short, loud, high-pitched tone of ***voice*** *(1:28, 1:46).*	*Her* ***voice*** *communicates comedy and a mood of playful mocking. This invites the audience to participate in Lyiscott's incredulous chuckling at the arbitrary and subjective nature of laws and "correctness" in English dialects.*

Taking the time to assess the mood of Lyiscott's poem will stretch students' understanding of what it means to make a claim about readers' emotional responses in individual lines of the poem as well as how those lines work together to create an

overall sense of mood for the poem. By developing an awareness of how both traditional and sound-specific elements create the mood of Lysicott's poem, students are able to gain a deeper understanding of their role as a reader, demonstrating students' emotional responsibility that the author is giving them and enabling them to perform the essential task of a close reading with integrity and skill.

Skill 8: Awareness of Tone

While mood refers to the feelings a text creates within the audience, tone refers to the author's feelings and how the author makes choices to "convey their own attitude towards a topic or subject" in that text (Öhman and Rossi 1). We consider determining the tone of a text to be more difficult when reading than identifying the mood because, while identifying mood may ask students to reflect on, assess, and analyze their own emotional responses or the author's intent for their reader responses, a study of tone prompts students to look outside themselves as readers. Identifying tone involves a form of perspective-taking in which students use an author's choices to more deeply understand an author's position and emotions regarding a text's topic and content.

While many of the close reading strategies used to determine mood and tone in a piece may be the same, the information that readers should be looking for when becoming aware of the tone of a text will be different. Of course, traditional elements will still be helpful; however, like mood, the tone of a sound text will be greatly impacted by the author's use of sound strategies. For example, a podcast or audio memoir recounting a personal anecdote about a difficult conversation may use the **sound effect** of a door slamming to communicate the author's sensation of being left behind or ignored. The choice to play intense, foreboding **music** underneath a radio public service advertisement authored by a substance abuse awareness group may communicate the seriousness with which that organization views this issue. The way a political speaker uses their **voice** in a public speech will provide important cues as to their feelings on the subject matter in their text. In an interview, a long, **silent** pause after a personal, invasive question can communicate that the interviewee feels uncomfortable or unsure of what to say. All of these sound strategies can also work together to create a sense of the author's tone in their text. Students who are reading to determine tone in a sound text will need to consider both the traditional elements used to assess tone as well as the impact of the sound strategies.

In Lyiscott's "3 Ways to Speak English," students will be able to use both generalized and sound-specific choices to decipher the tone of the piece.

TABLE 3.9: Examples of Close Reading for Tone in Lyiscott's "3 Ways to Speak English" Emphasizing Traditional Analysis

Evidence	***Discussion and Analysis***
Her repetitive use of the word "raped" throughout the poem.	*Lyiscott's diction choices are powerful in creating tone. With this particular choice, she communicates the sense of violation and violence that she feels regarding Western influences on her culture and linguistic heritage.*
Lyiscott's use of first-person point of view in the poem in tandem with the pronoun "you."	*This works to create an accusatory tone and suggest her sense of feeling wronged by and isolated from the larger Western academic network in which this conference was taking place.*

Again, the primary sound strategies available to listeners looking to interpret the tone of Lyiscott's poem are ***voice*** *and* ***vocal tones*** *along with* ***silence****. Table 3.10 demonstrates how students may analyze her strategic use of these sound strategies.*

TABLE 3.10: Examples of Close Reading for Tone in Lyiscott's "3 Ways to Speak English" Emphasizing Sound-Specific Analysis

Evidence	***Discussion and Analysis***
Lyiscott intensifies the impassioned, fierce tone of the piece as she shares how her cultural language patterns have been "raped away, along with [her] history" (2:59). As she says these words, her volume increases, and her ***voice*** *takes on a breathless, ardent, rumbling texture.*	*This generates a tone of emotional intensity and distress that escalates.*
Her ***vocal tone*** *abruptly softens, and she quietly says, "I'm so tired" (3:09), which she follows with a brief but poignant pause.*	*We would prompt students to consider how the contrast in Lyiscott's volume and* ***vocal tone*** *in these two pieces of evidence work together with the brief silence to powerfully create the tone of fatigue and pain in her piece, giving us insight into her emotional responses to some of the complicated and personal issues her poem addresses.*

Taking the time to identify, analyze, and understand an author's perspective and feelings in a particular text is not only critical to a thorough close reading, but it is also an important component of becoming empathetic and intentional readers who can hear the ***voices*** *of all authors.*

Skill 9: Identification of Theme

When making claims identifying a theme in a particular text and how that theme develops, students will want to consider a wide range of factors, including relevant genre norms, literary devices, the way a text is assembled, the rhetorical situation, the tone, and the mood of a piece. In the words of Zach Wright, "theme is slippery," and students need scaffolded support to feel confident in building this skill. We consider theme to be a universal message the author is constructing about humanity over the course of their text, a particular position on the human condition that the author wants the audience to reflect on and analyze after reading the piece. Asking students to make a claim identifying a theme in a text as well as how that theme develops is an excellent way to have students demonstrate the culmination of their analytical close reading skills.

Because a particular text can have multiple potential themes, this also provides an interesting opportunity for students to construct arguments around their individual readings of texts. Different students may identify differing, potentially even contradictory, themes. Engaging in discussion and argumentation around which themes exist, which are central and primary, which are perhaps secondary or localized to a particular excerpt of the text, and how those various themes unfold can be a powerful activity for students looking to practice intentional and rigorous close reading supported by textual evidence.

While it would be possible to identify and defend a variety of different themes in Lyiscott's poem, one that we think is primary and central would be the theme of how the power of language can become a tool of oppression.

TABLE 3.11: Examples of Close Reading for Theme in Lyiscott's "3 Ways to Speak English" Emphasizing Traditional Analysis

Evidence	***Discussion and Analysis***
Lyiscott frustratedly questions in her class, "Yo! Why dese books neva be about my peoples?" (0:57). She also regularly uses the pronoun "you."	*Lyiscott's addressing of her audience as "you" not only creates an accusatory tone but also establishes an othering or sociocultural separation that has taken place between "[her] peoples" and the audience as a result of the misuse of language's power and influence.*
Lysicott uses a figurative repetition of the word "raped."	*This furthers the thematic idea, communicating that language has been a harmful, oppressive, and violent force in her life and her communities.*
When considering Lyiscott's organization of her poem, she opens with anecdotes surrounding her own personal oppressions in her daily life and academic experiences, expands to a larger and more comprehensive observation on "broken English" (1:16), escalates to her desire for justice and knowledge in "every suburbia, and every hood" (2:01), finally culminating in a broader indictment of "your history" (2:44) and "the Eurocentric ideals of this season" (2:51). In the climax of intensity in her poem, she expands her use of the personal pronoun "I" to the more inclusive "our" when she claims "our current state is not a mystery" (3:07).	*As the organization of her claims and appeals escalates, Lyiscott indicates that her theme begins with her identification of how language has been used to oppress her personally and then progressively expands throughout the poem to develop the theme of language's power to oppress whole people groups throughout history.*

TABLE 3.12: Examples of Close Reading for Theme in Lyiscott's "3 Ways to Speak English" Emphasizing Sound-Specific Analysis

Evidence	*Discussion and Analysis*
We've previously discussed how, when pronouncing the word "raped," Lysicott's volume and pitch communicate connotations of pain and violence.	*We'd expect students to analyze how these choices help develop the idea that language can and has been used to oppress and harm her community.*
Considering Lyiscott's overall organization and structure of her poem is something that can be done using sound-specific features as well as more traditional content like the previous list describes. As Lyiscott opens with anecdotes, her tone of ***voice*** *is casual and her pace of speech is leisurely. The enunciation and tension in her* ***vocal tones*** *increases as she moves on to discuss the wider, more comprehensive impacts of language discrimination in her community. Her volume increases. At the height of intensity in her poem, her volume is at its loudest, her pace of speech is at its most rapid, and her enunciation is at its most pointed and jarring.*	*Her theme of the potential language has to oppress, particularly as she has seen it function in her life and community, develops clearly as her vocal delivery intensifies throughout the arc of her poem. With each new sphere of influence discriminatory language practices impact, Lyiscott's* ***voice*** *intensifies until she is fiercely claiming injustices committed against her people.*

By reading to identify a theme and how an author develops it, students are able to synthesize many of the prior reading skills. Theme also allows students to take a powerful message and meaning of the text and apply it to their future readings and their ideas about the world.

Skill 10: Identification of Rhetorical Appeals

In our opinion, the rhetorical appeals represent one of the most basic and foundational ways to identify and assess the overall function of a text and how it is behaving within its rhetorical situation. Andrea A. Lunsford and John J. Ruszkiewicz emphasize how these appeals have allowed students to meaningfully interpret complicated and nuanced texts for almost two millennia now (6). This skill will require that students lean on their understanding of the rhetorical situation, genre, various literary devices, overall structure, tone, mood, and theme in the piece. These will all work together to give readers the skills they need to identify intentional rhetorical appeals.

When identifying rhetorical appeals, much like tone, mood, and theme, particular excerpts, strategies, or lines within a text may rely on different individual appeals, but generally, a text as a whole will employ an overall primary rhetorical appeal. When asking students to identify and evaluate the rhetorical appeals within a text, we can ask them to make claims about either one!

Lyiscott's poem makes a variety of smaller rhetorical appeals in individual lines. As you read the analyses below, notice we are integrating evidence and cues that are both specific to the mode of sound as well as those that are not. Table 3.13 demonstrates how these cues work together.

TABLE 3.13: Examples of Close Reading for Rhetorical Appeals in Lyiscott's "3 Ways to Speak English" Integrating Traditional and Sound-Specific Analysis

Evidence	***Appeal***	***Discussion and Analysis***
She includes a variety of personal anecdotes, uses the "I" pronoun, and demonstrates her native fluency with a variety of English dialects	Ethos	*Lyiscott is asserting her credibility as someone who has personal, firsthand experience navigating the complexities of the racial, social, and cultural forces that govern the use of the English language.*
She remarks that "even 'articulate' Americans sound foolish to the British" (1:19).	Logos	*Here, she logically points out that our use of the English language is governed by human use and power.*
She also uses a hypothetical scenario of her professor using a traditional, standardized variety of English "on the block" (1:25) and sounding incorrect in the context of that different rhetorical situation. She points out that "even our language has rules" (1:38).	Logos	*She is logically arguing for the validity, scholarly value, and cultural significance of all English dialects.*
Around two minutes into her poem, Lyiscott escalates the intensity of her poem to a series of impassioned pathos appeals, delivered in a powerful, confident ***voice*** *and punctuated with intentional pauses. She claims a desire to "sing this from every mountaintop" (1:57), referring to her belief in the equality of all English dialects. Her speech increases in speed. Her lines become shorter, and her rhyme scheme becomes more intentional and rhythmic, creating a sense of momentum. She shares her personal emotions when code-switching and using a language that she "had to borrow . . . because [hers] was stole" (2:37). The emotional climax of her poem culminates in her emotional delivery and spitting enunciation of the words describing how her language "was raped along with [her] history. I speak broken English so the profusing gashes can remind us that our current state is not a mystery" (3:07). Her cacophonous delivery of these lines resonates with rage and pain before she abruptly transitions to the comparatively gentle and quietly spoken line, "I'm so tired" (3:10).*	Pathos	*Her desire to generate feelings of guilt, empathy, and anguish in her audience is clear as she allows the readers to experience the torrent of emotions that she associates with the Western use of the English language.*
She tells a story about how she "put 'tri-lingual' on her last job application" (3:47). The recording includes the quiet chuckles from the audience. She remarks that all three of her English dialects can help "diversify [their] consumer market" (3:53).	Patho, Logos, Ethos	*Her intonation clearly communicates that this is intended to be received as a joke, and her audience's laughter confirms this. She logically suggests that the variety in her English dialects allows her to communicate with various people, bringing more to the workplace. She asserts her credibility when she fluently demonstrates her ability to greet people in all three dialects.*
She closes on a pointed and poignant claim that she is "articulate" (4:09)	Pathos	*As she ends, she reminds the audience that the fantastically inspirational, devastating, and brilliant poem they have just witnessed came from a creator who has been systematically discriminated against by the way she and her community use the English language.*

Students can and probably will have varying opinions surrounding which lines rely primarily on which appeals, as many of these strategies and devices employ a combination of rhetorical appeals at any given time. This can make for incomparably valuable discussion in which students debate and defend their choices. The evidence they can and should use will span the entirety of the nine prior skills, considering who Lyiscott presents herself to be as an author, whom she is addressing, what argument she makes in service of what purpose, what genre she chooses to communicate her message, what literary devices she engages and how she does so, how she organizes and structures her argument, what tone she expresses, what mood she creates, and what overall theme her poem constructs and develops.

Ultimately, students should work toward a claim of what central rhetorical appeal this poem relies on. While the poem engages all three appeals at different times, which appeal is central? We would argue that Lyiscott's central appeal is a pathos one, intended to generate feelings of guilt, empathy, and passion for justice in the listeners. While logos and ethos appeals both exist, we argue that these exist to support the overall generation of these feelings in the audience, making pathos the primary appeal.

Conclusion

Chapter 3 Conclusion Audio

Chapter 3 Conclusion Transcript

4

How to Design Reading Activities Using Sound Texts

Introduction

Chapter 4 Introduction Audio

Chapter 4 Introduction Transcript

Choosing the Right Sound Text to Read

When you're designing a reading activity in any mode, one of the most significant decisions is choosing the text you and your students will be reading and using to practice the particular skills you are targeting. Reading activities in the mode of sound are no different. Because sound texts have their own unique characteristics and various genre norms, there are a few unique considerations to keep in mind as you make your choice!

Look for Transcripts

There are so many sound texts that come with ready-made alphabetic transcripts that it is a good idea to check if the sound text you are choosing offers that option. Most well-known songs, speeches, interviews, and podcasts will offer some form of transcript. Transcripts as an accompaniment to sound texts not only promotes accessibility and inclusivity for a wider range of students, but it also offers an organic way for students to experience the way the meaning of a text changes across different modes.

Regardless of whether or not the students you work with would rely on a transcript to fully access the meaning of the sound text you've chosen, all students benefit from the experience of reading transcripts alongside sound texts and engaging in discussions around what is gained and lost in each mode and how each mode reflects the content of the text differently. We are always interested to hear students share whether they emotionally and/or intellectually connected more with alphabetic transcripts or sound files; the resulting debates and discussions are treasure troves of firsthand learning about multimodal meaning making.

If you have a sound text you're particularly passionate about, but you can't find an accompanying transcript, don't despair! That text may still be the perfect choice for teaching reading skills in your class! In cases like these, depending on the needs of your class and the role the text plays in your overall unit, we recommend assigning the task of writing a transcript for the sound text. While this does blur the lines between reading and writing activities, students have to very carefully listen, analyze, and *read* the sound text they are transcribing before they can begin the task of creating a meaningful transcript. See the QR code for a link to a transcript-writing assignment we've created for you to use with your students.

Transcript-Writing Assignment

This can be an optional activity, group work, or a whole-class collaborative undertaking. We love having different small groups work to create their own transcripts of the same sound text so that we can come back together as a class to compare what each group created; students learn so much about modes and reading sound texts by exploring how and what the various transcripts created by their classmates capture and omit. Whether or not a particular sound text has a transcript to go with it shouldn't be the only determining factor for its usefulness in the classroom, but it's a valuable element to consider when choosing texts as well as how you plan to use those texts. No matter how you approach it, "transcripts of audio work hold equal value and weight to the original piece," and we believe firmly that integrating them alongside your sound reading work will only benefit students (Artz et al.)

Consider Unit Context

As with choosing texts to read in any mode, the roles those texts play in the larger classroom unit are going to be important factors. The way a particular text, in the mode of sound or not, fits into a unit will depend on a few different questions.

- What genre is your class reading?

Sound texts can be powerful supplementary tools to explore genre within a larger unit. For example, if your class is reading a memoir and developing an understanding of the rhetorical goals and genre norms of that memoir, choosing an audio memoir, such as a story from NPR's *Moth Radio Hour* or a clip of an author-narrated audio recording of their memoir, can launch important conversations about that genre.

Both Joy Harjo's memoir *Crazy Brave* and Trevor Noah's *Born a Crime* exist as traditional printed books; however, both texts also offer author-narrated audiobook versions. In these audiobooks, both authors reflect on their personal experiences as rhetorical speakers in important ways. Joy Harjo, also a musician and a poet, sings some of the traditional Muscogee (Creek) Nation songs and poetry from the book. Trevor Noah moves expertly between different accents, languages, and dialects as he reenacts significant interactions with family members and friends from his multicultural childhood, adding dimension and complexity to his memoir that cannot be accessed through the printed version. Reading these sound texts as part of a unit exploring the genre of a memoir will allow students to understand the nature and role of the genre, and the principle of genre in general, with much greater practicality and depth.

If you want to review some of the options available for sound texts in these different genres, check out our sound text library, organized by genre!

Sound Text Library

These options exist when reading a wide range of genres typically seen in the high school ELA classroom. Persuasive essays pair well with argumentative podcasts; poetry often can and should be performed orally; narrative genres like short stories or novels can be accompanied by immersive audio dramas with **sound effects** and **voice** acting. See the QR code in the margin for our Sound Text Library organized by genre or you can refer to the list of audio genres in Table 1 from 'Before We Get Started'. When designing reading activities using sound texts in your classroom, targeting a particular genre can be an excellent place to start.

- What topics is your class studying?

Something we love about sound texts is that they are wildly diverse and cover a bottomless range of topics and disciplines. Reading a fictional novel that features Latin American magical realism? NPR's *All Things Considered* offers an excellent, five-minute clip of reporter Katie Davis's 1984 interview with magical realist author Gabriel García Márquez, **layered** with recordings of Márquez's **voice** answering some of Davis's questions. Working on dystopian fiction by Ray Bradbury or Aldous

Interview with Gabriel García Márquez

"Concerning AI Ethics"

Huxley? The MIT (Massachusetts Institute of Technology) Review puts out a podcast called *In Machines We Trust* that explores developments of artificial intelligence in the average person's daily life; their episode "Concerning AI Ethics" is around twenty minutes long and perfect for asking students to consider the implications of robotics, technology, and morality in our current world.

You name it, and sound texts will cover it. From historical persons of interest to current events to historical eras to political topics to anything else you can think of, sound texts are a powerful way to bring rhetorical context and supporting information to any classroom unit.

- What **voices** and narratives is your curriculum design supporting?

"I'm Here" by Cynthia Erivo

We've written in earlier chapters about how sound texts are particularly powerful for inviting diverse **voices**, cultures, and identities into our classrooms. Whether these sound texts are honoring **voices** that resist the problematic Western ideas of "academic" English or integrating diverse cultural traditions into our work in ways that center a range of literacy practices, many genres of sound texts invite real and practical inclusivity into our ELA coursework. So, when designing reading activities using sound texts, we invite you to take this opportunity to assess which **voices** or perspectives are centered and which are not.

"Still I Rise" by Maya Angelou

If your classroom is reading the popular high school classic Harper Lee's *To Kill a Mockingbird*, we strongly encourage you to supplement the book with sound texts that center **voices** of color and stories of Black joy and success. This can include analyzing Cynthia Erivo's performance of the song "I'm Here" from *The Color Purple* or Maya Angelou's reading of her poem "Still I Rise." If an overview of your curriculum reveals that the majority of texts emphasize the isolating and linguistically limiting dominance of what Laura Greenfield refers to as "standardized" English, we suggest taking the time to have your students analyze and discuss a podcast episode like NPR's *Rough Translation* thirty-minute episode, "How to Speak Bad English"; this creates opportunities for students to consider how expectations around the English language are connected to power. Because sound texts so often meaningfully and respectfully integrate diverse **voices**, they can be powerful tools when designing reading activities with a goal of promoting cultural and racial equity in our learning communities.

"How to Speak Bad English" from NPR

Assess Text Complexity

We know from our long history as ELA teachers designing reading activities that not all texts are created equal in terms of complexity and challenge levels for students. When choosing the sound text to use in your reading activity, you'll want to have a sense of the level of complexity and difficulty it will present for your students. If this is a simple, formative assignment that students will complete together in class to develop new skills, a less complex text may be a better fit. If you are designing a summative, end-of-unit assessment that students will complete over several days, you may want to choose a more complicated text to give them a chance to demonstrate what they've learned.

Some metrics for assessing text complexity in sound texts will be the same as those in traditional alphabetic texts. You may even already have some favorite strategies that still hold true when choosing sound texts.

- The traditional Lexile level is a quantitative metric that measures text complexity based mostly on sentence length and the familiarity and frequency of the words in the text. This could be applied to certain sound texts as well; texts that use long, complicated sentences and unfamiliar, low-frequency words will present a higher challenge for students. However, even in the printed mode, the Lexile level metric cannot reliably measure the complexity of genres like poetry or song lyrics due to their irregular punctuation and sentence structure. This would mean that sound genres like music, performed poetry, and potentially certain audio dramas may not be able to be assigned a Lexile level. Whether or not you use the Lexile level, its general principle of considering sentence and diction complexity is good to keep in mind.
- The length of a text is always relevant when considering complexity. Just like in the traditional alphabetic mode, however, length does not always directly correlate to complexity. Short texts can be extremely abstract, **layered**, and complicated while lengthy texts can be extremely straightforward, literal, and easy to digest. However, regardless of internal complexity, longer texts simply take more time to read, particularly if the task you assign requires students to perform multiple readings of the text to analyze it. Consider how many minutes a single read-through or listening of your chosen audio text requires. And remember that, just as with alphabetic printed texts, you can always excerpt a sound text to lower the difficulty level for students.

Some of the ways you will determine the complexity of a sound text will be unique to this mode.

- In any text, the complexity of the structure is important to consider. While in printed alphabetic texts, structure can be indicated using different visual cues like fonts, headings, and paragraph breaks, sound texts will transition and organize using different tools. Structure in sound texts is often communicated using **music** or **sound effects** to indicate different sections, spoken transitions, or a narrated explanation of the overall trajectory of the text. As with any text, the more intricate the structure, the higher the complexity of the text, but it is important to remember that unless your students have a strong understanding of the ways in which sound texts enact transitions or major rhetorical moves, it may take some time for them to become familiarized with them. Starting to practice reading skills with simple, shorter sound texts is a good way to build familiarity with structure.
- The way that the five sound strategies (the ones we discussed in Chapter 2) are used in sound texts will be a mode-specific indicator of complexity.

  One of the sound strategies is **layering**, the interaction of two or more of the other strategies (**voice**, **silence**, **music**, or **sound effects**) at the same time. An example of this would be a particular musical score playing beneath character dialogue; the interaction between these two sounds would create a tension and meaning of its own. The degree of **layering** in a sound text will contribute to how difficult it is to analyze that sound text. A sound text with no **layering**, meaning that only one sound is playing at any given time, will be less complex. A sound text with some **layering**, perhaps two sounds occasionally overlapping, will require more interpretation. Some sound texts, particularly immersive audio dramas, can integrate very complicated **layering** with complete soundscapes featuring **sound effects**, dialogue, **music**, and pauses, all weaving in and out of one another. Texts like these, even very short ones, can be very challenging for students; we consider these to be fairly high complexity.

  Some of the sound strategies are less literal and more interpretive, making them more difficult to analyze. The strategy of silence, the absence of noise, a pause in the noise, creates the possibility of meaning; like figurative language, students will have to interpret this strategy in the context of the text in order to decide what the author's intention was. The same can happen when there is a juxtaposition between two sounds, as when a line of dialogue is seemingly peaceful, but intense, ominous **music** plays beneath it. Students will need to consider this juxtaposition in the larger context of the piece and interpret meaning from it. We discussed in Chapter 3 the potential for sounds to function as symbols, a particularly advanced literary device when working with sound texts; symbolic uses of sound will cause a sound text to be more complicated for students to interpret. Particularly if reading sound texts is unfamiliar to your students, they may need time to develop the ability to analyze some of these sound-specific strategies.

Of course, all of these elements for assessing the complexity of a sound text need to be considered along with the overall design of the reading activity, factoring in things like how much support you'll be giving as a teacher, how much time students will be given to complete the activity, and how difficult of a reading skill the activity will target. If you plan to complete the activity together as a class, offering clear and explicit guidance and support as the classroom teacher, perhaps also using a familiar and well-practiced reading skill followed by a more **layered**, difficult text may not actually feel as complex to students. If you plan to ask students to complete the work on their own, at home, over a short span of time, or to rely on a challenging new reading skill, even a simple, brief sound text may seem complex.

You know your students best, and you know what will challenge their reading abilities, engage their interests, and shape the classroom culture and ethos you hope to pursue. Our goal for this section is to offer ideas to consider as you select a sound text that best meets the unique needs of your ELA classroom.

Choosing the Targeted Reading Skill

When you're designing a reading activity, whether or not you've already selected the text you'll be reading, it's important to have an understanding of what particular reading skill you want the task to target. While, of course, any given activity will rely on multiple skills at a time, it's usually best to target one or two new skills for students to focus on. There have been and continue to be a wide variety of reading skill lists created by different organizations, and we are confident that you as an educator have a strong sense of the reading skills your students need the most work with.

To best explain how to design a sound reading activity around a target skill, we are going to rely on the list of ten close reading skills we outlined and discussed in the previous chapter. We don't believe this list to be comprehensive, but it does reflect some of the core reading skills that we prioritize in our own work with students when striving to educate and mentor dynamic, intuitive, and flexible twenty-first-century readers with the ability to interpret meaning from texts in any mode.

In the sections below, we've created ten different audio reading activities, one for each of the skills from our list. For each activity, we've chosen sound texts that we think are accessible, engaging, and appropriate for the target skill, and we've designed a simple, audio reading activity to strengthen the target skill.

A Note about Tying In the Common Core Standards

Although the following activities correspond with our list of ten close reading skills we previously outlined, we have also included references to the Common Core Reading Standards that each activity addresses; while educators everywhere have a wide range of feelings regarding the Common Core, we also recognize that many teachers are required to use these standards, so we wanted to make these activities as accessible and applicable as possible. If the Common Core isn't your thing, feel free to ignore those and move on; however, if you plan to use the standards we listed, we wanted to clarify a few points.

- The following activities reference the 9–10 reading standards. While we fully believe these activities can and should be used with students of any grade in high school, some may need to be altered slightly to meet the standards for grades 11–12 fully.
- We determined whether a skill was "Reading: Literature (RL)" or "Reading: Informational (RI)" based on the sound text we used for the activity. Many of these activities could easily address both "Literature" and "Informational," so don't let those distinctions limit your use of these activities.
- There isn't a perfectly matched Common Core Standard for each of the activities below. Some of the activities are not paired with a Common Core Standard because of the way we have designed the reading activity. For these activities, we believe that the targeted skill is foundational and necessary in order to fully and rigorously address the Common Core Standards. If identifying Common Core Standards in activity design is important to you, we encourage you to consider extension activities or modifications to these activities in order to tie them to the standard of your choice.

Let's Get into It: Ten Classroom-Ready Reading Activities in the Mode of Sound

We're finally ready for the practical part of this chapter! We'll walk you through each activity with some discussion and example student responses, and, if you use the QR code next to each activity, you'll find ready-made worksheets and rubrics to use in your classroom. We highly encourage you to use these activities however best supports you and your students. If you want to directly lift an activity exactly as it is with its pre-made worksheets and the sound text we've selected, we'd love that. If you want to heavily adapt an activity, choose a new sound text to practice with, or remake worksheets, we'd love that, too. What is most important is to try things out and see what works best for you and your classroom.

Assessment versus Grading

You'll see in our supplemental materials that we've given you single-point rubrics to use when assessing student work. If you've never seen a single-point rubric, we love them because they're simple, and they allow room for positive and constructive feedback around each of the major aspects of an assignment. One of the major differences between a single- and a multiple-point rubric is that the single-point rubric only describes the qualities of proficient student performance. This avoids "describ[ing] ahead of time all the ways to do poorly in detail" (Fluckiger 19). Christina L. Dobbs and Christine Montecillo Leider identify that "multiple-point rubrics commonly label student work that does not meet teachers' expectations with negative terms, such as 'unsatisfactory,' 'below basic,' 'unacceptable,' or 'insufficient.' Students might read these terms as a statement about their writing [or reading] potential or, even worse, as broader distinctions about their language" (64). The single-point rubric also does not "set limits on student achievement" by prescribing a predetermined "highest level" of performance on an assignment (Fluckiger 19). These rubrics are open-ended in their guidance, allowing students to surprise you with how they reach, and perhaps even exceed, the target goals.

The single-point rubrics we have created for you are not geared toward grading, however; they are not set up to focus on a particular grade or numerical evaluation of student work. Our single-point rubrics are about assessing students' work, giving them clear feedback, suggesting areas of growth, and identifying areas of strength. We view assessment as "a form of feedback to students regarding their progress" with a goal of "enhanc[ing] learning" (Marzano 5). Robert J. Marzano's research indicates that the most meaningful feedback students can receive "should be frequent, give students a clear picture of their progress and how they might improve, and provide encouragement" (11). Our single-point rubrics are designed to meet these requirements, and our personal classroom experience with these rubrics has been extremely positive. Additionally, Jarene Fluckiger's work with single-point rubrics points out that "descriptive feedback is more helpful than a number, a grade, a score, a ranking, or a single descriptive label" (20). If you wish to adapt these rubrics to assign a grade, you're welcome to do so, but we find that emphasizing assessment over grading aligns with our goals of viewing learning as a process rather than an end goal.

As an added benefit, single-point rubrics can be used as excellent tools for "responsible student self-assessment" as we prioritize giving students autonomy and ownership over their own literacy skills (Fluckiger 18).

You'll see that we've organized the activities around basic close reading protocols for each activity. Of course, we invite you to adapt these as needed; these protocols are based on our experiences in the classroom and our goal of prioritizing multiple full read throughs of a text as a necessary element of a thorough close reading. You'll also notice that, when discussing close reading in the audio mode, we move fluidly between the terms "listen" and "read"; this is because, when reading sound texts, listening is an inherent part of the process. Parsing the technical relationship between listening and reading when performing a close reading on a sound text falls a bit outside the scope of this book; we've chosen the word we think makes our intended meaning the clearest in each situation. Please also note that each step of the close reading protocols can be completed individually, in small groups, or together as a whole class. Occasionally, we will recommend one of these for a particular protocol step, but, as with most things in this book, we invite you to make the choice that feels right for your students. So, without any further delay, let's take a look at how some of these activities might unfold in a classroom setting.

Activity 1: Awareness of Author's Persona

Reading Activity 1 Materials

"Maman" by Sandra Kwawul

For this first activity, we ask students to read an audio memoir called "Maman" by Sandra Kwawul from NPR's *Moth Radio Hour*. In this audio memoir, the author candidly and somewhat comedically shares the experience of celebrating her birthday at a time in which, for a variety of reasons, she emotionally did not feel able to celebrate. This activity will prompt students to use textual evidence as readers of this text to develop an understanding of Kwawul's role and position as an author, her persona, and how that understanding impacts the audio memoir's overall meaning.

Common Core ELA Standard(s)	Description of Standard(s)
RL.1	Cite strong and thorough textual evidence to support analysis of what the text says explicitly as well as inferences drawn from the text.
Note: If you choose a text from an author who isn't from the United States, you will also address RL.6 **Objectives:** SWBAT read critically in order to identify and analyze an author's persona or personality, considering what an author's words and/or use of sound strategies communicate directly and/or indirectly about their position and role as author of the text. SWBAT identify evidence from the text in order to support their analysis.	

TABLE 4.1: Close Reading Protocol for Analyzing Author's Persona

First Listen	After or during this first read, students will complete **Part 1** of **"Awareness of Author's Persona Handout"** in order to answer some initial questions about the speaker. Some students may benefit from being provided with a word bank of adjectives. Additionally, teachers may find that some students respond with an observation, statement, or assumption about an author's culture or gender. Sometimes these responses can be supported using a close reading of the author's choices in the text, but we encourage educators to take this opportunity to challenge students on whether or not the text really does offer the information we need to draw those conclusions. We encourage educators to direct student answers to these questions by asking, "Has the author given us what we need to assume or conclude that?"
Second Listen	With their answers from **Part 1** in mind, students will complete **Part 2** of **"Awareness of Author's Persona Handout"** after their second listen in order to provide evidence for the claims they made about the author. As students work through **Part 2**, they may want to listen to the audio memoir again. We've included an example of **Part 2** below, completed with sample student answers, to give you an idea of the kind of work we look for from students completing this activity.
Third Listen	We strongly encourage teachers to push students to use sound strategies as evidence to support their claims in **Part 2**: tone of voice, pauses, and sound effects like sighs, laughter, or audience responses. If students get too caught up in transcribing *what* the speaker says without taking time to consider *how* she says it as well, they lose a large part of the benefit of working in the mode of sound. While this could be done during the second listen, we're big fans of encouraging students to do as many rereads as possible.

Awareness of Author's Persona Handout: Part 2—Sample Student Responses

Provide evidence to support the claims you have made about the author/speaker in Part 1.

	Evidence **Direct quotes and sound strategies**	**Analysis** **What does this show about the author/speaker? Why?**
What adjectives describe this speaker's personality?	• "I've been begging my friends to be here all month" (0:47) • Her best friend Gloria remembers her birthday and comes to celebrate with her sister and gifts (2:48) • "Suddenly we're all enjoying and having a good time" (4:06) • "My birthday is about the people in my life" (4:15) • Her relationship with Gloria gives her hope (5:25)	The author is motivated by her friends and her family. Even in her darkest time, her best friend remembers her birthday and comes to celebrate her, something that gives her hope and revives her desire to live joyfully. Her relationships are core to who she is.

What adjectives describe this speaker's current emotional state?	• Laughs (0:22, 0:55, 1:16) • "I was not expecting to go first" (0:28) • "my heart is beating out of my chest" (0:42)— said breathlessly • "I'm shaking" (0:49— said in a nervous, high-pitched voice • Sighs and says "okay" to prepare to begin story (0:54)	She is feeling anxious about performing. She keeps laughing nervously, and she admits that she didn't think she would be the first one. She tells the audience that she's shaking, and she audibly sighs and prepares herself before beginning her story. Her voice and sounds and words all communicate a feeling of anxiety.
What do we know about this speaker's background?	• "My parents gifted me a herd of siblings" (1:44) • Her mom died when she turned 15 and it was very hard for her (4:28)	She comes from a large family, something she enjoys, and she lost her mother young.
What do we know about what this speaker wants?	• "Recently I was listening to the podcast, and they said that if your name is picked first, statistically you are less likely to win tonight, but that's okay" (0:30) • She wants to live fully and celebrate her life along with her mother's life. She has the audience sing happy birthday to her (6:30) and thanks them, laughing (6:46)	She has been paying attention to how different speakers win the competition. She is paying attention to whether or not she wins. By singing happy birthday with the audience at the end and laughing along with them, she shows us that she wants to continue to celebrate her life and her mother's life joyfully.

The activity ends by having students synthesize their understanding of the author's persona in responding to the **Part 3** of **"Awareness of Author's Persona Handout"** prompt about the persona's impact on the text overall; students can respond to this question in writing or through discussion.

Activity 2: Awareness of Audience

Reading Activity 2 Materials

In this activity, we ask students to analyze two different radio advertisements, both of which are attempting to sell cars to their listeners. The first advertisement, for Infinity luxury cars, targets their advertisement to a very specific demographic, while the second, for Dodge Ram pickup trucks, shares the goal of selling a car but aims their advertisement at a different target audience. This activity invites students to use textual evidence to build an understanding of how an intended audience can impact an author's choices in a text and, by extension, the overall message of that text.

Infinity Luxury Cars Advertisement

Dodge Ram Trucks Advertisement

Common Core ELA Standard(s)	Description of Standard(s)
RI.1	Cite strong and thorough textual evidence to support analysis of what the text says explicitly as well as inferences drawn from the text.
Objectives: SWBAT read critically in order to identify and analyze choices authors make to directly and/or indirectly profile and address the intended audience of a piece. SWBAT identify and analyze evidence from the text in order to support their claims, including a consideration of how sound strategies are deployed to target a particular listener demographic.	

TABLE 4.2: Close Reading Protocol for Audience Awareness

First Listen	After or during this first listen, students will complete **Part 1** of **"Awareness of Audience Handout,"** which has students consider who the audiences are of each advertisement and what they're like, using evidence to support their claims. Teachers should, whenever possible, encourage students to answer these questions using sound strategies as evidence; however, if students need some time to warm up to that, the work they complete during the second listen will prompt them to rely more heavily on sound strategies. We also think it's important, as with the author's persona activity, to acknowledge that some students may find themselves unintentionally making claims about a target audience's belief system, race, etc., that may not be supported by the text. We encourage students not to make assumptions that can't be substantiated by the text but also not to make any assumptions that may be based on stereotypes. Particularly when we are listening to an author's spoken language, "the disinformation and misrepresentation that get distributed about dominant languages and marginalized languages and dialects" can prompt problematic reflections (Baker-Bell 15). Proactive classroom discussions can provide opportunities for you as an educator to prompt students to return to the text and challenge them to analyze and support their claims with clear and direct evidence, looking for personal bias in their own interpretations.
Second Listen	After students answer the questions in **Part 1**, they will answer a second set of questions in **Part 2** of **"Awareness of Audience Handout"** that require them to look more closely at the evidence that supports their responses. For students who didn't feel comfortable or ready to start examining sound strategies as supporting evidence, these questions have been specifically developed to challenge them to do so, ensuring they are able to engage with the text and the mode of sound fully. Students may find that in order to answer the questions with evidence, they may need to listen to the text a few more times, too! We've included an example of **Part 2** of **"Awareness of Audience Handout"** below, completed with sample student answers to give you an idea of the kind of work we'd hope to see from students.

Awareness of Audience Handout: Part 2—Student Sample Responses

Answer the following questions using evidence from the texts to support your answers.

1. How are the tones of voice in each advertisement reflective of the different audiences?
   a. The tone of voice in the Infinity ad is a soft-spoken British man who sounds proper and classy, suggesting an audience that enjoys things that are luxurious and cultural.
   b. The tone of the speaker in the truck ad is a gruff-sounding man who is speaking in a low, hyper-masculine voice, suggesting that this audience values social displays of masculine strength and power.
2. How is the content in each advertisement reflective of the different audiences?
   a. The Infinity advertisement repeats the word "luxury." They assume the listeners have been to wine-tasting by saying that "the aroma is full-bodied, the flavor is decadent" (0:04) when referring to the test-drive event.
   b. The advertisement for the Dodge truck uses words like "tough" and "trustworthy" and references to the kind of "guy" the listener is, assuming that traditionally masculine working men would be most interested in these vehicles.
3. How is the music in each advertisement reflective of the different audiences?
   a. The infinity advertisement uses smooth, repetitive music that sounds like it belongs in an elevator in a hotel lobby. This might reflect an audience that considers themselves sophisticated and cultured.
   b. The music in the Dodge advertisement is loud, aggressive electric guitar music that is reminiscent of the rock genre, suggesting an audience that is no-nonsense, strong, and fearless.

Using their answers to these questions, students should be able to construct a profile of the intended audiences for each of these sound texts, something that will be invaluable when interpreting other elements of the texts.

Reading Activity 3 Materials

Activity 3: Identification of Argument

This activity asks students to determine the central argument of a review of the new *Legend of Zelda* game from NPR's *All Things Considered* and then outline the main points that develop and support that argument. Reviews like this one or ones from NPR's *Pop Culture Happy Hour* are particularly useful for having students practice this skill because they make a clear argument and can be found for any relevant and engaging game, movie, television show, etc. You can choose whatever your students are excited about at the moment!

"The new Zelda game, *Tears of the Kingdom*, lives up to the hype"

Common Core ELA Standard(s)	Description of Standard(s)
RI.2	Cite strong and thorough textual evidence to support analysis of what the text says explicitly as well as inferences drawn from the text.
Objectives: SWBAT read critically in order to identify and analyze the central argument of a text as well as how the author supports and develops that central argument with evidence and reasoning. SWBAT identify evidence, including sound strategies, from the text in order to support their analysis.	

TABLE 4.3: Close Reading Protocol for Identifying an Argument

First Listen	After the first listen, we recommend students try to solidify what they believe the author's main argument is. The graphic organizer provided in **"Identification of an Argument Handout"** offers some scaffolded steps for doing this.
Second Listen	After students have identified what they believe the main argument is, they should continue to complete their outline, focusing on the claims that support their identified central argument. The graphic organizer provided in **"Identification of an Argument Handout"** guides students through the process of identifying the supporting claims that make up the argument of the text; teachers should feel free to adapt this activity outline to include as many or as few supporting claims as needed. Also, if you feel your students don't need this much support, you can simply ask them to outline the central argument of the podcast and let them approach that task with a higher degree of choice and flexibility. If you choose this route, we do encourage you to require that your students include direct evidence from the sound text to back up their outlined points. Students will likely need to complete multiple listens as well as to pause and replay sections in order to include evidence in their responses. We've found it can be helpful to remind students that sound strategies can be as equally important to the development of an argument as the words are. You'll likely notice that **"Identification of an Argument Handout"** includes an extension option for students, asking them to identify and analyze the counterclaim of the text. This can be a great way to help students see an additional strategy that authors can help develop and strengthen their arguments. We've included an example of an outline using **"Identification of an Argument Handout"** below to give you an idea of what students might create.

Identification of an Argument Handout—Student Sample Responses

Central Argument: What is the author's central argument in the podcast?

The new *Legend of Zelda* game maintains the high quality of the game series.

Introductory Information: What kind of background or context info does the author provide to get the listener into their argument?

- General Zelda Game Series Info
  - First game came out in 1986
  - 37 years of the game
  - Millions of players
  - 30 different Zelda games
- General plot information from the game's storyline
- Zelda game music playing under the narration
- New game information
  - For Nintendo Switch
  - Called "The Legend of Zelda: Tears of the Kingdom"

Point 1:

- What is the author's first point to support their argument?
  Zelda games are something that, once people start, they love.
- What evidence does the author use within this point?
  People who get into Zelda, it becomes a lifelong thing for a lot of them."
  —Keza MacDonald (1:16)
- What kind of evidence does this author use? (anecdote, statistic, quote, etc.) Why is this an effective choice for this point?
  This fact is supported by data, which is effective because, if you're someone who isn't familiar with the game, it demonstrates how addictive the game has become over the decades it has been available.

Point 2:

- What is the author's first point to support their argument?
  The game is very immersive and easy to lose yourself in.
- What evidence does the author use within this point?
  "I started playing Zelda when I was seven, and it was the first video game that I had played that felt as rich and as deep and as interesting as the fantasy novels that I loved at the time, like Narnia. And I think that's what Zelda still is now. It feels like somewhere you can take a holiday." —Keza MacDonald (1:17)
- What kind of evidence does this author use? (anecdote, statistic, quote etc.) Why is this an effective choice for this point?
  This is a personal anecdote from a video game editor from a major publication, so she's trustworthy, and she shares her experiences with the game.

Optional Extension—Counterclaim:

- Does this text include a counterclaim?
  Yes
- If the author includes a counterclaim, what is it?
  It isn't the best-selling series by Nintendo. Mario and Pokémon made significantly more money.
- If the author includes a counterclaim, how does the author refute this counterclaim?
  The game design is well respected by designers, developers, and gamers. It's a masterpiece.

In addition to the extension option to consider as a potential counterpoint, we also recommend teachers explore an extension activity in which, after completing outlines, students compare their outlines, noticing where they differ in their assessment of the supporting points or central claim. This can make for an interesting discussion, inviting students to advocate for their understanding of the argument by referring to the text to support their outlined answers.

By completing this activity, students are able not only to identify an argument but also to see how an author develops that argument with evidence and reasoning. Once students complete this outline, they will have all of the necessary components to provide, either written or orally, a clear and objective summary. For teachers who wish to offer an additional challenge to students, once they have completed this activity, it is an appropriate time for them to reflect on the author's purpose for this podcast: what does the author hope this argument achieves or does in the world?

Reading Activity 4 Materials

Activity 4: Awareness of Genre

This activity asks students to explore the concept of genre by identifying genre norms, particularly within the genre of poetry, and examining how those genre norms can be altered by the mode of a text. Students will read two poems, "Echo," an alphabetic poem, and "Closer Captions," a spoken-word poem, both by Raymond Antrobus. Both of these poems explore ideas and themes revolving around his deafness. In this activity, students will compare and contrast the genre of a poem as it appears when written in printed letters versus what it is like when written with sound.

"Echo" by Raymond Antrobus

"Closer Captions" by Raymond Antrobus

Unlike our prior activities, this one doesn't include any Common Core Standards. This is because the Common Core doesn't explicitly list genre awareness as a necessary reading or writing skill, but we think this is an unfortunate oversight, particularly since we believe several Common Core Standard skills rely on students having at least a basic understanding of the genres in which they are reading. Genre awareness is a fundamental skill that students will need in order to identify, understand, and analyze the more complex aspects of a text, so while the Common Core may not agree, we think explicitly teaching students to understand and analyze genre will make them more critical and thoughtful readers and writers.

Objectives: SWBAT read critically in order to identify and analyze the genre choices that an author makes. SWBAT identify how genre norms can change when an author composes in the audio mode as compared to the alphabetic mode.

TABLE 4.4: Close Reading Protocol for Genre Awareness

<table>
<tr><td>Before Listening</td><td>Teachers may find it helpful to provide students with the definition of genre norms; we define genre norms as features or characteristics of a text that readers expect to see in a particular genre.

We recommend taking a moment to ensure that students have a basic understanding of genre as a concept, as well as some of the reasons a particular text may deviate from those genre expectations. If you have your own materials for reviewing the concept of genre with students, we encourage you to use them before beginning this activity. Additionally, if you're looking for content to support designing a more in-depth or comprehensive review of genre, we encourage you to revisit our "Genre Awareness" section from Chapter 2: The Fundamentals of Studying Sound Texts.

Once you are confident that your students have a baseline understanding of genre, norms, and how these both develop in response to their contexts, have students brainstorm a list of genre norms, which we usually divide into two categories:
• norms that will appear in almost every single poem
• norms that only appear in some poetry

Poetry is a large genre with many subgenres, and all genres have norms that only appear under certain conditions. Organizing your brainstorming this way provides students some space to debate and consider what truly makes something a poem and why genre expectations aren't more fixed. Students may need some examples to get them started on a genre norms list, which is why we'd encourage teachers to complete this "before listening" step as a whole class. We've listed this step as Part 1 of "Awareness of Genre Handout."</td></tr>
<tr><td>First Listen</td><td>Students will read the alphabetic poem and the sound poem each at least once all the way through. Students will answer specific questions about each poem in Part 2 of "Awareness of Genre Handout" in order to begin considering how each either meets or doesn't meet their expectations for the genre.</td></tr>
<tr><td>Second Listen</td><td>After students have responded to the questions, they will take their understanding of genre norms and each poem a step further by completing a compare-and-contrast Venn diagram of the two poems from Part 3 of "Awareness of Genre Handout" as they complete a second (and maybe third) listen.

Students may need some modeling of what to include in the Venn diagram; teachers can model some responses with the class before asking them to continue on their own, or teachers can prompt the class with questions to get them started. These questions can include:
• Does the alphabetic text structure the stanzas or words in a particular way on the page that can't be communicated in the recording?
• Does the spoken word poem use a particular vocal quality that the written poem isn't able to use?
• What aspects of the genre of a poem appear the same or in similar ways in both texts?

We've included some responses we'd expect to see from students in the model of Part 3 of "Awareness of Genre Handout" below.</td></tr>
</table>

Awareness of Genre Handout: Part 3—Student Sample Responses

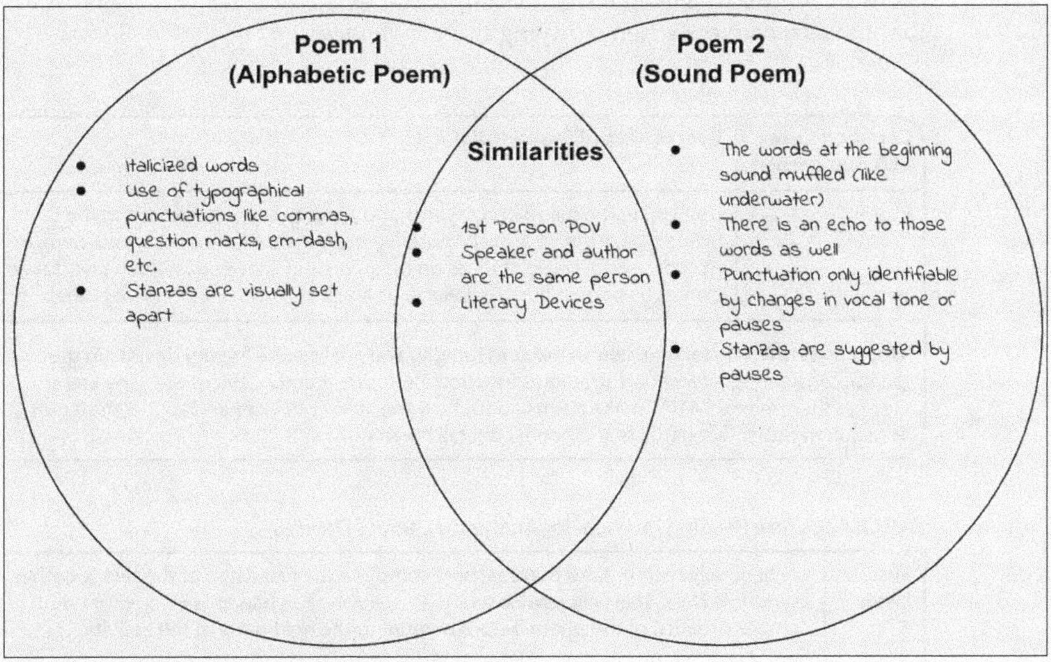

FIGURE 4.1: Genre Comparison Venn Diagram

This activity concludes by having students go back to the original brainstormed list of genre norms for poetry to see if their expectations have changed at all using **Part 4** of **"Awareness of Genre Handout."** Teachers may choose to have a whole-class discussion in which students alter and add to the original brainstorm on the board. By having students look back at the original list the class created, teachers demonstrate to students that genre isn't static and can be altered by the mode in which the genre is written.

Reading Activity 5 Materials

Activity 5: Interpretation of Literary Devices

In this activity, students will listen to the spoken-word poem "How To Translate a Joke" by Emi Mahmoud in order to analyze her use of literary devices, considering her intent behind each device along with how her devices impact the overall meaning and/or purpose of the poem. While this activity could be done with any literary genre, we particularly like using poetry because it's often a genre we find students are a bit more nervous to read. Listening to the poet verbally perform their poem adds a layer that can often make students feel a little more confident about interpreting meaning from their reading.

"How to Translate a Joke" by Emi Mahmoud

Additionally, while we prioritize transcripts with all reading activities in the mode of sound, we particularly recommend that teachers try to use sound texts that have transcripts when studying literary devices.

Common Core ELA Standard(s)	Description of Standard(s)
RL.4	Determine the meaning of words and phrases as they are used in the text, including figurative and connotative meanings; analyze the cumulative impact of specific word choices on meaning and tone (e.g., how the language evokes a sense of time and place; how it sets a formal or informal tone).
Objectives: SWBAT read critically in order to identify and analyze the literary devices in the poem, considering how sound strategies function alongside literary devices or as the literary devices themselves. SWBAT make claims about how the literary devices and sound strategies function together in regards to the poem's overall meaning.	

TABLE 4.5: Close Reading Protocol for Analyzing Literary Devices

First Listen	We generally recommend that teachers complete the first listen of the text together as a whole class. This way, you ensure that everyone has had at least one (or two) complete read(s) of the poem before beginning the next parts of the activity. We also wait to give students any handouts or further instructions until the second listen; we've found this encourages students to focus on nothing other than listening and noticing what strikes them. Sometimes we ask students to simply listen during the first reading and then to take generalized notes on what stands out to them in the second listen. Teachers can consider giving more structured, scaffolded note-taking guidance or handouts for students to support their initial listens to the poem; however, we strongly encourage that teachers keep this part simple.
Second Listen	During their next listen(s) of the poem, students will use **Part 2** of **"Interpretation of Literary Devices Handout"** to annotate the transcript with an emphasis on any literary devices they hear. The first step on the activity handout asks students to identify the literary devices in the poem as well as *why* they believe it is that particular literary device. We've found this is particularly beneficial for when students may make mistakes; when students explain their reasoning, we can better help them figure out where their error may have originated. Some students may benefit from being given a word bank of literary devices they can look for. We've included a word bank in our differentiated materials; however, if you have one you usually provide students or that reflects your recent work with them, that's even better.

Third Listen	Once students have identified the literary devices in the poem, in **Part 3** of **"Interpretation of Literary Devices Handout,"** they will be prompted to describe the sound strategies they hear during the literary devices in Mahmoud's poem. This step can help students take their analysis of a literary device and its impact a step further, leveraging the mode of sound to help students grasp how literary devices infuse meaning into a text. This is also the section in which students will reflect on how literary devices appear differently in different modes. It is up to the teacher whether this consideration happens implicitly or explicitly; students may simply notice these things on their own, but teachers can choose to prompt a discussion around how a particular metaphor spoken after a dramatic pause might appear differently in the mode of sound than on the printed page.
Fourth Listen	Students will complete the organizer with **Part 4** of **"Interpretation of Literary Devices Handout"** by synthesizing the work they've done in the prior steps of this activity, analyzing the purpose of the literary devices alongside accompanying sound strategies in order to explain how the combination of these things work together to impact the text overall. We've found that this step really helps students who may be struggling with the purpose of literary devices; the added layer that sound strategies provide can be tremendously helpful in articulating the impact for some students. The model below provides samples of students' responses we'd expect during each listen of the activity.

Interpretation of Literary Devices Handout Parts 2–4—Student Sample Responses

Transcript	**Literary Device (Part 2)** What literary device is Mahmoud using? Explain why it is this literary device.	**Sound Description (Part 3)** What sound strategies do you notice being used in conjunction with the literary device?	**Analysis (Part 4)** What is Mahmoud's purpose in using this literary device? How do the sound strategies used with the literary device impact the meaning overall?
... He walks up to a woman selling flowers: "Do you have any flowers, you rose?" She melts. Gives him flowers and a kiss.	Metaphor—She does not literally melt Anaphora—The last three stanzas begin with "He walks..."	She speaks brightly, quickly, and in a chipper voice. She is speaking lightly, comedically.	She is creating the light, comedic tone of the joke. She is creating a sense of playfulness. She is continuing the playfulness of the joke, emphasizing how skilled this village playboy is. He can approach any woman and figuratively take her life with his smoothness.

He walks up to a third woman. "Do you have any sugar, sugar?" She practically dies. Gives him sugar and kisses him twice. The playboy comes back. "Your turn, stud."	Metaphor—She doesn't die	She is chuckling lightly as she says this.	
The man apprehensively walks up to a woman selling dairy and says: "Do you have any milk, cow?" Realize that humor transcends all boundaries.	Anaphora—There are a series of phrases here that begin with either "realize" or "that"	She is speaking lightly, brightly, comedically; however, she says the last line, "Realize that we call women cows in every language," in a slower, lower pitch.	She is creating a contrast between the laughter of the joke and the darkness beneath it. The anaphora emphasizes the contrast in lines and tones.
That laughter is a language that knows no borders. That this joke that I learned in Arabic makes perfect sense in English and French and in any other language. Realize that we call women cows in every language. Realize that humor leaves little room for questions, even less room for victims, and even less room for apologies. …	Anaphora—She is continuing to begin phrases with the word "realize" Repetition—"less room" emphasizes shared fear	Her tone has turned more severe and sharp, less comedic. She is punctuating these words with her voice.	By maintaining the word "realize" but changing the tone of her words and repeating the claustrophobic "less room." she is emphasizing that the joke with which she began the poem is actually not so funny.

Once students have completed the organizer, teachers may consider asking them to engage in a whole-class discussion or to write an explication essay in order to synthesize and share their takeaways from this activity.

Reading Activity 6 Materials

Activity 6: Awareness of Organization and Structure

For this activity, students will listen to "The Kids Take the Climate Change Fight to Court" by *The New York Times's The Daily* in order to analyze how the organization and structure of this podcast episode impact the overall argument. The text we've chosen for this activity features a clear argument and is reasonably short for a podcast; however, if teachers have a text they want students to analyze that is longer or more complicated *or* if students are just getting started with this skill, it may be beneficial to have them first complete an outline identifying the overall argument (see Activity 3) of the text before attempting these more analytical questions about the argument's organization and structure.

"The Kids Take the Climate Change Fight to Court" from *The Daily*

Common Core ELA Standard(s)	**Description of Standard(s)**
RI.3	Analyze how the author unfolds an analysis or series of ideas or events, including the order in which the points are made, how they are introduced and developed, and the connections that are drawn between them.
RI.5	Analyze in detail how an author's ideas or claims are developed and refined by particular sentences, paragraphs, or larger portions of a text (e.g., a section or chapter).
Objectives: SWBAT read critically in order to identify and analyze how an author develops their argument, including analyzing the kind of evidence used, the order in which points are made, the manner in which the text transitions between these points, the way the podcast is introduced and concluded, etc., as well as how sound strategies create or support each of these elements. SWBAT analyze how these choices impact the overall argument of the piece and its effectiveness in reaching its audience with its argument.	

TABLE 4.6: Close Reading Protocol for Awareness of Organization and Structure

First Listen	Either during or after the first listen, we recommend students start their analysis of the text by clearly identifying the central argument of the text, the first question in **"Awareness of Organization and Structure Handout."** Understanding the central argument is critical to understanding how and why a text is organized and structured in a particular way, so we think it's a good idea to check in with students to see that they're on the right path before they continue their work.
Second Listen	During their second listen, students will answer the rest of the questions in **"Awareness of Organization and Structure Handout."** They may choose to work through the text slowly during this second listen, pausing to analyze or answer questions at regular intervals or when a shift occurs in the argument's trajectory or tone. Teachers should also feel free to tackle only a few of these questions, or even to tackle them one at a time, in order to emphasize a particular element of argumentative writing. We've included a model below of the kinds of answers we'd expect students to come up with.
Third Listen	Once students have completed the questions, we recommend having them listen to the text in its entirety one final time so they can step back and observe the functional parts they have been identifying and analyzing unfold the way the author(s) intended.

Awareness of Organization and Structure Handout—Student Sample Responses

1. Is the central argument of the podcast explicitly stated or implied? Explain your answer. Why do you think the authors chose this?

   At the beginning of the podcast, the host clearly states, "Today, my colleague David Gelles explains why the case could be a turning point, and what a win in Montana would mean for the future of the climate fight" (1:00). She is referring to the court case a group of students is bringing against the state of Montana to reduce the use of fossil fuels. This is a fairly explicit claim that these students have the potential to meaningfully impact environmentalist efforts in the U.S. I believe the authors chose this because they feel their message has a moral importance and is not subjective or up for interpretation. They want their audience to be very clear on the argument they are making.

2. At what point in the podcast is the listener entirely clear on the authors' central argument? Why do you think the authors made this choice?

   The host makes this clear very near the beginning of the argument. It helps give a sense of importance and relevance to the rest of the podcast's content. It gets listeners interested. It also shapes the way they understand the upcoming claims.

3. How do the authors choose to open the podcast and introduce the main topic? Why?
   a. What words do they use?
      i. They give the date of the episode because a new episode comes out each day
      ii. They introduce their main guest, David Gelles
   b. What sound strategies do they use? (music, voices, sound effects, silence, layering)
      i. They use the recognizable *Daily* intro theme song
      ii. They introduce the two main voices of the host and the interviewee
      iii. There is a pause after Gelles says "Held v. Montana" to emphasize that this is going to be central to the discussion
      iv. They use music to transition out of the intro and into a discussion with one of the young people
4. How do the authors choose to conclude the podcast? Why?
   a. What words do they use?
      i. The host and interviewee discuss the significance of this case potentially winning, what it might impact
      ii. The host thanks the interviewee
      iii. The host summarizes what has been happening with the active and ongoing trial
      iv. The host also adds some more updates on what is going on in the world before ending the episode
   b. What sound strategies do they use? (music, voices, sound effects, silence, layering)
      i. They transition into the conclusion with music
5. If you had to divide the podcast into sections or parts, how many parts would it have? Why did the authors create this structure, and why are the parts in the order in which they are?
   a. Introduction of topic and interviewee
   b. Interview with Lander Bussey
   c. Overview of the legal argument/interview with Julia Olson
   d. Host's counterpoint—is it fair to hold the government accountable?
   e. Introduction of the Montana case specifically, with Montana's unique constitution and the addition of this language
   f. Discussion of the state government in Montana's response to the lawsuit
   g. Discussion of the likelihood of this case succeeding
   h. Conclusion

   This order introduces the topic and the personal, more remarkable elements of the story. like how it is being driven by young people passionate about environmentalism. The host uses the counterpoint to segue into sections that consider the state of Montana's legal position and the likelihood of the case succeeding. This arrangement is interesting and naturally starts with the individual stories of the students involved, expanding out to consider the implications of this case on a national and global scale.

Once students have answered these questions, teachers may consider having a class discussion about what choices the author made that were particularly beneficial in developing the argument and/or what choices the author could have changed to make the argument stronger. This takes the skills a step further for students, asking them to evaluate the development of the argument as well as the argument's ability to accomplish what students determine to be the author's purpose for the text.

Activity 7: Interpretation of Mood

Reading Activity 7 Materials

For this activity, which takes place in several steps, students will listen to the trailer for QCODE's *Carrier*, making a prediction about the mood of the audio drama, and then do the same with Apple Podcast's written description of the audio drama; the activity ends with students comparing their two predictions. Through this activity, students are able to understand different ways that authors create moods.

Trailer for QCODE's *Carrier*

Common Core ELA Standard(s)	**Description of Standard(s)**
RL.5	Analyze how an author's choices concerning how to structure a text, order events within it (e.g., parallel plots), and manipulate time (e.g., pacing, flash-backs) create such effects as mystery, tension, or surprise.
Objectives: SWBAT read critically in order to identify and analyze the choices an author makes in order to develop the mood of their text, including their words and use of sound strategies as well as the interplay between the two. SWBAT identify evidence from the text in order to support their analysis.	

TABLE 4.7: Close Reading Protocol for Analyzing Mood

Before Listening	Because we've found that students can struggle to differentiate mood and tone, we suggest going over the definition of mood before beginning this activity. We define mood as the feelings the author creates within their audience or, as Öhman and Rossi put it, mood refers to the feelings the author's choices in the text create in the reader or "the atmosphere that the author creates [for the reader] through their word choices, style, and use of imagery," along with other literary devices (1). Additionally, some students may benefit from having a word bank for different moods they may encounter; we have a word bank available in our differentiated materials, but, of course, you can use your own, too!
First Listen	To begin the activity, students should listen to the trailer once all the way through. After this first listen, teachers may have students jot down how they feel after listening to the trailer, but this isn't a requirement.
Second Listen	Students will then listen to the trailer again. During this second listen, students will analyze the text, using the organizer in **Part 1** of **"Interpretation of Mood Handout,"** both the words and sounds, in order to predict the mood of the audio drama. It's likely that students will need to replay and pause in order to com-plete their analysis. The final question in this part of the activity could be answered in writing or through discussion. We've provided a model of **Part 1** of **"Interpretation of Mood Handout,"** with student answers you might anticipate seeing below.

Interpretation of Mood Handout Part 1—Student Sample Responses	
	Evidence **What You Hear in the Trailer**
Voice Include *what* is said and *how* it is said	The main character's voice sounds stressed; she is also expressing financial need and struggling to get ahold of her father: "At this point, I really don't know what else I can do" (1:00). The action seems to be mysterious. "What the hell is this place" (1:23), said in a confused voice. "I hope you know what you're doing" (1:38), said over the phone. "A sealed trailer, yeah, that could be anything" (1:42). Later in the trailer, the main character's voice begins to sound more frantic, more panicked. She stutters on the phone call (1:57). At 2:20, the speaker is breathless, panting, struggling in panic to speak.
Sound Effects	Realistic sounds of being on the side of a highway, sounds of a large shipping truck, sounds of a phone ringing to indicate that she is trying to get ahold of her father and various professional contacts. Sound effects generally tell the listener where the main character is and what she is doing. A loud metallic bang in the back of the truck after a pause of silence suggests something large and live.
Music	There is slow, quiet, foreboding music playing underneath the first part of the episode. At 2:20, the music intensifies, becomes faster and more anxious.
Layering	The highway and truck sound effects are taking place underneath the sounds of the conversations between the characters and over the phone, creating a sense of being immersed in the scene. As the trailer progresses, the layering becomes denser with music and sound effects and conversations, all taking place on top of each other.
Silence	After the sound effects of the main character walking around to the back of the truck and opening the doors to her truck, there is silence in the back of the truck. Even though suspenseful music is playing, the silence as she opens the truck creates anxiety. The trailer cuts to total silence after an increase in volume, layering, and intensity at 2:28, creating a sense of a cliffhanger.
Now that you have considered the choices the author makes in the trailer, what do you predict the mood of this audio drama will be? Use evidence to support your response. We would expect students to answer with mood words like suspenseful, intense, tense, anxious, or frightening, using any of the evidence from the above table to support their claims.	

Once students have completed their mood prediction based on their reading of the audio trailer, they will be given the opportunity to practice the same skills with an alphabetic text with a similar rhetorical purpose to the audio trailer. While the second part of this activity doesn't have students reading sound texts, students will have benefitted from their prior practice with the audio trailer. Students may find themselves tuning in to specific words because the audio trailer primed them to consider certain details. This will also help students develop the skill of reading to determine mood in a variety of different modes. After reading the alphabetic text, students will complete **Part 2** of **"Interpretation of Mood Handout,"** which again requires them to make a prediction about the text's mood. Teachers can choose to have students complete this section in writing only or have students also engage in a discussion.

This activity concludes with **Part 3** of **"Interpretation of Mood Handout"** by asking students to compare the mood predictions they made for the audio trailer and the written description. This can lead to an interesting discussion about mood and how students identify and interpret mood, particularly as it appears in different modes. When answering this last part as a whole class, we love to see students argue for their different mood predictions, using evidence from the texts to support their claims.

Reading Activity 8 Materials

Activity 8: Interpretation of Tone

In this activity, students will listen to an excerpt from a 2013 episode of Oprah Winfrey's podcast *Oprah's Super Soul*. In this excerpt, she interviews Beyoncé Knowles about her first Super Bowl halftime performance in 2013, where Beyoncé reunited with the other members of her old band, Destiny's Child. Students should pay particular attention to the discussion between the two women in order to determine the tone of the interview. Interviews are a particularly interesting genre to use for this activity because they afford students the opportunity to practice their tone skills by looking at both the interviewer and the interviewee.

Excerpt from interview between Oprah Winfrey and Beyoncé Knowles on *Oprah's Super Soul*

Common Core ELA Standard(s)	Description of Standard(s)
RI.4	Determine the meaning of words and phrases as they are used in a text, including figurative, connotative, and technical meanings; analyze the cumulative impact of specific word choices on meaning and tone (e.g., how the language of a court opinion differs from that of a newspaper).
Objectives: SWBAT read critically in order to identify and analyze the choices an author makes in order to develop the mood of their text, including their words and use of sound strategies as well as the interplay between the two. SWBAT identify evidence from the text in order to support their analysis.	

TABLE 4.8: Close Reading Protocol for Analyzing Tone

Before Listening	As we mentioned earlier, because students can struggle to differentiate between mood and tone, we suggest going over the definition of tone before beginning the activity. We define tone as the feelings or attitude the author has about the topic of their piece or, as Öhman and Rossi put it, tone refers to how the author makes choices to "convey their own attitude towards a topic or subject" in that text (1). Additionally, some students may benefit from a word bank of tone words; our differentiated materials include one that teachers can use, but if you have one you usually use, that's great!
First Listen	To begin the activity, students should listen to the interview once all the way through. After this first listen, students will likely be able to answer the first question in **"Interpretation of Tone Handout,"** which asks them to identify the main subject or topic of the interview.
Second Listen	Students will then listen to the interview again; during this second listen, they will answer the remaining questions in **"Interpretation of Tone Handout,"** which help them analyze the tone of the interview. Students will likely find themselves needing to replay and pause the interview in order to answer the questions thoroughly. The final question requires students to find evidence to support their claim about tone; teachers should remind students to use both words and sound strategies as evidence. We've provided a model with student answers you can anticipate seeing below.

Interpretation of Tone Handout—Student Sample Responses

Answer the following questions below, giving at least one piece of evidence to support each of your responses:

1. What is the subject of this interview question that Oprah Winfrey asks Beyoncé?

   Oprah and Beyoncé are talking about how Beyoncé felt about her halftime performance at the 2013 Super Bowl.

2. How does Oprah Winfrey feel about this subject?

   Oprah is excited to discuss this with Beyoncé, and she seems to feel very supportive and proud of Beyoncé's accomplishments and relationships with her prior bandmates.

3. How does Beyoncé feel about the subject?

   Beyoncé seems to feel empowered, proud, and confident about her performance.

4. Given your answer to the previous question, what is the tone of this interview?

   The tone of the interview is supportive, encouraging, and celebratory.

5. What evidence, both words and sound strategies, support the tone you answered in the previous question?

   - Oprah's question implies that Beyoncé's performance was a huge success when she asks when Beyoncé knew that she "got this." She says this assertively and confidently, reassuring Beyoncé that the audience all saw her confidence.
   - Beyoncé's answer is immediate. There is no pause because she does not need to consider her answer. She says she knew immediately that "she had it."
   - She repeats "I knew I had it" twice with increasing volume and intensity, communicating a sense of sureness.
   - Beyoncé answers by breathlessly saying "oh my God," drawing out the exclamation to stress how much she enjoyed and took pride in that moment. Beyoncé laughs lightly as she affirms Oprah's statement, reliving her feelings by quoting her own inner monologue at the time in an excited, intense voice, referring to her bandmates as "my girls."

While students could end their tone practice here, they could also have a class discussion or do some writing to synthesize their findings.

Activity 9: Identification of Theme

For this activity, students listen to Wireless Theatre's audio drama "On Three" in order to determine the main theme and explain how it is developed over the course of the narrative. We have chosen an audio drama to use with this activity to help demonstrate the ways in which audio dramas can be a powerful multimodal tool for helping students master the complicated literary skill of theme identification; however, this activity could work with a wide range of audio genres, as the concept of theme is broadly applicable. While identifying theme in other genres of texts may also require students to consider elements like historical or social context, author's persona, and target audience, for this particular text, we will be emphasizing the skills of identifying tone and literary devices as tools to identify a theme. As we mentioned in Chapter 3, we see determining a theme in a text as a culminating skill that relies on some of the prior skills we've discussed so far, most notably the skills of interpreting literary devices and tone, so we recommend that students have some level of proficiency or mastery over these skills before attempting this activity.

Reading Activity 9 Materials

"On Three" by Wireless Theatre

Additionally, regardless of the genre teachers choose to use with this activity, we recommend that texts be broken up into smaller chunks; for example, we've broken this audio drama up into several scenes. Chunking a text can be a great way to scaffold activities, and it also encourages students to spend more time considering each part of the text. Teachers may choose to chunk or break up the text for students, complete this step as a whole class, or ask students to determine the best way to break it up.

Common Core ELA Standard(s)	Description of Standard(s)
RL.2	Determine a theme or central idea of a text and analyze in detail its development over the course of the text, including how it emerges and is shaped and refined by specific details; provide an objective summary of the text.
Objectives: SWBAT read critically in order to identify and analyze the theme of the text as well as the choices an author makes in order to develop that theme, including consideration of when and where sound strategies are used in theme construction. SWBAT identify evidence from the text in order to support their analysis.	

TABLE 4.9: Close Reading Protocol for Analyzing Theme

Before Listening	Theme can be a particularly complicated concept, and, even if students have studied it before, we recommend beginning this activity with a review of theme. We define theme as a universal message about humanity that the author is constructing over the course of their text, a particular position on the human condition that the author wants the audience to reflect on and analyze after reading the piece. If you as an educator have a particular definition you favor or that reflects the work you've done thus far with your students, we encourage you to use it. Giving students a moment to discuss and fully revisit this definition before attempting this activity may support a more thorough analysis of the theme of this audio drama.
First Listen	We recommend students complete a full listen to the audio drama before getting into the bulk of the activity. Students could jot down their thoughts about the theme or major ideas, but this is optional. We recommend you keep work to a minimum during the first listen of the audio drama so that students have a chance to entirely immerse themselves in the listening experience and resist the urge to remove themselves from the listening process in an effort to take notes or keep up with a worksheet.
Second Listen	During their second listen, students will complete an organizer, which can be found in **"Listening for Sound Strategies: Theme Handout,"** in which they will analyze the sound strategies in the audio drama and the impact of those strategies on each scene as a whole. Although this step does not explicitly discuss or refer to theme, we begin with it because an understanding of sound strategies and how they appear in the text is essential for making claims and drawing conclusions about tone and various literary devices. Teachers should encourage students to listen multiple times, including pausing and replaying parts that seem particularly important. Teachers may even consider having students complete this step with a jigsaw in which one student per group is responsible for a specific sound strategy, which they then share with their group members.
Third Listen	Students will use their responses from **"Listening for Sound Strategies: Theme Handout,"** in order to complete this next step in **"Elements of Theme Handout."** While students could complete this part without an additional listen and refer to their earlier responses solely, we love to encourage an additional listen when we can! To complete **"Elements of Theme Handout,"** students will use their previous findings to make claims about the tone and literary devices used in the audio drama. Again, this step doesn't explicitly deal with theme; however, we believe these steps are critical to a thorough analysis of theme and its development. Using their claims and analysis about tone and literary devices, students will then answer questions, which will guide them to make a claim about the main abstract idea of the text.

The work students will have done thus far has prepared them to analyze more fully the abstract idea that they will go on to use to formulate a theme; **"Determining Theme Handout"** asks students to consider their previous work in order to support this next step. We have provided a word bank of various abstract ideas that students could be given; however, we encourage you to create and use your own if ours doesn't feel like a good fit! Once students have determined the abstract idea that their close reading best supports, they can use that to determine the main theme of the text. This may be a good point to clarify with students the difference between an abstract idea and a theme. A brief discussion of the differences between the two may help students complete this step more successfully. We included a model below of the **"Determining Theme Handout"** with answers we might expect from students.

Determining Theme Handout—Student Sample Responses

Reflect on your overall close reading of "On Three" by answering the questions below. Give evidence to support your answers.

1. What ideas, images, devices, or techniques appear repeatedly throughout the text? Give examples.

   There will be many potential answers to this question, but potential responses include: Death/ Loss, the List, Laughter.

2. Considering your answer from the prior question, do those ideas, images, devices, or techniques evolve or remain the same? Explain your answer.

   Depending on their answers to question 1, student responses here could vary. However, we'd expect them to mention how the laugh at the end demonstrates a change from the discussion of her laughter in the therapist's office. The list also evolves as they cross off the last line, showing a progression in their healing journey.

3. Does the story have a message or moral? If so, what is it? Support your answer.

   Again, there will be many potential answers to this question, but potential responses include:

   - *When you love someone, they are always with you even if they can't be physically.*
   - *Love can help us conquer all hardships and fears.*
   - *No matter how hard things get, we need to support those we love and help them through it.*

Now that you've completed a thorough analysis, what is the main abstract idea of the text? Remember, an abstract idea refers to a major idea or topic of the text and is generally something conceptual or intangible.

Abstract Idea

There will be many potential answers to this question, but potential responses include: Loss and grief, love, hope, connection

In order to determine the theme, combine the abstract idea with what the author is suggesting about it.

Theme

Depending on the students' choice of an abstract idea, potential answers could include:

- Grief is a reminder of how much we loved, and through our processing of our loss, we can find peace and love.
- Love and loyalty can overcome tragedy.
- There is always hope, even in deep darkness.

It may be useful to discuss with students how a single text can have multiple themes or that there can be major as well as minor themes in a text. Students may present different answers to the above section, and they may all be correct. The argument students are making is not only for the theme they identify but also that their identified theme is central or primary in some way, a major theme. While this may create a sense of competition, it is important for students to argue for the centrality of the theme they have chosen because, particularly in longer texts, multiple coexisting themes can be identified.

To complete this activity, students will respond to the prompt in the **"Analyzing Theme Handout"** that asks students to synthesize their work in the prior steps to demonstrate their understanding of how the theme they have identified develops over the course of the text. This step can be completed as a group discussion, a graphic organizer, an outline, a more traditional alphabetic essay, or a wide range of classroom activities. The main priority in this part of the activity is to prompt students to use the information they gathered from each step of the activity to trace the author's evolution, construction, and development of the theme.

Analyzing Theme Handout—Student Sample Responses

Finally, write a response in which you identify the main theme in the text and explain how the author develops it. Use evidence from the audio drama, particularly the materials you gathered from the previous handouts, to support your answer; remember to consider the particular sound strategies used and how they impact the text overall.

There is a wide range of potential answers to this prompt; however, in their response, students could explain things like...

- To support the theme of grief as a product of love and a path to peace
  - Repeated examples of love between the husband and wife, between the parents and the son, as seen in conversations, pauses, sound effects
  - Beginning and ending the narrative in the same location and scene, despite everything that has happened, demonstrates the characters returning to love and joy, even when it is frightening or hard
  - The symbol of the wife's laughter, which is absent in the beginning, then appears in a memory, and then appears in real time, demonstrates how healing can happen through grief
- To support the theme of hope in darkness
  - The beautiful instrumental music playing as the woman describes the scene and includes a vision of her son demonstrates that she is seeing beauty even in a frightening situation, even when she still misses him
  - In all four scenes, even though they each have a tone of sadness, the husband and wife's love for one another appears clearly through their conversation, sound effects, and actions

To conclude this activity, teachers may consider having a class discussion about the themes students found and analyzed or having students write a literary analysis essay.

Activity 10: Identification of Rhetorical Appeals

In this activity, students will listen to Michelle Obama's last remarks as First Lady in which she addresses the youth of the United States, encouraging them in very specific ways. This activity will ask students to identify the rhetorical appeals she chooses and consider why and how those appeals work to make Obama's speech effective.

Reading Activity 10 Materials

Michelle Obama's Last Remarks as First Lady

We have chosen a speech by a well-known public figure as the genre of audio text for this activity because rhetorical appeals are most powerful as tools when considered within the larger rhetorical situation (author, audience, purpose, etc.). Speeches by well-known public figures offer students lots of accessible, relatable opportunities to consider the context within which the text exists. However, this activity can work with a wide range of audio genres; it is our belief that all texts in all genres, modes, and disciplines appeal to their audiences in some way. We encourage you to adapt this activity for use with nonfiction such as informational texts like interviews and podcasts; we also encourage you to consider how this activity might work with literary texts, including poetry, music, or audio memoirs.

As we mentioned in Chapter 3, we view the identification and analysis of rhetorical appeals as a cumulative skill that relies on some of the prior skills we've discussed in this chapter. In order to effectively identify and analyze rhetorical appeals in a text like a speech, students will need to have an understanding of the author's persona, their target audience, identification of an argument and/or purpose, and awareness of organization and structure, as well as potentially many others. We recommend that students have some degree of confidence and familiarity with these skills before attempting this activity.

<table>
<tr><th>Common Core ELA Standard(s)</th><th>Description of Standard(s)</th></tr>
<tr><td>RI.6</td><td>Determine an author's point of view or purpose in a text and analyze how the author uses rhetoric to advance that point of view or purpose.</td></tr>
<tr><td colspan="2">Objectives: SWBAT read critically in order to identify and analyze the choices an author makes in order to construct targeted rhetorical appeals in a speech, using evidence from the text, including sound strategies, and contextual information from the rhetorical situation to support their identification and analysis.</td></tr>
</table>

TABLE 4.10: Close Reading Protocol for Identifying and Analyzing Rhetorical Appeals

Before Listening	It may be helpful to give students a refresher on the three rhetorical appeals and how they work before tackling this activity. We find that offering examples is the best way to help students recognize these appeals, and using audio examples will best prepare them to approach this particular activity head on. We've created a brief summary table in the **"Rhetorical Appeals Review Handout"** as an optional support tool to give students a quick warm-up on their rhetorical appeals knowledge; however, this is not essential to the activity. If you have your own materials for reviewing the rhetorical appeals with students, we encourage you to use them before beginning this activity. Additionally, if you're looking for visuals and content to support designing a more in-depth or comprehensive review of the rhetorical appeals, we encourage you to revisit our "Rhetoric" section from Chapter 2: The Fundamentals of Studying Sound Texts.
First Listen	As always, we recommend that teachers have students listen to the speech in its entirety at least once before starting the handouts. During this first listen, students could jot down their thoughts about Obama's goals or major ideas, but this is optional. We recommend you keep work to a minimum during the first listen of the speech so that students have a chance to entirely immerse themselves in the listening experience and resist the urge to remove themselves from the listening process in an effort to take notes or keep up with a handout.
Second Listen	During the second listen, students will complete an organizer in the **"Rhetorical Situation Awareness Handout"** that asks them to identify the rhetorical situation, which students must understand before they can analyze Obama's use of rhetorical appeals. Much like we suggested in Activity 9, we find students enjoy completing this organizer as a jigsaw in which each individual member of a group listens for their assigned element of the rhetorical situation, focusing on its role in the speech as a whole and then sharing their findings with their group in order to determine together Obama's purpose. Students will then answer questions related to her central goal based on their responses in the organizer. Additionally, as an extension option or opportunity for differentiation for this part of the activity, we also personally enjoy asking our students to look outside of the audio text in order to complete basic research into the rhetorical situation using simple internet searches as one of the tasks of this activity. In a scenario like this one, students can learn basic information about Michelle Obama's life, what was happening politically and socially in the United States in the same week or month as this speech, and a variety of other similar pieces of information. This extension option works best when students are already equipped with an understanding of basic research and source-evaluation skills. The overall activity can be completed effectively without this addition; however, this outside research can deepen and enrich the way students read and rhetorically analyze the text as well.
Third Listen	Once students have a firm understanding of the speech's rhetorical situation and purpose, they will be ready to move on to an analysis of the rhetorical appeals using the organizer from the **"Rhetorical Appeals Handout."** This "third listen" may not be a complete listen, and it's very likely that students will frequently need to pause and replay sections of the speech in order to complete their work. The organizer from the **"Rhetorical Appeals Handout"** below provides a model of student answers for a portion of the speech.

Rhetorical Appeals Handout—Student Sample Responses			
Evidence A direct quote from the speech (words and sounds); this should include a timestamp. Note: Remember, the sound of *how* she says something is just as important to *what* she says.	**Rhetorical Appeal** When you hear Obama use a rhetorical appeal, identify which appeal you hear (ethos, pathos, or logos).	**Analysis** Why did you identify this line as the appeal that you did? What did Obama say and how did she say it that made you choose that appeal?	**Serving Her Purpose** How does using this appeal in this way help accomplish the purpose you identified in the Rhetorical Awareness Worksheet? Why is this appeal a good fit for this rhetorical situation?
"I can think of no better message to send to our young people in my last official remarks as First Lady" —She emphasizes "official" by increasing her volume and slowing down the word a bit (0:04–0:11). …	Ethos …	She is establishing her credibility as First Lady; this is a role that she takes seriously and that holds power. …	She is establishing herself as an authority and reliable speaker, someone the youth of America can and should trust. …
"For all the young people in this room and those who are watching, know that this country belongs to you—to all of you, from every background and walk of life." —She pauses after "belongs to you" and puts an emphasis on the word "all" by changing her pitch and slightly cracking her voice (0:14–0:26).	Pathos	By emphasizing "all," she is making her audience feel included and seen. Given the context of her speech, this would be particularly emotional for her audience, who are likely feeling tension with the new admin.	Her audience is more likely to respond to her message if they feel that they are part of the community and legacy she has created. She is including them in order to generate a sense of personal investment.
"If you or your parents are immigrants, know that you are part of a proud American tradition." —She gets louder and puts an emphasis on the word "proud" by increasing her volume and slowing down the word a bit (0:27–0:33). …	Pathos …	The new admin and current political discourse has largely villainized immigrants, so this is Obama pushing back on that. She purposely includes immigrants as part of America's history, and an important and positive part of it, to make any immigrants or immigrant children feel seen and valued. …	Obama's position is closely tied to the well-being of the country. By encouraging pride and civic action alongside a feeling of patriotism, she is encouraging young Americans to stay involved in politics, even if they do not feel included with or represented by the upcoming elected officials. …
Her voice continues to crack with emotion as she says, "And know that I will be with you, rooting for you and working to support you for the rest of my life" (7:14–7:19).	Ethos	She asserts her commitment to the youth of the country by promising to be with them and help them.	Showing that her audience has her commitment, she helps her audience feel supported in their fight.

With a strained voice, like she's starting to cry, she says, "So, I want to close today by simply saying thank you. Thank you for everything you do for our kids and for our country. Being your First Lady has been the greatest honor of my life, and I hope I've made you proud" (7:50–8:06).	Ethos and Pathos	Calling herself "your First Lady," she builds her credibility as someone who has worked for the people, and she furthers this point when she says she "hope[s she's] made [the audience] proud." Her crying voice and her gratitude would likely make her audience feel appreciated, valued, and connected to her.	By sharing her gratitude and servitude, she humbles herself in front of her audience, which helps the audience feel like more of an equal in this continued fight, a fight that they will work on together.

It is helpful to note that the text we've chosen to use with this activity, Obama's speech, primarily makes use of ethos and pathos appeals, without much use of the logos appeal. When completing this activity by reading a different audio text, it's important to consider that not all texts make use of all three rhetorical appeals. If you choose a different text to use with this activity, you may find that you or your students identify little or no evidence of one or more of the three rhetorical appeals. In this scenario, we recommend, after students identify and analyze the rhetorical appeals in the text, giving them the opportunity to consider the following prompt: "If a rhetorical appeal does not appear in the text, explain why you think the author chose to omit that appeal. Use your work from the **"Rhetorical Situation Awareness Handout"** to explain your answer." While this isn't essential, it will offer another chance for students to connect their analysis of the rhetorical appeals to the overall purpose of the text within its rhetorical context.

When students have an identification and analysis of the rhetorical situation, **"Rhetorical Situation Awareness Handout,"** and rhetorical appeals, **"Rhetorical Appeals Handout,"** they are ready for the final step, which asks students to synthesize their earlier work in order to analyze Obama's use of rhetorical appeals. For the final step of this activity in **"Rhetorical Analysis Handout,"** students can respond to the questions in writing or during discussion. We've included a model of student responses on next page.

Rhetorical Analysis—Student Sample Responses

1. Which of the three rhetorical appeals does Obama open her speech with? Given the rhetorical situation, why do you think she chose to open with that appeal?

   Students may answer with either ethos or pathos or a blend of the two. While ethos is the immediate appeal that we think students would see, given her emphasis on her position as First Lady, some students may choose pathos because she talks about the idea of who the country belongs to and who belongs in the country, appealing to emotions of unity, pride, and solidarity. Opening by jointly invoking her position as well as emotions of pride and connection not only establishes her reliability and authority but also engages the audience in a sense of camaraderie with her as she concludes her remarks. We would expect students to consider elements of the rhetorical situation in this answer, including her position as a First Lady about to step down, her audience of America's youth, and her rhetorical purpose in this speech.

2. Which of the three rhetorical appeals does Obama close her speech with? Given the rhetorical situation, why do you think she chose to close with that appeal?

   Obama uses a combination of both ethos and pathos in her closing, so students may choose to focus on both or emphasize one. Concluding with these two appeals leaves her time in her position with a tone of thankfulness and humility while creating a sense of pride in her listeners. When considering how this would impact her speech's effectiveness, we would expect students to consider elements of the rhetorical situation in this answer, including her position as a First Lady about to step down, her audience of America's youth, and her rhetorical purpose in this speech.

3. Of the three appeals, which do you think is primary in Obama's speech? Explain why you chose the appeal you did.

   Likely, students will argue that pathos is the primary rhetorical appeal for this speech. However, students may also choose ethos. In this speech, the two often intertwine. Students may choose to support their answers with the number of appeals used or the significance and influence of the appeals used with an understanding of the rhetorical situation in which the speech took place.

4. Consider your answer to Question 3 in light of the rhetorical situation for this speech. Why do you think Obama chose to make this her primary rhetorical appeal? How would that appeal be most effective?

   Reasons students may give for why she chose pathos might include:

   - *This is her final speech, which would be emotional for people who liked her and her husband.*
   - *People who supported the Obamas were likely worried about the change that comes with a new administration.*
   - *Although she doesn't explicitly state it here, it's obvious she also has anxieties about the new administration and their politics.*

   Reasons students may give for why she chose ethos might include:

   - *This is her final speech as First Lady, so she's emphasizing this position.*
   - *Given the new administration coming in and their very different political views, she'd likely want to emphasize her position, particularly as the first Black First Lady of America.*

For teachers who want to take this a step further, natural ways to continue this work could include asking students to write rhetorical analysis essays analyzing Obama's choices or to write argumentative essays justifying their own choice of primary rhetorical appeal in the essay.

Conclusion

Chapter 4 Conclusion Audio

Chapter 4 Conclusion Transcript

5

The Fundamentals of Writing Sound Texts

Introduction

Chapter 5 Introduction Audio

Chapter 5 Introduction Transcript

The Writing Process

Before getting into the individual writing skills that the mode of sound can help students access, we think it's important to take time to acknowledge that writing in any mode is a process. We believe firmly that students need to experience and grapple with "how writing evolves from the time when there is . . . not a single word . . . until there is final published" content (Murray 27). Understanding this can often be one of the biggest gifts we can give to our students.

Because of this, the next chapters are going to spend some time on what that process can look like in the audio mode in particular. You can expect some students to be familiar with parts of this process from their experiences with traditional printed texts or texts in other modes. However, you can also expect that aspects of the process of composing an audio text will be entirely unique to this mode and potentially very unfamiliar to students. We want to open this chapter with a discussion of some of the elements of the writing process that might be unique to the mode of sound, as well as elements that will remain the same.

As we discuss some of these aspects of the sound writing process, we'd like to take a moment to note that, in any mode, different students may work better with different types of writing processes. Donald M. Murray suggests that "the process of writing changes with the writing task, the writer's experience with that writing task, and the thinking style of that writer" (27). We'd also like to add that the process may change with the writing mode as well; the same student may approach visual composition differently than audio or alphabetic. So, particularly when composing in a new mode, we encourage you to allow students some choice in how they approach the process of composing their own sound texts, familiarizing them with options but allowing them to reflect on their practices and identities as writers and begin a process of making writerly choices for themselves.

Brainstorming and Prewriting

This step will have a lot in common with the writing processes students have been through before; performing this phase of the writing process for a sound text should feel fairly familiar. Strategies such as outlining, freewriting, and using word maps to brainstorm the text can and should all be part of this process. Even when writing a sound text, this phase of the writing process will most likely involve pen and paper or typed brainstorming materials. Students may gather at a whiteboard to map out their plans for the text. Below we have a few samples of the pen-and-paper brainstorming materials we've generated for students; however, these brainstorms can take any form, including traditional outlines or bulleted lists. Students may also wish to create a traditional printed script as part of their prewriting process after brainstorming and/or outlining. All of these things will feel familiar to students who are more used to working in traditional printed modes.

Some of the factors students are considering when brainstorming and prewriting a sound text will also be the same as factors they consider for their essays or other traditional printed writing assignments. Brainstorming and workshopping ideas for a good sound text means thinking about diction, tone, and which genre best fits their rhetorical situation. Students will need to consider their organizational structure and how best to arrange and present their information, potentially creating an outline. This phase of the writing process will also often consider the use of any literary devices. All of these familiar elements go into the brainstorming and planning phase of writing a sound text, meaning that not only will students bring some confidence and experience to the table when writing sound texts, they will also develop and strengthen key skills when drafting a sound text that they can then directly apply when writing in a different mode or for a more traditional printed text.

However, some elements of the brainstorming and prewriting phase of the writing process will be unique to the mode of sound. While considering the tone and purposes of the text they are writing, students will need to think about how they plan to use some of the sound strategies to create their desired tone and achieve their purposes. Some students may decide they need **sound effects**, and their brainstorming and preparation portion of the writing process may require them to consider how to gather the sounds they will need. Students may need to consider access to interviewees, recording equipment, and editing software as they map out their plans. Other writing processes may find a need to use **music** in the sound text, and then the drafting process may require students to consider copyright and legality issues (we will cover how to discuss this with students later in this section). Planning where to employ **silence**, which **voices** to use, and how to **layer** these sounds together is all unique to the process of writing using sound. Teachers may wish to use specific worksheets to scaffold this process for students, particularly if students are new to working in the mode of sound. Our next chapter will give you plenty of examples and ideas to review for the kinds of materials you can offer students to support their brainstorming and prewriting process.

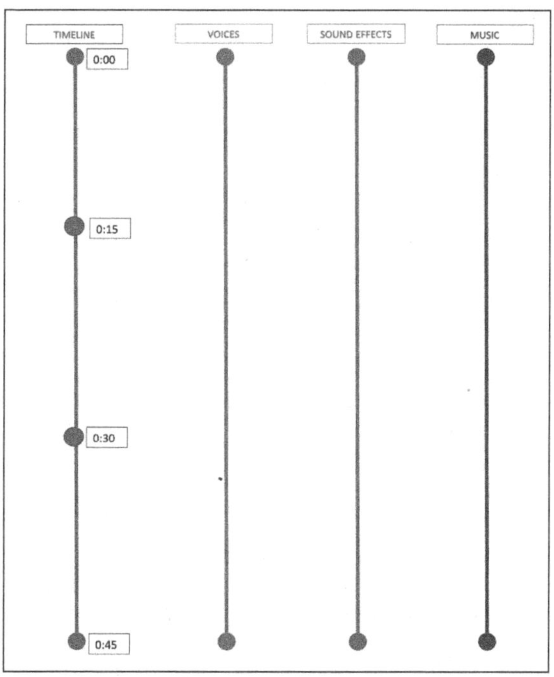

FIGURE 5.1: Timeline Prewriting Device

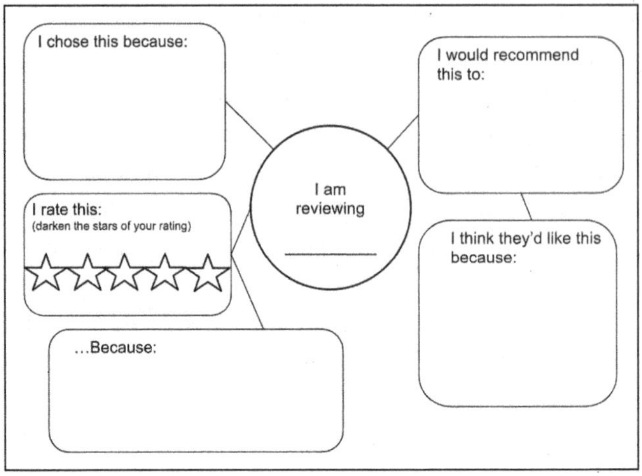

FIGURE 5.2: Review Podcast Organizer

Storyboard Template for Audio Drama

Scene 1:

- Setting:
- Characters present:
- Summary of any dialogue:
- List of sound effects, music, or silences to plan for:
- Estimated length of scene in minutes and/or sections:

Scene 2:

- Setting:
- Characters present:
- Summary of any dialogue:
- List of sound effects, music, or silences to plan for:
- Estimated length of scene in minutes and/or sections:

FIGURE 5.3: Storyboard Template

Drafting

Taking plans from the prewriting phase of the sound text writing process, whether those be outlines, word maps, or freewrites, and beginning the step of assembling them into a draft is intimidating. This is a difficult step in the writing process, regardless of the mode in which students are working. In any mode, this process involves connecting different ideas and elements of the text into a unified whole. When doing this with a traditional printed text, it usually involves sitting down in front of a computer screen and assembling and grouping ideas into sentences and paragraphs and then arranging those sentences and paragraphs to create the typed text.

When drafting in the mode of sound, students will still be assembling ideas and elements of their text into a whole, but these will take the form of recorded sounds instead of typed or handwritten words. This means students will be gathering and recording sounds and editing a sound file, piecing together the elements from their prewriting process into a single sound text. The interviews, **sound effects**, and **music** that students decided on in the prewriting process will need to be recorded, gathered, and imported into an editing software where students can arrange, edit, and **layer** them as needed. The scripts and outlines that students created will need to be translated into sound and arranged in the audio file. The end product of this phase of the process should be a single text; when writing using sound, that text will be an audio file.

The technical part of the drafting stage when writing a sound text is probably the most unique to this mode, and this is largely

Ethical Interviewing Practices!

Holding and recording interviews may or may not be a part of your students' drafting processes; however, interviews are common ingredients in sound text genres like podcasts and audio news broadcasts. Interviews sometimes even function as sound texts in their own right.

If your students' prewriting and drafting begins to suggest that interviews will be one of the elements in their sound texts, it's a good idea to prepare them with some basic interview etiquette to ensure that their interviews are fair, ethical, and respectful. Some simple principles we teach our students include:

- It is essential that the interviewee fully understands that they are being recorded and that they consent to the recording being used in the way you plan to use it. Discuss the logistics and general purpose of your project with your interviewee beforehand, particularly letting them know where the finished sound text will be shared.
- It is the interviewer's responsibility to listen with respect to an interviewee's answers, creating space for the interviewee to answer honestly and thoughtfully. Good interviews are "more like a conversation than a rapid-fire question-and-answer session" (Rodrigue and Stedman 157). Consider how to create an inviting, conversational dynamic with your interviewee.
- Interview questions should not be leading. This means that questions should not be unfairly biased or stacked so as to lead to particular answers or outcomes that may or may not truly reflect the interviewee's perspective.
- Do your research before your interview. Know who you are interviewing and what their position and relevance is to your topic or subject. Don't rely on them to explain basic information to you.
- When editing the recording of your interview, it is unlikely that you will use every word. When choosing which clips of the interview to use, be careful to include enough context so as not to misrepresent or incorrectly frame your interviewee's words. Make sure that, after your editing, the interview reflects what your interviewee meant to say.

because of the equipment needed to record and create the sound texts. Drafting a sound text will require students to make choices about equipment and software (more on this shortly). Students may need to practice recording in different spaces or in different ways to make sure their sounds are clear. Depending on availability, they may try using different microphones and recording devices in order to achieve the desired effect. Once students are editing their sound file, they may prefer one editing software over another. While there are some ways to minimize the need for students to delve too deeply into the technology and equipment end of writing using sound, we like to encourage students to play with this part of the drafting process as much as possible, as it asks them to consider their text draft in different ways, and it develops lifelong skills with finding, learning, and using digital tools.

Revision and Editing

Once student writers have created at least a first draft, the process of receiving feedback, editing, and revising a sound text will also have both familiar and sound-specific elements to it. Just like traditional printed writing, teacher and peer feedback is important and can take the form of written notes, brief conferences and conversations, and sharing impressions of what the student authors' purposes appeared to be in the draft.

However, the way this feedback is gathered may be different. Instead of having peer editing sessions in which students read one another's essays, teachers may need to facilitate listening sessions in which peers can hear each other's work. Feedback from peers and teachers will most likely include timestamps so that comments can be specific and clear. Chapter 6 will include some guided peer review activities as well as some direction on how you as an educator can give productive feedback on a student's draft of an audio text.

Once student writers have received feedback on sound texts, responding to that feedback through revisions will most likely also differ from the traditional writing experience. Instead of using a word-processing program on a computer to rearrange paragraphs or adjust wording and grammar, which is likely the scenario we and our students see most often in the writing process, revisions of a sound text may ask student writers to rerecord interviews or gather different **sound effects** or **voices**. While students may need to rearrange portions of the sound text in ways that are similar to rearranging paragraphs in a traditional printed text, this rearranging process will most likely look different for a sound text. Moving sounds in a sound file will ask students to do some editing, smooth transitions, balance volume, and ensure that **layering** is effective and clear. Instead of scanning lines of text to consider copying and pasting words or adding lines, students who are returning to edit an audio file are listening to their work and considering different sounds to copy and paste or add.

The Nuts and Bolts of Sound Writing Technology

As we mentioned earlier, one of the elements of the writing process when working with the mode of sound that will likely differ the most from what educators and students are used to will involve technology. The use of sound-specific equipment will probably have the largest impact on the drafting, revising, and editing steps; however, depending on how students' approach their work, the tech can become important at any phase.

Because the technology—that is, the hardware and software—around recording, editing, and producing sound texts is evolving so rapidly, we have decided to refrain from getting into too much depth or specificity here. We're pretty sure that if we wrote up any how-to guides or software-specific references, they'd be out of date by the time the book was printed and on shelves. Instead, we've created some practical generalized guidelines for those of you who might be somewhat new to creating your own sound texts with students.

When we talk about the technology required to compose in the mode of sound, there are usually two categories of equipment we're referring to: recording and editing.

- Tools needed to record generally refer to whatever device(s) you and your students are using to capture sounds from the world around you to include in your sound texts, whether that be a student's spoken narration, a **sound effect**, or ambient noise.
- Tools needed to edit generally refer to software students will use on their computers to gather, arrange, and modify the sound files they gather.

TABLE 5.1: Tools for Writing with Sound

Recording Tools	Editing Tools
a. Phones—Whether Apple or Android, if your students have access to mobile phones, either their own or their family's, almost all smartphones have basic recording functions that students can export and email to themselves. b. Laptops—Most laptops come equipped with fairly sophisticated built-in recording equipment. If your students, or even one student in the group, has access to a laptop with a built-in microphone, they'll be able to record high-quality content through GarageBand, QuickTime, or a variety of free downloadable applications. c. Microphones—If your school has access to recording equipment or Makerspace audio tools, it can be a great experience for students to get hands-on time recording using podcasting microphones. We understand that this is not an option available to most classrooms; however, some schools do have this capability.	If you hop on Google and search "best free audio editors," you'll find a dozen different "top 10" lists, each featuring some exciting new up-and-coming options. We've had very good personal luck with choosing some highly rated new editors and giving them a try! This is how we came upon some of our current favorites. You may also find that students have software they are familiar with, can locate themselves, and/or would like to use. In general, we recommend allowing students to compose with their software of choice if they demonstrate a preference. It may mean that you have to ask them to explain some of the controls to you, but this is a great opportunity to decenter yourself as an authority in the classroom and allow students to take the reins of their learning processes. Selection of Audio Editing Software Options

Whether for recording or editing, the digital tools students are using to write across all modes are evolving rapidly. There is a huge benefit to fostering confidence in students when it comes to approaching a new digital composition tool and asking them to develop the skills required to use the tool effectively. Both the Common Core and NCTE's *Definition of Literacy in a Digital Age* emphasize fluency with digital composition tools as a critical element of literacy skills. If you and/or some (or all) of your students are unfamiliar with a particular tool, this presents a great opportunity to learn collaboratively as a class, working together to discover the affordances and constraints of digital composition tools.

Generally, regardless of which audio editing software you choose, there will be some similarities in the interfaces and visuals. Below are three screenshots from three different audio editing softwares: GarageBand, Audacity, and Podcastle.

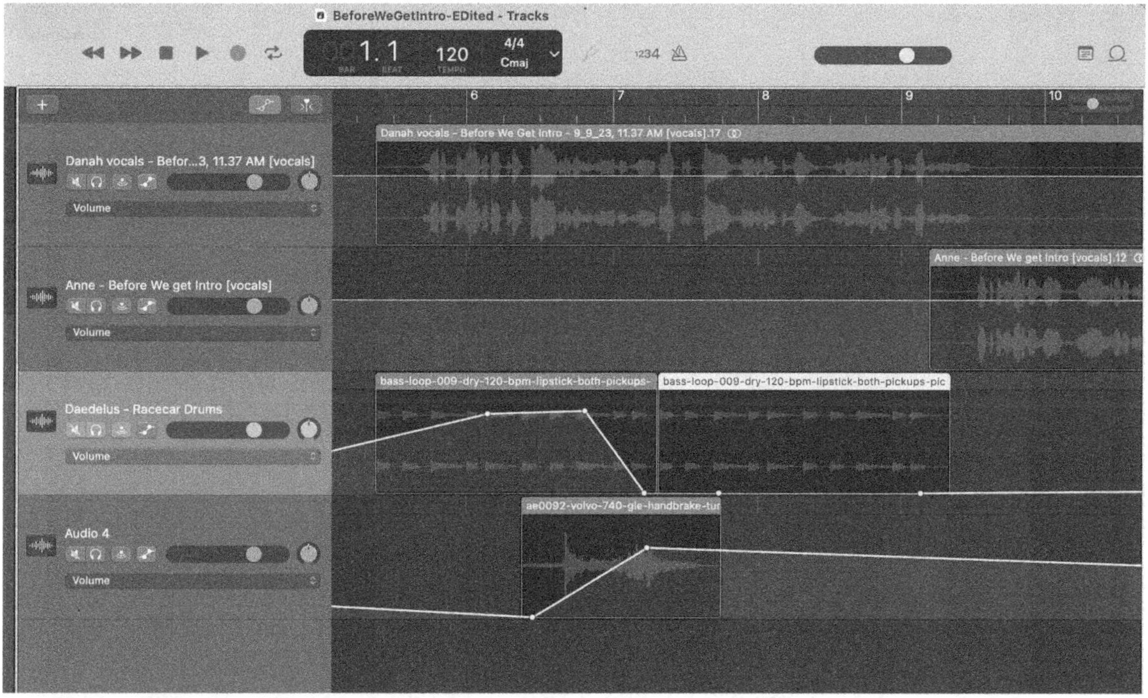

FIGURE 5.4: GarageBand User Interface

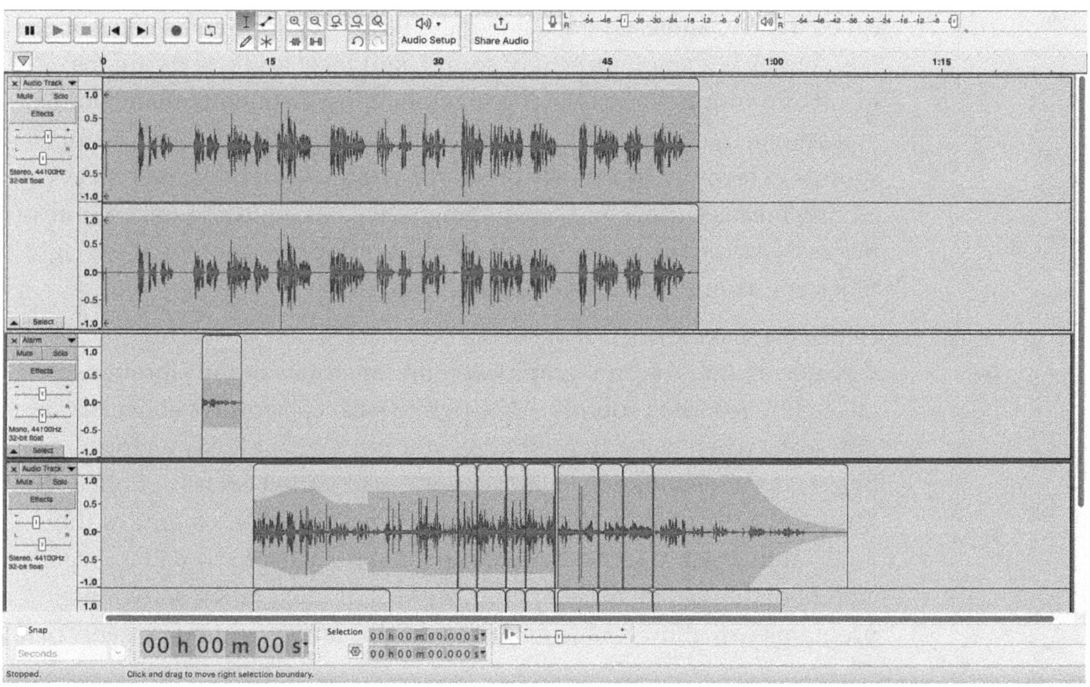

FIGURE 5.5: Audacity User Interface

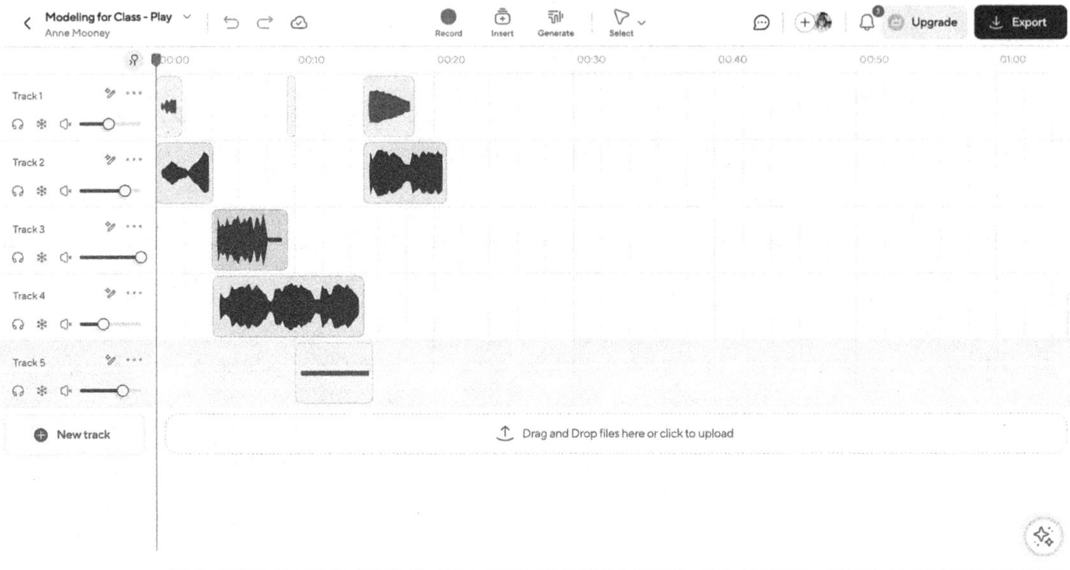

FIGURE 5.6: Podcastle User Interface

You'll notice that all three interfaces have:

- *Multiple separate rows, each with their own controls.* Each of these rows is called a track, and each track generally houses its own respective sound file. A track is a single stream of sound, and most audio texts are the result of multiple tracks playing together. Most frequently there will be at least one track for each speaker, and then an additional track(s) for sounds to **layer** in, like **music** or **sound effects**. Generally, the process of editing means cutting and/or moving as well as adjusting the volume on pieces of each track around so that they overlap one another at the right times and volumes to create the desired effects.
- *Horizontal soundwaves that appear on each track.* These are called waveforms, and they are graphical representations of the vibrations created by recorded sounds. Although the screen captures above are in grayscale, when using the software, you can see that the waveforms are blue in GarageBand, purple in Audacity, and varied colors in Podcastle. The height of a peak in a waveform corresponds to the volume of the audio at that point, so a very large spike in the waveform will indicate a point of marked increase in volume. Most audio editing software programs will allow you to zoom in and out on particular segments of a

waveform so that you can visually identify particular lines or moments of silence in a recording. This helps you locate where individual lines, words, or sounds start or stop so that you can edit precisely.

So, while the controls and color schemes will vary from software to software, the mechanics and layout of an audio editing software are fairly consistent. You should be able to see a series of tracks arranged on top of one another, each with their own waveform that you can use to identify particular moments in the individual recordings. In a way, once you become comfortable with the editing process in one audio editing software, moving to another is just a matter of learning the new buttons and controls. We aren't here to oversimplify the process, but we do believe that the mechanics and technology of writing in the mode of sound aren't as daunting as they might initially appear.

Sourcing, Copyright, and Fair Use

When it comes to writing, regardless of mode, it's essential that our students confront the issue of ethical use of sources and plagiarism. Student writers need to engage the complicated question of integrating and working with the texts of others when writing their own in ways that are honest and give appropriate credit. When working in the mode of sound, copyright and fair use become some of the central concepts we use to address the idea of source use and plagiarism.

- **Copyright** refers to the rights that an author has over their own original work. This can apply to texts in a variety of modes including visual, audio, or alphabetic, but copyright ownership allows the author to maintain control over the way their work is reproduced, copied, distributed, displayed, performed, shared, etc. It allows authors and creators to treat their work as intellectual property from which they can make money if others wish to use it. Only a copyright owner has the ability to give permission to use their work.
- **Fair use** refers to situations in which authors can use copyrighted materials without getting permission from the owner of the copyright. The goal of fair use is to encourage creativity, play, remixing, and creative expression without financial limitations. What exactly fair use covers can be complicated, and we don't think students or educators need a comprehensive understanding of fair use to be able to take advantage of its opportunities to use copyrighted work.

The main takeaway we want educators to understand about copyright and fair use policies is this: *When writing in their own classrooms, educators and students have free rein through fair use policies; as long as the audio texts that educators and students create are only written and shared within the classroom, copyright permissions aren't something you have to worry about.*

However, if you or your students plan to publish audio texts publicly, submit them to public competitions, or in any way share these texts with an open audience, then it might be time to consider whether the audio text in question still falls under fair use or whether you and your students need to get into the business of obtaining copyright permissions. We certainly have stories of students who have emailed copyright owners, explaining their assigned projects and asking for permission to use copyrighted content. It's not unheard of for copyright owners to grant students the right to use original work cost-free; an email response to a student request is legally sufficient. However, obtaining copyright permissions is more often a costly and complicated affair. We find it easiest to simply tell students up front that we won't be publicly sharing the sound texts they create in this class; our work with audio texts is for educational purposes to help them grow in their writing skills.

In our own work with audio texts, even when we are relying on fair use policies, we take citing the work of others seriously. In most audio texts we assign our students, we require an accompanying list of sources. We want to emphasize that fair use policies mean that students and educators don't have to financially pay to use copyrighted content; they don't mean that the responsibility of correct citation disappears. Depending on the kind of writing students are doing, sourcing may include research citations, song credits, the source information for a snippet of dialogue students pull from a feature film, etc.; the list can be fairly extensive. Essentially, we ask that if students use something in any mode that they themselves did not originally create, they cite where it came from. We actually find that this discussion of citation and sourcing material in any mode helps students return to their work of citing alphabetic texts with a higher degree of understanding of the purpose and significance of correct sourcing when writing.

As a sidenote, when writing in the mode of sound, we often take the opportunity to teach our students about creative commons licenses. A creator or author who chooses to give their original work a creative commons license is giving permanent permission to the public to use their work. This means that anyone in any situation can use what would otherwise be considered copyright-worthy work freely in original texts and compositions. Students can take advantage of huge libraries of creative commons licensed materials online; there are databases of **sound effects**, **music**, images, etc., that have all been given creative commons licensing and are free for the taking. As educators, we feel strongly that students still need to cite and give appropriate credit for these materials. But giving students a quick heads-up about creative commons materials can be an easy way for them to create complicated audio texts that they can share publicly without the concerns of copyright infringement.

Artificial Intelligence and AI Tools

Any teacher of reading and writing today is familiar with the ongoing and rapidly evolving discussion about the tools and options students have available to them through AI technology. We would be remiss if we didn't at least mention these tools as we consider different ways to approach the writing process when working with sound. When it comes to the audio mode, AI can be very powerful. Various softwares and apps can generate scripts and talking points in the alphabetic mode, even recommending where to place **music** and **sound effects**. AI technology has familiarity with genres in the audio mode, including podcasts, radio ads, speeches, and many others; it can generate content in many of these sound-specific genres. Beyond that, some algorithms can process a huge array of sound files to simulate human **voices** in order to generate singing or speaking **voices.** AI **voice** generators can convert written text into audio files of artificial human **voices** speaking or singing. While this list is not comprehensive, we are confident that, by the time this book is published, a whole new wave of AI possibilities will have become available to anyone writing with audio. One of the few things on this topic that we know for sure is that if you and your students end up using content in a text that was generated by AI-powered software, that content will need to be appropriately cited, giving the AI-powered generator credit for the work it contributed.

How these AI-powered resources and developments impact your classroom and your students' writing processes is ultimately up to you. We won't pretend to have the answers, and we doubt any real answers exist at this present time, given the rate at which AI technology along with our understanding of its applications is expanding. For the time being, we are using the word "tools" to describe these developments because that is how we view them. They are tools that can be used to accomplish certain goals, just like grammar editing and spelling correction software, dictionaries and thesauruses, and various other tools students are already using in their writing processes. As our understanding of these tools and their possibilities grows, teachers will need to make informed decisions for themselves and their classrooms regarding if and/or how to use AI technology with their students. If you are comfortable talking with students about how these tools can both enhance as well as limit their writing, then students can absolutely explore integrating these tools into their writing processes. If these tools feel as if they will derail or distract your students from the writing skills you need them to develop, then we recommend you have that discussion with your students and consider holding work sessions in class where you can monitor their use of such tools. Whatever happens in the education community's ongoing journey to understanding the role of AI in the ELA classroom, we believe it is essential that students understand AI technology as a set of tools that has the potential to support as well as limit their writing processes; however, regardless of the tools student writers choose to use, they are still personally responsible as individuals for understanding and responding to the rhetorical situation in which they are composing and making choices as writers. Additionally, when talking with students about AI, it's important to acknowledge the devastating environmental impact associated with its use and encourage students to make informed choices with their tools within a global context.

There's a lot to consider when discussing what the writing process may look like in the mode of sound. To sum up some of the aspects of the audio writing process, we've created the table below.

TABLE 5.2: Summing It All Up

Element of the Writing Process in the Audio Mode	What do we expect students to be familiar with based on their preexisting writing experience and knowledge?	What do we expect students to find unique to the process of composing in the audio mode?
Brainstorming and Prewriting	• Pen and paper strategies, including outlining, freewriting, word maps, etc. • Consideration of familiar elements such as diction, tone, genre, organization, etc.	• Planning for gathering and use of sound strategies (sound effects, music, silence, voices, and layering) • Technical considerations such as recording equipment and editing software • Consideration of copyright and/or fair use
Drafting	• Synthesizing plans from the brainstorming and prewriting phase into a single draft text	• Assembling recorded sounds as opposed to alphabetic words • Working with sound editing software as opposed to a word processor • Gathering sounds with recording devices

TABLE 5.2: Continued

Revision and Editing	• Teacher and peer feedback both important • Similar review formats, including written notes, conferences and conversations, and sharing impressions of student authors' purposes and intentions	• Instead of reading drafts, students and educators need time and space to listen to texts • Feedback and comments from reviewers need accompanying timestamps for clarity • Revisions based on feedback will require edits and rearrangements of sounds as opposed to words
The Nuts and Bolts of Sound Writing Technology	• Recording tools are usually available on devices students already have access to and regularly use in their writing processes, like smartphones or laptops	• We do not expect students to have experience selecting or using tools for recording or editing sound texts
Sourcing, Copyright, and Fair Use	• Consideration of citation and giving proper credit when integrating the work of others	• Consideration of copyright and fair use policies if or when planning to publicly publish audio texts
Artificial Intelligence and AI Tools	• Consideration and discussion around how to use assistive writing technology and tools when composing original texts	• Consideration and discussion around AI technology's ability to create work specific to sound genres as well as artificial sounds • Appropriate citation of any content explicitly generated by AI that appears in the final draft

Let's Try It Out: A Research Podcast Writing Assignment

To give you some idea of how the writing process might unfold when composing an audio text, we're going to outline a sample audio writing assignment below so that we can discuss how a student might approach the process of completing it. We're choosing what we hope is a familiar audio genre, a podcast episode, for this sample assignment; maybe you've even read or written this genre with your students already. While we promise to get into more adventurous and avant-garde genres in the next chapter, we think it's a good idea to get started with a well known and loved genre with which we most likely all have some basic experience.

Sample Sound Writing Assignment: Research-Based Argumentative Podcast Episode (eight to ten minutes)

Take a position in response to the following question by drafting, writing, and recording an 8–10-minute podcast. Your answer should include some basic research from at least three sources to support your position. When choosing your sources, you should use at least one interview or cited recording from an outside source. Include an MLA works cited page outlining any materials you used to research and/or compose your podcast episode.

What is a rule you disagree with, and why?

When we ask our students to complete writing assignments like this one, we require that students receive approval for their topic before proceeding with the writing process. This allows us to preview student choices to ensure that all content is appropriate. This is entirely optional, but we recommend it as a measure to prepare yourself to deal competently and ethically with sensitive, nuanced, or contentious topics.

While each student's writing process will look different, and each teacher may choose to guide their students' writing processes in different ways, we would expect to see some of the elements outlined in Table 5.2 in a writing process responding to this assignment statement.

This podcast episode assignment and the discussion we've included here represent a general idea of how the writing process might look when students are writing an audio text. Up to this point in the chapter, we've been focusing on the process of writing in the mode of sound and how the audio mode might shift and reshape the way students approach the writer's process. These ideas will remain relevant as we move on to discuss the ten writing skills we believe are core to a high school student's literacy. The next section of this chapter will focus on how we can use writing sound texts in the classroom to foster key writing skills in ways that are engaging and powerful for our students. Each writing assignment should ask students to engage fully in a process of brainstorming, prewriting, drafting, revising, and editing, regardless of the writing skill it emphasizes, so we hope you'll keep the first part of this chapter in mind as we move on in our discussion.

TABLE 5.3: Students' Writing Process and Considerations for Podcasting

Brainstorming and Prewriting	To begin the writing processes, students will need to make preliminary central choices such as which rule they plan to disagree with, why, and basic ideas about how they would like to present this information. Students may wish to brainstorm these ideas on a whiteboard, shared Google Doc, or pen and paper. Teachers may also wish to scaffold this brainstorming with worksheets or guided discussions. If you'd like to preview some of the materials we've generated for you to use with students at this step in the writing process, feel free to take a peek at Chapter 6's materials. Once some of the central choices have been made, we encourage students to consider their rhetorical situation. Who are they addressing in their podcast? Other students? Members of a particular social, cultural, or political group? Who are they speaking as in the podcast, and what unique take does their position bring to the discussion? Students, with an idea of their rhetorical situation, can go on to make choices about tone and which sound strategies they plan to use. They may wish to consider how they plan to structure and organize their podcast episode and how many speakers they will feature. Again, teachers may scaffold elements of this process with worksheets. At this point, some students may choose to create a rough script or basic outline of the contents of their episode, noting which sound strategies will be used at which timepoints in the podcast episode. This script or outline can also be used to estimate the general length of the episode to see if students need more or less material. For scaffolding at this step, teachers may provide graphic organizers to help students consider which sound strategies they will use and in what general order they will arrange their information. Teachers can also require that students complete and submit an outline or script of their episode in order to ensure that students are moving through the writing process in ways that support a meaningful writing experience. If you are concerned about students using AI and would like to discourage that, emphasizing process at this step in the assignment will go a long way. Asking students to show their brainstorming and prewriting work in explicit ways will lessen the temptation to inappropriately use AI technology. As students near the end of their brainstorming and prewriting process, we encourage them to make a list of sounds they will need to gather based on what they have decided. This may include interviews, **sound effects**, and/or **music**, but this list is an important part of the process that students will need before transitioning into the drafting phase of the writing.
Drafting	At this point in the process, students will begin recording the individual elements of their podcast episode and gathering sounds. Depending on the style of the episode, this can include a narrator, interviews, archival clips, discussions, etc. Students will need to have chosen any **music** or **sound effects** and generally scripted any dialogue. Once all the necessary sounds have been gathered, students can then import those sounds into a chosen sound editing software where they can arrange and **layer** them according to the materials they created during the brainstorm and prewriting phase of this process. They are ready to move on to the next step of the writing process when they have compiled their sounds into a single audio file draft that they can share with you or their peers. We recommend requiring that the first draft be within one minute of the target time range in order to be considered a true draft, ready for review.
Revision and Editing	For students whose podcast episode drafts are at this phase in the process, a group peer review can be particularly beneficial. For this activity, students will need to use headphones to listen to one another's podcast episodes and provide pointed feedback. We recommend teachers prompt students on how to respond to one another's podcast episodes, asking them to consider factors like clarity of message, use of the five sound strategies, transitions, and quality and relevance of supporting research. Students should offer one another specific feedback with timestamps to support areas of strength and needed improvement in each other's episodes. Students working on second and third drafts of their podcast episodes will need to spend time revisiting their earlier drafts and prewriting materials in light of comments they receive from their peers and teacher in order to clarify their message and supporting research by adjusting their choices in the text.

Copyright and Fair Use	This element of the process will depend on how you as the educator plan for students to use their texts. If you've chosen to indicate that, for copyright reasons, students will not be sharing these podcast episodes outside a school setting, then that is the extent of the conversation you need to have. You can release your students to the world of audio resources and not give copyright a second thought. If you want to engage students in a larger discussion around these ideas or if you're planning on releasing student episodes publicly for something like the NPR Student Podcast Challenge, then you may have set a requirement that students use only original sounds. They can integrate **sound effects** or **music** if they like, but it has to be content they created for this episode. You may also choose to introduce students to the idea of a creative commons license so they can have access to a wider range of sound resources without the concern of copyright infringement. Whether you decide to keep the podcast within your classroom and allow students unlimited options or you ask them to follow specific rules for a publishing source, it's important to remind students to cite any and all sources and resources they use.
Artificial Intelligence and AI Tools	Similarly to copyright and fair use, teachers can decide how much of a role they'd like AI to play in the writing process for an assignment like this. With the rapidly expanding landscape of AI technology, there's a range of degrees of involvement teachers can choose when integrating AI into student writing processes. Students can prompt AI-powered software to assist in their brainstorming process, help locate sources, generate ideas for scripts or overall text structure, brainstorm the effects of different audiences or tones on a particular text, edit grammar or sentence structure, or to stand in as a speaking **voice** in the text if students prefer an artificial **voice**. Frankly, the information and knowledge around this technology from an educational perspective is limited enough for us to refrain from taking a stance on how it should be used in the classroom; we all as educators will be making difficult decisions around the use of AI technology over the next few years.

Core Writing Skills

In order to be considered strong, effective, and flexible writers capable of responding to a wide range of real-world situations, students need a level of confidence and comfort with a variety of individual writing skills.

Although the Common Core Standards features its own list of nationally recognized writing skills that all students should master, we will continue to base our discussions on our own list of skills. This list, shown below, integrates some broader categories as well as our own practices working with ELA students as well as the mode of sound.

It is our experience that these writing skills are often linked to reading skills. For example, if students are adept at identifying tone and mood in their close readings, they are usually going to demonstrate higher ability levels when it comes to creating a sense of tone and mood in their own writing. Accordingly, you will recognize these skills from Chapter 3: The Fundamentals of Reading Sound Texts—here, we have adapted this list slightly to apply the skills to writing as opposed to reading. However, this means that our intentional ordering of these skills still applies.

TABLE 5.4: Core Writing Skills

#	Skill	Description
1	Crafting Author's Persona	The first three skills ask students to assess their rhetorical situation and make choices as an author that best suit their context. We view these choices as foundational to beginning the drafting process for any text, which is why we have listed them first.
2	Addressing an Audience	
3	Crafting an Argument	
4	Making Genre Choices	The next three skills address choices student writers will make after having assessed their rhetorical situation. With an understanding of their roles as authors, their target audience, and their central purpose or argument, students can then make thoughtful choices regarding which genre norms to follow, how to leverage literary devices to benefit their text, and how to organize their writing to maximize impact on the reader.
5	Integrating Literary Devices	
6	Making Organizational and Structural Choices	
7	Conveying Tone	The final four skills are, much like when reading, the higher-level cumulative skills that require students to have developed some dexterity with the prior six skills. Crafting tone and mood in a text all rely on an author's use of literary devices, genre, and organization. Student writers will have to consider these preliminary skills in their efforts to convey particular tones or moods. You may notice that while Chapter 3 lists mood first and then tone, here we list them in the opposite order. This is because we believe that, when writing, crafting mood is the higher-order skill. We believe it is easier for students to communicate and establish their own feelings as opposed to considering the perspective and creating reactions of their target audience, which is required for crafting a particular mood. Finally, establishing theme and employing rhetorical appeals asks students to synthesize all the prior skills in this list. The writerly tasks of intentionally constructing and developing a theme as well as strategically employing various rhetorical appeals in a particular text are extremely sophisticated; it may take students years to develop a sense of expert comfort with these skills. This is why we place them last on the list, as some of the more ambitious skills to work toward in a student's literacy journey.
8	Crafting Mood	
9	Crafting Theme	
10	Employing Rhetorical Appeals	

Just as with reading, we acknowledge that these skills are not specific to the mode of sound. Again, this is intentional; these are skills students will need when writing in any mode and for any purpose. Our goal in this chapter is to demonstrate how the mode of sound has a unique potential to foster these writing skills in powerful ways for a wide range of students. We will also discuss how these skills appear when writing sound texts in particular, noting where they are different from traditional printed texts.

Let's Try It Out (Again): Returning to the Research Podcast Writing Assignment

In order to tie our discussion of these ten writing skills back to practical, applicable content, we're going to return to the sample research-based argumentative podcast assignment we just discussed. We'll review the assignment below and then go on to discuss how this assignment can be used to target each of the ten writing skills we've listed.

> *Sample Sound Writing Assignment: Research-Based Argumentative Podcast Episode (eight to ten minutes)*
>
> Take a position in response to the following question by drafting, writing, and recording an 8–10-minute podcast. Your answer should include some basic research from at least three sources to support your position. When choosing your sources, you should use at least one interview or cited recording from an outside source. Include an MLA works cited page outlining any materials you used to research and/or compose your podcast episode.
>
> What is a rule you disagree with, and why?

For a writing assignment like this one, we use a rubric like the one below.

TABLE 5.5: Sample Podcast Episode—Assignment Rubric

Areas for Growth	Elements to Assess	Areas of Strength
	Assignment Requirements • Episode falls within time limits (eight to ten minutes) • Episode responds directly to the prompt, taking a clear position on a particular rule and explaining that position • Includes a list of MLA-formatted sources for all research and borrowed sounds	
	Process • Student engages fully in the writing process: brainstorming, drafting, and responding to reviews	
	Research • Episode references at least three sources to support the central claim • Episode uses at least one of the following: interview or cited recording from outside source	
	Editing Quality • Volume is consistent and balanced • Transitions and cuts are clean and clear • Recordings are clear with minimal background noise and interference • Speakers are easy to hear and understand	
	Creativity and Aesthetics • The podcast episode makes innovative and effective choices, both with content as well as use of sound strategies • The episode's presentation of content and use of sound strategies is aesthetically pleasing, consistent, and demonstrates effective design choices • The episode is engaging, interesting, and unique	

This represents a basic, generalized rubric for this assignment; as we discuss each of the ten writing skills and how this assignment can target them, we'll suggest a line or two that you might add to this rubric to emphasize each particular skill. We do not recommend using any particular assignment to target more than one or two skills at a given time. While any particular writing assignment in the mode of sound may have students relying on more than one or two skills, we wouldn't be assessing more than one or two at once. Students won't be able to develop multiple new writing skills simultaneously, but we can offer some suggestions on how to emphasize particular individual skills with this assignment, depending on where your students are in their writing journeys.

As we discuss how this assignment can be used to develop each individual writing skill below, you'll notice that these explanations aren't quite classroom-ready. We haven't created handouts or materials for teachers to use. We have ready-made classroom activities and materials in the next chapter, but for this chapter, we just want to briefly talk through how these writing skills function when using the mode of sound and what it looks like to discuss them with students.

In general, we find teaching any and all of the skills below works best when students submit reflection work throughout the writing process. It's not always enough to have students make effective writerly choices; students also need to reflect on why they made those choices. Reflective writing before, during, and/or after creating the final draft of an audio text like this podcast episode can be a powerful element in a writing process for a student looking to develop these skills.

Skill 1: Crafting Author's Persona

Establishing the position and role as an author in any text is a foundational skill for a writer to help them decide which choices to make. While every student writer has a complex and nuanced personal identity that is too vast to appear entirely in any given text, they can and should choose a particular persona for every text they write. We consider an author's persona to be the role or **voice** they intentionally choose and project throughout a text. This may include elements of a student's identity, but it is the student's choice to emphasize elements of that identity when projecting their persona in a text. A skilled writer knows how and where to make choices that clarify their role in relation to the text in order to better communicate their goals, argument, or message.

For some genres, the author's persona doesn't feature as explicitly or prominently in a text; for example, an author's persona would appear clearly in a persuasive political speech but may be more implicitly integrated into the plot in the case of a poem or a narrative. We believe that an author's persona always plays a role in a text; however, if you're choosing to emphasize this writing skill with students, assigning particular genres may work better than others.

When it comes to writing with sound, students have a unique set of tools at their disposal for asserting the persona they wish to project. A student's ability to use their own literal **voice** in a text is a powerful tool for asserting persona. Not only can students use their **voice**, vocal expression, and vocalizations to communicate their feelings and position, they can also choose to integrate diverse language and dialects of the English language to communicate their position. **Sound effects** can capture a wide range of student positions, giving glimpses into student identities with recordings of conversations and sounds that only a student in that particular position would have access to or familiarity with. **Music** has the unique ability to reflect various cultural, ethnic, social, or religious identities; student use of **music** in a composition can convey huge amounts of information about that student's relationship to that identity. Well-positioned **silence** may help establish a student author as feeling isolated or repressed in a particular context. Each of these sound strategies offers unique ways for students to consider how they appear as authors in their own texts.

When writing this podcast episode, a student's persona will become relevant in how and why they oppose their chosen rule. If they are choosing to object to a school's dress code, their persona as a student comes into play. If they are choosing to object to a minimum drinking or voting age, their position as an underage citizen of the US becomes relevant. If they decide to object to a social or cultural rule about behavior or dress, a student could be considering integrating the role their gender, ethnicity, culture, religion, or sexuality plays in their position and persona as an author.

Once a student has chosen the elements of their persona that they would like to communicate in their podcast episode, they will have to consider the following questions:

- *How does this persona impact the way I speak? Are there any particular words I will or won't use? Are there any particular emotions I will convey around particular topics?*
- *How does this persona impact the sounds I use in this episode? What kind of* ***music*** *or* ***sound effects*** *might represent me and my position?*
- *Are there any details about my persona that I need to explicitly or implicitly share with my audience so that they understand my position and role?*

In a scenario where you assign this writing task to students in order to target and develop the skill of establishing and crafting a persona, we suggest adding the line from Table 5.6 to the generalized rubric in Table 5.5.

TABLE 5.6: Rubric Assessment for Author's Persona

Areas for Growth	Elements to Assess	Areas of Strength

	Author's Persona
	• Episode clearly establishes the author's personal stake in the rule
	• Author uses at least two of the following sound strategies to communicate their persona in the text:
	  ◦ Voice
	  ◦ Sound effects
	  ◦ Music
	  ◦ Silence
	  ◦ Layering	

Skill 2: Addressing an Audience

An awareness of the intended audience will impact several subsequent author choices, so we value working on this skill with students early on to help them position their texts within their rhetorical situations. Cheng-Yueh Jao notes that having a sense of their intended audience is necessary for student writers "to fulfill readers' expectations and requirements" (2), and Beaufort argues that audience awareness is an important step in students' "learning to be flexible writers" (15). When writing in a classroom setting, we often find that students assume their audience to be their teacher. While this will always be partially true, if students only practice writing skills with an intended audience of their teacher, their ability to respond with sophistication and nuance to a real-world audience will be stunted. Assigning work in which students intentionally address groups of people other than their writing teacher will not only lead to high-quality end-products, it will more importantly foster a sense of rhetorical awareness in student writers. Given the culturally relevant nature of various sound genres, we find writing audio texts to be a natural way for students to explore this skill.

The mode of sound offers unique approaches to targeting a particular audience in student writing. Multilingual students may use **voice** and language to establish their audience; integrating multiple languages into their episode can clearly suggest who the content is for. Certain colloquial language patterns can direct a message toward social groups, and jargon or disciplinary language can communicate a particular audience. **Sound effects** work on familiarity; the listener has to be familiar with the sound, so a student may choose a **sound effect** that is most familiar and meaningful to their target audience—no one knows the sound of a particular creaky door like the class that uses that door every morning. All schools' class change bells evoke a certain emotion, but if a student is aiming their message at their school community, using their school's specific bell will evoke a powerful response. **Music** has very strong cultural, ethnic, and social ties. Certain audiences can and will relate to particular songs and musical styles more than others. The options available to students in the mode of sound are plentiful and invite creative ways of targeting particular audiences.

For this podcast episode, we encourage students to consider a range of audiences. Perhaps the student is arguing for their chosen rule to be changed, addressing the individuals or organizations in power over the rule. Perhaps the student is arguing for more individuals in their position to recognize the injustices or shortcomings of their chosen rule, addressing their peers or others in similar situations. Perhaps the student is arguing against an unofficial social or cultural rule, in which case they may direct their message to groups in positions of power in those social or cultural systems. The possibilities are endless, and we encourage educators to use this opportunity to prompt students to seriously consider who they want to address with their podcast episode and why.

Once students have chosen their intended audiences, they will have to consider the following questions among others:

- *How will this choice of intended audience impact the way I speak? Are there any particular words I will or won't use? Are there any particular emotions I will need to convey around particular topics?*
- *How does this audience impact the sounds I will use in this episode? What kinds of* ***music*** *or* ***sound effects*** *will my intended audience find meaningful?*
- *Will I be explicitly sharing who my intended audience is, or will I be hinting at it with various cues throughout the episode?*

In a scenario where you assign this writing task to students in order to target and develop the skill of establishing and addressing a particular audience, we suggest adding the line in Table 5.7 to the generalized rubric in Table 5.5.

TABLE 5.7: Addressing an Audience

Areas for Growth	Elements to Assess	Areas of Strength

	Target Audience
	• Episode clearly establishes who the author is addressing in their episode
	• Author uses at least two of the following sound strategies to communicate their intended audience in the text:
	    ◦ Voice
	    ◦ Sound effects
	    ◦ Music
	    ◦ Silence
	    ◦ Layering	

Skill 3: Crafting an Argument

We discuss this briefly in Chapter 3, but we subscribe to the belief that all texts in all modes and genres make arguments, implicit or explicit. We believe that an important part of authoring a text is understanding what argument you are making. Accordingly, we like to target the skill of argumentation specifically in a wide variety of modes and genres. However, if your approach to teaching writing holds that only particular genres make arguments, we encourage you to assign those genres to address this skill.

One of the unique affordances the mode of sound offers students working to develop this skill is the range of evidence available to support various claims. When choosing evidence, students can still choose traditional information that they can share verbally in their text, but they can also consider things like interviews, **sound effects**, **music**, clips from archival sources, and many others. For example, if a student claims their dog loves a particular song, they can include a recording of their dog howling along to that song as evidence. In an alphabetic text, such a claim would need a very different kind of evidence.

For this assignment, we've chosen a prompt and genre that make a clear and explicit argument. The student will choose a particular rule and disagree with it, fundamentally arguing that the rule is inadequate. Students may choose to support that argument in a variety of ways. They may argue that the rule is unethical, ineffective, outdated, or irrational. As they construct the plans for their podcast episode, they will have to consider exactly what argument they are making and how they plan to make it. When emphasizing this skill, we guide students to think about their central claim and then the series of supporting claims and evidence they plan to use in constructing their case against their chosen rule.

In a scenario where you assign this writing task to students in order to target and develop the skill of crafting an argument, we suggest adding the lines from Table 5.8 to the generalized rubric in Table 5.5.

TABLE 5.8: Rubric Assessment for Crafting an Argument

<table>
<tr><th>Areas for Growth</th><th>Elements to Assess</th><th>Areas of Strength</th></tr>
<tr><td></td><td>Central Argument<ul><li>Episode clearly argues a central claim that asserts which rule is inadequate and why</li><li>Episode contains at least three claims to support this central claim. Each of these claims presents and discusses its own evidence</li></ul></td><td></td></tr>
<tr><td></td><td>Evidence<ul><li>Evidence for each supporting claim is clear and relevant</li><li>Each piece of evidence has its own analysis, directly explaining how this evidence demonstrates the individual supporting claims and central claim</li><li>Author uses at least two of the following sound strategies in their evidence choices:<ul><li>Voice</li><li>Sound effects</li><li>Music</li><li>Silence</li><li>Layering</li></ul></li></ul></td><td></td></tr>
</table>

Much as in the corresponding reading skill of understanding argument from Chapter 3, we sometimes differentiate between an author's purpose and their argument in a text. For educators who want to challenge students, a rewarding extension activity can ask them to identify their purpose in the text and discuss how their argument would accomplish that purpose with their intended audience. Educators can choose to add a line in the rubric to assess a student's ability in this area.

In their podcast episode, a student may argue that a particular rule is unethical in order to support the purpose of prompting a particular audience to change this rule. The same argument that a particular rule is unethical could also be used to support a different purpose, perhaps to encourage peers to boycott the rule. Asking students to consider their purpose in addition to their argument in their writing process will prompt them to make even more specific and targeted choices in their composing.

Skill 4: Making Genre Choices

Making writerly choices regarding genre is a deeply challenging skill for students, particularly when genre is so often and easily understood as a list of static rules to follow or "simply a matter of filling in the blanks" (Dirk 251). When students write, we want them to have the awareness and flexibility regarding genre that allows them to choose which genre norms to follow and which to ignore. We want our student writers to have a sense of authority and power in their writing that allows them to make meaningful choices instead of feeling beholden to genre structures that come from some theoretical and detached sources of authority and power beyond them.

We've mentioned in earlier chapters that we view writing in the mode of sound in particular as offering a bevy of opportunities to develop this kind of genre awareness, and we encourage educators to intentionally target this skill when assigning audio writing tasks to your students. The menu of genres available to teachers working in the mode of sound is expansive, creating lots of exciting options for students.

A podcast episode can be a great genre to begin with when writing in the mode of sound because the genre is fairly well defined yet also naturally incorporates a high degree of flexibility. Students will be familiar with podcasts as a genre, which means they will also be familiar with the many liberties authors take within this genre. Podcast episodes can range anywhere from a few minutes to a few hours. They can integrate one speaker or many. Some make heavy use of the sound strategies of ***sound effects****,* ***music****, and* ***layering****, while others rely almost entirely on* ***voice****. Despite being a generally established genre, the podcast episode still invites students to make choices within the genre category.*

In a scenario where you assign this writing task to students in order to target and develop the skill of making choices regarding genre, we suggest adding the lines from Table 5.9 to the generalized rubric in Table 5.5.

TABLE 5.9: Rubric Assessment for Making Genre Choices

Areas for Growth	Elements to Assess	Areas of Strength
	Essential Genre Expectations • Episode has a clear introduction, sharing the title, the speaker(s), and the main idea • Episode has a clear conclusion • Episode has a clear central idea and consistent tone and mood • Episode meets time expectations for length	
	Optional Genre Expectations • Episode features at least one of the following occasionally occurring genre expectations for a podcast episode: • An interview with a guest speaker ◦ A thank you to sponsors ◦ Transitions between sections of the podcast through music or sound effects ◦ A theme song for the intro and outro • Episode makes use of at least two of the sound strategies: • Voice • Music • Sound effects • Silence • Layering	

For an extra challenge, you can ask students to consider why someone might deviate from the genre expectations in a podcast episode. You can even add a line to the rubric requiring one aspect in which the podcast episode subverts or undermines genre expectations. In order to get the most out of this extension option, we strongly recommend you have students reflect on why they chose to deviate from that genre convention and how it contributed to their overall argument and purpose. The goal is for students to explore genre expectations with a sense of control and power over their choices, understanding how, when, and why their choices will impact the way their text works in the world.

Skill 5: Integrating Literary Devices

As we mentioned in Chapter 3, the term "literary devices" can refer to an immense range of literary techniques, elements, strategies, and constructions. Just like when reading to identify and interpret literary devices, when we ask students to use literary devices in their own writing, we don't usually spend much time on the categories and terminology. Instead, we try to emphasize for students that literary devices, when used intentionally and carefully, can amplify the meaning, effectiveness, and complexity of their writing. So, while we may use certain terms when exploring how writing in the mode of sound can foster a student writer's ability to integrate literary devices into their work, we don't get particularly specific or technical with our students. If you are an educator who is passionate about the terminology and theory behind literary devices, we fully encourage you to integrate that passion into your sound writing assignments.

Exploring the use of literary devices in the mode of sound can be an illuminating experience for students. While some traditional alphabetic literary devices can feel intimidating, inaccessible, or perhaps even a little contrived, many of the audio literary devices will be familiar to students and may come more easily to them. A student may balk at the idea of integrating a symbol into their short story, but we find that students feel more readily able to use a **sound effect** that symbolically captures an emotion or idea, such as the sound of a kiss representing dating relationships or the sound of the classic iPhone alarm representing the daily grind. While repetition may feel uncomfortable to students in their poetry or essays, the notion of a looped song or sound bite is something they will have likely heard before. By giving students experience using sound-specific literary devices, we often create opportunities for them to more meaningfully understand literary devices in general and how to integrate them into their writing.

Choosing to plan for literary devices that will appear in your text as you write it is a complicated element of the brainstorming, prewriting, and drafting steps of the writing process in any mode. Some students may need more scaffolding in this area; this can include a list of literary devices to choose from or guidance in a larger conversation about your students' goals or purposes for the pieces and how particular literary devices can help them accomplish those goals or purposes.

When preparing to write this podcast episode, it will be helpful for students to begin the literary device brainstorm by considering some of the skills leading up to this one. Does their position as an author lend itself to any particular devices? Will their audience respond particularly well to any particular devices? Are there any devices that help students make their argument or accomplish their goals in a text? Are there any devices that are more commonly seen in podcast episodes?

In a scenario where you assign this writing task to students in order to target and develop the skill of integrating literary devices, we suggest adding the line from Table 5.10 to the generalized rubric in Table 5.5.

TABLE 5.10: Rubric Assessment for Inclusion of Literary Devices

Areas for Growth	Elements to Assess	Areas of Strength
	Inclusion of Literary Devices • Episode integrates at least three literary devices • Literary devices are effectively used and serve the larger purposes of the text as a whole • Author considers the use of at least one of the following sound strategies in all three of their literary devices: ◦ Voice ◦ Sound effects ◦ Music ◦ Silence ◦ Layering	

Skill 6: Making Organizational and Structural Choices

Once a student has established their argument and its rhetorical situation and once they understand the genre in which they are writing, they can begin the process of planning how to lay out what William Strunk and E. B. White refer to as "the shape" of their text (26). Strunk and White establish "the first principle of composition" to be the ability to "foresee or determine the shape of what is to come and pursue that shape" (26). This decision process will ask students to lay out the individual components of their composition and design how those components will assemble into the text as a whole.

For the podcast episode, students will most likely begin their drafting with an established, central claim about the rule they plan to argue against. This claim will have several supporting claims, each with their own associated evidence; this is all part of Skill 3, crafting an argument. When exercising the skill of making decisions concerning structure and organization, students strategically decide how and in what order to present the information in this argument.

One of the primary decisions in this process will be how and where to place the central claim of the episode. Students may choose to frontload their episode with an explicit statement of their argument; depending on their author's persona or their target audience, a direct, clear, and confrontational structure may be more effective. However, students may also choose to structure their argument more inductively, leading their audience through a series of claims and evidence that ultimately culminates in a clear claim near the end of the episode. This may be more effective for an audience that is unlikely to agree with them or that may have emotional reactions to their central claim; this slow-burn structure may give the student time to make their case before triggering opposition.

When it comes to supporting claims, students will need to consider what order in which to present their claims and how to transition between them. Some scenarios

call for starting with the strongest supporting claim and evidence while others may call for an episode that opens with a more emotional claim before transitioning into increasingly practical and logical fact-based claims. If the student's argument contains a counterpoint, it is important to consider where this will fall in the argument. Is it an obvious concern that should be addressed up front in the episode, or is it a more nuanced claim that should be acknowledged just before the conclusion of the episode?

Once the student has a sense for the overall "shape" of their text (Strunk and White 26), they can begin to consider questions of transitions and segues in order to facilitate the assembly of these individual parts in the order in which they've decided.

This summary is just a small overview of the decisions students can explore regarding organization and structure when completing this assignment. In the next chapter, we'll walk you through an assignment equipped with some more explicit guidance on how to coach students through these decisions.

In a scenario where you assign this writing task to students in order to target and develop the skill of making organizational and structural choices in their text, we suggest adding the line from Table 5.11 to the generalized rubric in Table 5.5.

TABLE 5.11: Rubric Assessment for Organization and Structural Choices

Areas for Growth	Elements to Assess	Areas of Strength

	Organization of Claims
	• The placement and presentation of the central claim of the episode is effective and meets the needs of the audience and the author
	• The order and presentation of the supporting claims and corresponding evidence in the episode is effective and meets the needs of the audience and the author
	• If a counterpoint is present, it and its supporting evidence is integrated seamlessly and logically into the argument's overall trajectory
	• Transitions between individual elements of the overall text are smooth and help a reader understand the larger purpose and direction of the text as a whole
	• Author integrates at least two of the following sound strategies into organizing and communicating the structure of their text, whether that relates to introductions, conclusions, transitions, and/or a different organizational component:
	  ◦ Voice
	  ◦ Sound effects
	  ◦ Music
	  ◦ Silence
	  ◦ Layering	

Skill 7: Conveying Tone

Developing the skill of conveying tone asks students to communicate their own emotions about the subject of their text. As we noted earlier, while mood is listed before tone as a skill in Chapter 3, we've listed tone first here because we see mood as a slightly more complex writing skill given its requirement to consider others' thoughts and not just our own.

Some elements of conveying a tone when writing audio texts will feel familiar to students based on the writing they will have worked on before; elements like diction or point of view work to communicate particular emotional positions in both traditional alphabetic texts as well as in audio ones. Sound texts, however, do not have access to some of the visual cues that traditional alphabetic writing often relies upon to convey tone; punctuation, syntax, font, etc., aren't available to students writing in sound. Students looking to convey a particular tone in a sound writing assignment will instead have to lean more heavily on the five sound strategies. The **sound effect** of heavy breathing in an audio memoir can help establish an author's anxiety in a situation. The choice to play peaceful instrumental **music** during a particular narration may convey a sense of the author's comfort and sense of calm around an idea. Particularly if the author uses their own **voice** in the audio text, the way the author uses their **voice** as they deliver particular lines will give readers strong and specific information about the author's emotions. If the author is using their own **voice**, the choice to pause in a spoken line, allowing a moment of **silence,** can convey feelings of discomfort or deep sadness with a particular topic. Students will need to lean into these strategies individually or in combination with one another as they think about how they want their readers to react to their writing.

In this podcast episode, students will need to consider the rule they've chosen to disagree with and how that rule truly makes them feel. We expect students to choose tones like indignant, frustrated, powerless, misunderstood, or isolated; these are all reasonable emotional states to hold in response to a rule with which they disagree. Once students have chosen a tone to convey in their writing, they may need to engage some of the prior skills to brainstorm what choices would best communicate that tone. They should consider the following questions among others:

- *How will this choice of tone impact the way I speak? Are there any particular words I will or won't use? How will my* ***voice*** *sound as I deliver the lines in the recording?*
- *How does this tone impact the sounds I will use in this episode? What kinds of* ***music*** *or* ***sound effects*** *will communicate my emotions? How can I use* ***silence*** *to convey my emotional position?*

- *Will I be explicitly sharing my emotional position with my audience, or will I be hinting at it with cues embedded throughout the episode?*

In a scenario where you assign this writing task to students in order to target and develop the skill of conveying tone in their text, we suggest adding the line from Table 5.12 to the generalized rubric in Table 5.5.

TABLE 5.12: Rubric Assessment for Conveying Tone

Areas for Growth	Elements to Assess	Areas of Strength
	Conveying Tone • Episode clearly and consistently communicates the author's particular emotional position throughout its duration • The tone conveyed in the text fits logically with the author's persona as well as for the episode's intended audience, purpose, and genre • Episode intentionally uses at least two of the following sound strategies to convey the chosen tone: ◦ Voice ◦ Music ◦ Sound effects ◦ Silence ◦ Layering	

Skill 8: Crafting Mood

Mood refers to the feelings that a student writer aims to create in their readers through their choices in a text. Student writers will need a strong sense of their target audience and how that target audience will react to various cues regarding a particular topic. The author will also have to consider their persona and tone in the piece and how the audience might react to someone in the student's position.

Much like tone, while there will be many familiar strategies for communicating and establishing a mood in a student-authored text, the mode of sound and the five sound strategies will offer a unique range of tools for students to practice creating a mood in their writing. Certain **sound effects** have particular emotional impacts on certain audiences; for members of the medical community, the sound of an ambulance siren may generate strong emotions of urgency or intensity, whereas that same sound might create a sense of security or reassurance for an audience who regularly deals with illness at home. Student authors can use **music** to create emotions in their listeners, foreshadowing a dark turn of events by generating a sense of unease with spooky **music**. The human **voice** has a high degree of power over how audiences feel—a whisper can evoke interest and a sense of intimacy while a sharp shout can create a sense of anxiety or tension in listeners. A long **silence** can prompt listeners to feel suspense or unease. A variety of possibilities become available when students **layer** these different strategies together.

In writing this podcast episode, students may choose to target a wide range of moods; their choice of mood will most likely be impacted by the audience they've chosen to target and their argument in and purpose for the episode. If the episode is addressed to administrators regarding a sexist dress code policy, for instance, it is likely that students will want their readers to feel a sense of shame, responsibility, and perhaps even anxiety at being held accountable. However, if a podcast episode addresses that same sexist dress code policy but aims its message and goals toward other students in the school, a student writer may be looking to generate a mood of camaraderie, indignation, and empowerment. Once a student has selected a mood to target, they can consider a variety of their writerly choices in the podcast episode to see how those choices work together to craft the student's intended mood. They will have to consider the following questions among others:

- *How will this choice of mood impact the way I speak? Are there any particular words I will or won't use? How will my* ***voice*** *sound as I deliver the lines in the recording?*
- *How does this mood impact the sounds I will use in this episode? What kinds of* ***music*** *or* ***sound effects*** *will my audience respond to most strongly? How can I use* ***silence*** *to prompt my audience to respond in the way I am intending?*

In a scenario where you assign this writing task to students in order to target and develop the skill of crafting mood, we suggest adding the line from Table 5.13 to the generalized rubric in Table 5.5.

TABLE 5.13: Rubric Assessment for Crafting Mood

Areas for Growth	Elements to Assess	Areas of Strength
	Crafting Mood • Episode clearly and consistently generates a particular emotional reaction from its listeners throughout the duration • The mood created in the text fits logically with the author's persona as well as for the episode's intended audience, purpose, and genre • Episode intentionally uses at least two of the following sound strategies to craft the intended mood: ◦ Voice ◦ Music ◦ Sound effects ◦ Silence ◦ Layering	

Skill 9: Crafting Theme

As with our list of reading skills, we place this writing skill as one of the final ones in our list because it requires students to synthesize several of the prior skills. As we established in Chapter 3, we consider theme to be a universal message that student authors construct about humanity throughout their text, a particular position on the human condition that the student wants their target audience to reflect on and analyze after reading their text. Asking students to intentionally construct a theme within their text is an excellent way to have students demonstrate the culmination of their writing skills.

When we ask students to consider how they want to make use of a theme in their podcast episode, we ask them to consider what larger message about humanity they want a listener to take away from that episode. What is their overarching message beyond their objection to their chosen rule? For example, a student may object to their school's cell phone policy, but their larger theme and message might be about the importance of preserving students' choices or the ways in which technology actually connects us.

Once a student has selected a theme for their episode, we ask them to work backward and select a certain number of skills they will weave together to support the construction of that theme. We may offer them a list of options and require a minimum number of choices. That list includes elements like literary devices, tone, mood, genre, title, and organization. Once students have selected the elements they plan to use to construct their theme, they will need to focus on each element individually, potentially even returning to some of the prewriting questions or strategies they used when developing prior skills. For example, if a student has chosen a theme of the importance of preserving student choice in schools, they might go on to choose a tone of independence and individuality in order to work toward constructing that theme in their podcast episode. That student then may return to the questions we pose in our description of Skill 7: Conveying Tone:

- *How will this choice of tone impact the way I speak? Are there any particular words I will or won't use? How will my* ***voice*** *sound as I deliver the lines in the recording?*
- *How does this tone impact the sounds I will use in this episode? What kinds of* ***music*** *or* ***sound effects*** *will communicate my emotions? How can I use* ***silence*** *to convey my emotional position?*
- *Will I be explicitly sharing my emotional position with my audience, or will I be hinting at it with cues embedded throughout the episode?*

The student then repeats this process for the other elements they chose to target their chosen theme.

In a scenario where you assign this writing task to students in order to target and develop the skill of crafting theme, we suggest adding the lines from Table 5.14 to the generalized rubric in Table 5.5.

TABLE 5.14: Rubric Assessment for Crafting Theme

<table>
<tr><th>Areas for Growth</th><th>Elements to Assess</th><th>Areas of Strength</th></tr>
<tr><td></td><td>Choice of Theme<ul><li>The theme created in the text fits logically with the author's persona as well as for the episode's intended audience and purpose</li></ul></td><td></td></tr>
<tr><td></td><td>Crafting Theme<ul><li>Episode clearly and consistently constructs a particular central theme throughout the duration</li><li>Episode intentionally uses at least two of the following elements to craft the intended theme:<ul><li>Literary devices</li><li>Tone</li><li>Mood</li><li>Title</li><li>Genre</li><li>Organization and Structure</li></ul></li><li>Episode intentionally uses at least two of the following sound strategies to craft the intended theme:<ul><li>Voice</li><li>Sound effects</li><li>Music</li><li>Silence</li><li>Layering</li></ul></li></ul></td><td></td></tr>
</table>

Skill 10: Employing Rhetorical Appeals

As our tenth and final skill, this skill is the key to teaching students to think critically about the strategies and approaches they use to write effective texts that accomplish particular goals in the world around them. We want our students to understand that good writing can truly act upon its audience within certain rhetorical situations. In our opinion, an intentional and strategic use of the rhetorical appeals represents one of the most basic and foundational ways to direct and construct the writing of a text to ensure that the text functions in a particular way. Doing this requires student writers to engage their understandings of rhetorical situations, genres, literary devices, overall structure, mood, tone, and theme in a text. These skills all work together to give students the skills they need to write dynamic, relevant, and powerful texts that make things happen.

When planning to use rhetorical appeals in their writing, students will need to be aware that particular excerpts, strategies, or lines within a text may employ individual appeals, but generally, a text as a whole will employ a primary rhetorical appeal overall. We consider it valuable to ask students to focus on either one of these or both. They can try to integrate at least one of each appeal into individual parts of a particular text, or teachers can ask them to focus on a single overall rhetorical appeal, or for an extra challenge level, teachers can request both.

When considering how rhetorical appeals will factor into the composing of their podcast episode, students will first need to consider their rhetorical situation. What persona will they be taking on? They should use ethos appeals to assert this. Who is their target audience? Are they more likely to respond to pathos or logos appeals? Ultimately, what is their argument and purpose for the podcast? How can various rhetorical appeals be leveraged to accomplish this goal?

Once students have done preliminary work on establishing their rhetorical situation and how it will impact their use of rhetorical appeals, they will next need to consider how other writing skills can be used to make appeals. A hurt, pained tone shared from the persona of a vulnerable student may elicit a response of sympathy from some audience in a powerful pathos appeal. The literary devices of repetition or polysyndeton when sharing particular statistics might stress the factual severity of an issue, emphasizing a key logos appeal. Students will need to spend time brainstorming how they can leverage their various writerly skills to get the most out of their rhetorical appeals.

After completing the brainstorming and prewriting necessary to plan for their use of rhetorical appeals, students are ready to begin their drafting, working to intentionally integrate as many strategically positioned rhetorical appeals into their episode as possible.

In a scenario where you assign this writing task to students in order to target and develop the skill of employing rhetorical appeals, we suggest adding the lines from Table 5.15 to the generalized rubric in Table 5.5.

TABLE 5.15: Rubric Assessment for Employing Rhetorical Appeals

Areas for Growth	Elements to Assess	Areas of Strength
	Choosing Rhetorical Appeals • Episode clearly and consistently employs a central rhetorical appeal throughout, occasionally supported by other appeals AND/OR • Episode clearly employs all three rhetorical appeals at different times throughout the episode	
	Employing Rhetorical Appeals • Episode intentionally uses at least two of the following skills when employing rhetorical appeals: ◦ Genre ◦ Literary devices ◦ Organization and structure ◦ Mood ◦ Tone ◦ Theme • Episode intentionally uses at least two of the following sound strategies in their rhetorical appeals: ◦ Voice ◦ Music ◦ Sound effects ◦ Silence ◦ Layering	
	Considering Rhetorical Situation • The rhetorical appeal(s) in the text fits logically with the author's persona as well as for the episode's intended audience and purpose	

Conclusion

Chapter 5 Conclusion Audio

Chapter 5 Conclusion Transcript

6

How to Design Writing Activities Using Sound Texts

Introduction

Chapter 6 Introduction Audio

Chapter 6 Introduction Transcript

Planning for an Audio Writing Activity in Your Curricula

When designing an audio writing activity for your students, we find it can be most generative to start with where you think the activity will fit into your coursework. This will provide you with a large amount of the supporting information you'll need to design the details of the activity. We consider a few of the following factors when doing this.

Pairing Reading and Writing Assignments

One of the greatest factors to consider when assigning a writing activity in any mode is how much experience the students have with reading the kind of writing we're going to ask them to do. This can include genre, mode, topic, or a variety of other factors. We view reading models to be an important element of giving students the support they need to successfully develop their writing skills. This is a big part of the reason we use similar lists for the ten reading and writing skills that students and educators should prioritize. Each writing skill has a corresponding reading skill that models the skill before asking students to attempt it themselves. In order for students to fully understand how to establish persona, craft a mood, or integrate rhetorical appeals, they first need experience reading texts that successfully do this. Students need to observe how successful authors employ those skills so they can analyze and consider how they wish to develop that skill in their own writing.

Particularly when you pair model reading assignments with upcoming writing assignments, you can make students aware that they can and should "read like a writer" (Bunn 71). Mike Bunn suggests that we help students develop the ability "to figure out how the text [they] are reading was constructed so that [they] learn how to 'build' one for [themselves]" (74). The value in preparing students to write by asking them to read model texts holds true for any mode but particularly for the mode of sound because we are assuming that most students will not have much experience writing in this mode. Preparing to write in a new mode and a potentially new genre increases the need for students to interact with high-quality models in their reading beforehand.

With this in mind, there are a few elements to consider as you plan for how and where a sound writing activity best fits into your classroom.

Unit Context

If you want to integrate a sound writing activity into your coursework, it's important to consider the role it will play in the unit in which you plan to assign it. This may include asking some of the following questions:

- **What genre is your class working with?** Whether you are reading or writing in a specific genre, asking students to write texts in that same genre will not only ensure they have the sufficient genre knowledge to make smart writerly choices, but it will also allow them to deepen their understanding of the genre as readers. Even when reading or writing genres in the traditional alphabetic mode, it can be generative for students to attempt to write in the same genre but in a different mode. Reading fiction lends itself to composing audio dramas; reading memoirs pairs well with audio memoirs; and nothing deepens a student's engagement with the genre of poetry like having them create their own audio poems. Both of us as educators ask students to write and record argumentative podcast episodes as a means of teaching argumentative academic essays because the process of organizing ideas into the audio mode of a podcast closely mirrors the sometimes stale and rote process of writing an academic essay.

- **What reading skill(s) is your class working on?** Earlier in this chapter, we mentioned reading skills as an important preliminary support for writing skills. The opposite is also true. For students struggling to recognize literary devices or to understand how to identify the audience in their reading, taking the time to use the mode of sound as an avenue to explore integrating literary devices or targeting an audience in their own writing can open their eyes to whatever is standing between them and success in that reading skill.

Assessing the Complexity of a Sound Writing Task

When designing any writing activity in any mode, teachers also need to consider the complexity of the activity and the difficulty level it will present students. This helps teachers make decisions around how much time to dedicate to the activity, whether the work should be completed individually or in groups, where most of the work will take place, how much scaffolding to provide, and a variety of other choices inherent in assignment design.

Some aspects to consider when attempting to gauge the complexity of a writing task in the mode of sound in particular:

- How familiar students are with the genre and mode of the writing activity will make a big difference. If your class has just completed a unit on sound and performance poetry, asking a student to write an audio poem will feel less daunting to them. However, that writing task becomes more difficult if your class has just completed a unit on traditional printed poetry but has only read one or two audio poems.
- The length of the sound text teachers assign is extremely relevant. With sound writing activities, we almost always find that less is more. Asking a student to craft a 3–5-minute podcast episode filled with clear transitions, succinct arguments, and some **layered** sound strategies is a generative and challenging task. Asking students to maintain that same quality for a podcast episode with a target length of twenty to thirty minutes becomes exponentially more challenging. The practical concern of editing alone on a writing activity of that length will create a huge challenge for students, not to mention the hefty teacher task of assessing twenty to thirty minute podcast episodes.
- More significant than length of the assigned text is the complexity of the sound text itself. Longer sound texts don't always mean more complexity and challenge for students; in fact, we find the opposite to be true more

often. A 30-second text packed with **layered** and complicated sound strategies and meanings can be extremely difficult to write, whereas students may have an easy time holding and recording an open-ended 30-minute discussion on a particular topic. This will depend entirely on how teachers write the assignment statement. Writing activities in the mode of sound that require complex, abstract use of sound strategies (required sound symbols, background **music** playing simultaneously with dialogue and/or **sound effects**, extensive use of **silence,** etc.) or complicated structures and ideas (assigning an emerging audio genre with undefined expectations, deviations from traditional alphabetic writing structures and genres, etc.) are going to be more challenging for students, regardless of length.

Of course, all of these factors will be impacted by other elements of the assignment design, such as how much time and support students will be given as they work. You know your students best and are the best person to evaluate how much difficulty a sound writing activity will present to them.

Choosing the Targeted Writing Skill

One of the most essential components of designing a writing activity in any mode is selecting the skill your activity will target. While any given writing activity will ask students to use multiple writing skills at the same time, when designing a writing activity, we ask students to focus on one or two new skills.

To best explain how to design a sound writing activity around a target skill, we are going to rely on the list of ten close writing skills we outlined and discussed in the previous chapter. Again, we don't believe this list to be comprehensive, but it does reflect some of the core writing skills we prioritize in our own work with students when striving to educate and mentor dynamic, intuitive, and flexible twenty-first-century writers with the ability to craft effective and sophisticated texts in response to a range of rhetorical situations.

In the sections below, we've created ten different audio writing activities, one for each of the skills from our list. For each activity, we've assigned writing in genres and on subjects that we think are accessible, engaging, and appropriate for the target skill, and we've designed some prewriting, reflection, and assessment materials to support that activity. As you go through each skill's activity, you will likely notice the potential for an activity to target more than that specific skill; while we've chosen to highlight certain skills with certain activities, we encourage teachers to adapt these activities in ways that best meets the needs of their students.

A Note about Tying In the Common Core Standards

Although the following activities correspond with our list of ten writing skills we previously outlined, we have also included references to the Common Core Writing Standards that each activity addresses; while educators everywhere have a wide range of feelings regarding the Common Core, we also recognize that many teachers are required to use these standards, so we want to make these activities as accessible and applicable as possible. If the Common Core isn't your thing, feel free to ignore those and move on; however, if you plan to use the standards we listed, we wanted to clarify a few points.

- The following activities reference the 9–10 Common Core Writing Standards. While we wholeheartedly believe these activities can and should be used with students of any grade in high school, some may need to be altered slightly to meet the standards for grades 11–12 fully.
- While we have matched each activity in this chapter to at least one Common Core Standard, not all of the Common Core Standards we've chosen directly relate to the skill we're targeting. We have found that the Common Core Standards do not fully address some of the foundational and necessary writing skills that we target in this book; however, we still chose to tie each activity to a relevant Common Core Standard in order to support educators who feel strongly about using or are required to use those standards.
- Just by virtue of the way we have designed the activities in this chapter as well as the nature of composing with sound, all of the activities in this chapter meet the following Common Core Standards. We have not listed these with each individual activity out of a desire to avoid repetition, but any activity from this chapter will also target the following Common Core Standards for writing.
    - W.4—Produce clear and coherent writing in which the development, organization, and style are appropriate to task, purpose, and audience.
    - W.6—Use technology, including the internet, to produce, publish, and update individual or shared writing products, taking advantage of technology's capacity to link to other information and to display information flexibly and dynamically.
    - W.10—Write routinely over extended time frames (time for research, reflection, and revision) and shorter time frames (a single sitting or a day or two) for a range of tasks, purposes, and audiences.

Getting the Most out of the Audio Writing Activities

Before we get into the classroom-ready audio writing activities we have for you, we want to give you some ideas about what to expect and how to get the most out of this section. While there will be several similarities to the way we laid out Chapter 4's reading activities, this chapter's presentation of the writing activities will also be a little bit different.

Writing as a Process

As we discussed at length in the previous chapter, we believe wholeheartedly in the critical importance of approaching and teaching writing as a process. Accordingly, for each assignment, we have included the assignment statement and an assessment rubric as well as a series of process materials in order to help you and your students walk through the prewriting, drafting, and reflection steps of writing in the mode of sound. You'll notice that the rubrics we've created for each assignment are single-point rubrics, focused on assessment and feedback as opposed to numerical grades or linear ranking (more on this shortly!). This design choice is part of our effort to emphasize the process of writing, encouraging reflection as well as meaningful editing and revision.

As always, we encourage you to consider all the process materials included with these activities as open to modification and tweaking. If we offer a list of brainstorming freewrite questions to prepare students to begin drafting, and you think your students would respond better to those prompts in a group discussion or as a word association activity, we truly hope you feel free to adapt the materials to suit your needs. If you want to adapt our single-point assessment rubrics to integrate a numerical or letter grade system, we encourage you to do so as well. Our supplemental materials are there to support you, however you need.

For the reflection materials in all ten activities, we have formatted those as lists of reflection questions; however, unlike the other materials in these activities, we have not given explicit instruction on how to use those questions. This is because there is a wide range of reflection activities that can be assigned based on the questions we've provided. Teachers can ask students to give individual responses through a reflection letter, essay, or freewrite and open response. Students may reflect in pairs or in small-group discussions. Teachers may also decide to use these reflection questions to facilitate a peer review when navigating the editing and revision stage of the writing process.

Writing Collaboratively

We also believe firmly in the power of collaborative writing. This brings an incredible amount of value to students in helping them understand writing as a social, communal process; it also asks students to engage in discussions and debates around their writing, negotiating meaning as they go and emphasizing the process of composition. Despite the fairly broad consensus on the power of collaborative writing for a wide range of student needs (NCTE's "Position Statement on Writing Instruction in School," Qiang Zhang, Yana Landrieu et al., etc.), practically speaking, it can be difficult to find productive and clear ways to integrate this into our classroom writing instruction.

Several sound genres lend themselves naturally to collaborative writing. The process of writing a sound text like a radio advertisement, an audio drama, or a podcast episode actually functions much more successfully when it relies on collaboration within a group of students. The task of composing a sound text often requires various roles: brainstorming, sound editing, speaking parts in the text, gathering **sound effects**, etc. Negotiating these activities in groups working on a common text "offers students the chance to co-construct texts, pool their language and idea resources, and thus complete more linguistically complex and grammatically accurate texts" (Zhang 64).

Not all genres of sound texts lend themselves equally to collaborative writing; however, you will find that several of the upcoming activities are designed to function well when assigned to groups of students. We include recommendations for assignments that invite collaborative writing in different ways, and we encourage you to explore the capacity that writing in the mode of sound has to create opportunities for authentic, generative, and organic group writing.

The Role of Alphabetic Scripts in the Sound Writing Process

A major question that plays a role in the design of any sound writing assignment is to what extent students should write out alphabetic scripts for their sound texts before beginning to record. Of course, as part of the prewriting process, students create outlines, talking points, and main ideas for their sound texts, but how much of what students will say verbatim in their sound text should be scripted out beforehand?

Our answer is unfortunately vague in that it simply depends! It depends on your students—some students may feel more comfortable and grounded when reading from a prepared script while others may prefer the freedom to ad-lib and speak freely. It also depends on the genre in which students are writing; some genres invite thorough, formal scripts more than others. An audio drama with its roots in theatrical performance genres lends itself to a clear script, potentially even including stage directions and guidance for **voice** actors; an audio poem should almost always be fully drafted beforehand with a fairly high level of clarity, as the genre of poetry emphasizes the significance and meaning of each individual word. However, other genres, like podcasts, can sound too stiff or formal when heavily scripted; the podcast genre generally invites more conversational, spontaneous interactions between speakers. There are many factors to consider. We have included some guidance and recommendations in this chapter's discussion of each activity as to what role we think scripts should play in the drafting process, but only you know the best fit for you and your students.

Pairing Audio Reading and Writing Activities

As we mentioned earlier in this chapter, we believe a significant element of developing a strong grasp of particular writing skills in any mode is reading good models by authors who demonstrate sophisticated use of that skill. Correspondingly, we believe that one of the best ways to wrestle with the complexity of certain reading skills is to try creating those effects in our own writing. This is a big part of why we've used the same reading and writing skills in Chapter 4 as well as in this chapter, designing our sound activities around those skill lists. Between Chapter 4 and this chapter, each of the targeted skills in the skill lists we've given will come with a classroom-ready audio reading activity (Chapter 4) and an audio writing activity (this chapter).

Whenever possible, we recommend pairing an audio writing activity from this chapter with an audio reading activity from Chapter 4. We have designed many of the audio writing activities in this chapter to use the same sound genre as the audio reading activity that corresponds with the targeted skill. Table 6.1 summarizes the activities from this chapter that will pair well with Chapter 4's reading activities due to their use of matching sound genres.

TABLE 6.1: Pairing Audio Reading and Writing Activities

	Writing Skill	Shared Genre for Reading (Chapter 4) and Writing Activity (Chapter 6)
1	Crafting Author's Persona	NPR's *Moth Radio Hour* Memoir
2	Addressing an Audience	Radio Advertisement
3	Crafting an Argument	Review Podcast Episode
4	Making Genre Choices	*These activities won't pair as easily, as the reading activity relies on the genre of poetry and the writing activity relies on the audio genre of a voicemail*
5	Integrating Literary Devices	Poetry
6	Making Organizational and Structural Choices	Informational Podcast Episode
7	Conveying Tone	*These activities won't pair as easily, as the reading activity relies on the genre of an interview and the writing activity relies on the audio genre of a speech*
8	Crafting Mood	Audio Trailer
9	Crafting Theme	Audio Drama
10	Employing Rhetorical Appeals	*These activities won't pair as easily, as the reading activity relies on the genre of a speech and the writing activity relies on the audio genre of an audio tribute*

Materials to Support the Following Activities

In the following ten activities, we have generated skill-specific and activity-specific process materials to support you and your students. As you review the upcoming activities, we also want to offer you three supporting resources that you can feel free to use or omit in your own classroom editions of each activity.

Self-Editing an Audio Text Checklist

- The QR code, **Self-Editing an Audio Text Checklist**, in the margin will take you to a technical self-editing checklist. For students and teachers who are new to writing in the mode of sound, it can be hard to know what to look for from a technical perspective when reviewing and giving feedback on a student-authored sound text. Of course, we are looking to see that students are exercising the targeted writing skills we've chosen, but the technical aspect of writing in the mode of sound is important to the quality of a text as well. This checklist is something you and your students can use to assess work and to guide editing choices during the drafting phase.

Peer Feedback Activity

- The QR code, **Peer Feedback Activity**, in the margin will take you to a peer feedback activity that students can complete as part of their writing process. We understand that peer feedback can feel daunting and that some students may not see the value in the feedback they receive. To help with this, we have tried to create peer feedback guidelines with focused questions that clearly and simply direct student attention to the most useful areas for feedback and response. We believe that intentional, honest peer feedback is important to any writing process, but we find that the peer review process is particularly effective when working in the mode of sound. Students interact with sound texts daily, so they bring a wealth of outside experience, knowledge, intuition, and instinct to the practice of giving feedback on sound texts. We've even found in some cases that because students feel some confidence and authority when working with certain sound text genres, they participate more fully in the peer review process in ways that help them understand the value in peer feedback in general, even for the traditional alphabetic mode. Of course, we recommend talking with students beforehand about the most effective language to use when giving feedback; we generally encourage our students to use respectful language and to focus their feedback specifically on the content that the feedback questions prompt them to. We ask students to always add "because" statements to the end of their feedback, pushing them to use evidence from the text to support their observations.

- We mentioned in "Chapter 4: Designing Reading Activities" that asking students to write alphabetic transcripts for completed sound texts is a meaningful writing activity that engages both the alphabetic and audio modes while also challenging students to consider a range of rhetorical choices. This also makes for an excellent writing activity when used with completed student-authored sound texts. Students can generate transcripts for their own sound texts or for sound texts their peers created. Not only does this encourage intentional close reading as well as thoughtful writing in students, but it also goes a long way in promoting inclusivity in our classrooms and curriculum design. Assigning work with transcripts emphasizes the importance of making sure our work is available to everyone. The QR code, **Transcript-Writing Assignment**, in the margin links to the materials for a writing assignment that asks students to transcribe a sound text, one either they or a peer has authored or a published text that you have chosen.

Transcript-Writing Assignment

Let's Get into It: Ten Classroom-Ready Writing Activities in the Mode of Sound

Now, on to the practical part of this chapter! We'll walk you through each activity with some discussion and example student responses, and, if you use the QR code next to each activity, you'll find blank ready-made worksheets, process documents, and rubrics to use in your classroom. We highly encourage you to use these activities however best supports you and your students. If you want to directly lift an activity exactly as it is with its premade worksheets and assignment statement, we love that. If you want to heavily adapt an activity, choose a new sound genre to practice with, or remake worksheets, we love that, too. What is most important is to try things out and see what works best for you and your classroom.

So, without any further delay, let's take a look at how some of these activities might unfold in a classroom setting.

Assessment versus Grading

You'll see in our supplemental materials that we've given you single-point rubrics to use when assessing student work. If you've never seen a single-point rubric, we love them because they're simple, and they allow room for positive and constructive feedback regarding each of the major aspects of an assignment. One of the major differences between a single- and a multiple-point rubric is that the single-point rubric only describes the qualities of proficient student performance. This avoids "describ[ing] ahead of time all the ways to do poorly in detail" (Fluckiger 19). Christina L. Dobbs and Christine Montecillo Leider identify that "multiple-point rubrics commonly label student work that does not meet teachers' expectations with negative terms, such as 'unsatisfactory,' 'below basic,' 'unacceptable,' or 'insufficient.' Students might read these terms as a statement about their writing [or reading] potential or, even worse, as broader distinctions about their language" (64). The single-point rubric also does not "set limits on student achievement" by prescribing a predetermined "highest level" of performance on an assignment (Fluckiger 19). These rubrics are open-ended in their guidance, allowing students to surprise you with how they reach, and perhaps even exceed, the target goals.

The single-point rubrics we have created for you are not geared toward grading, however; they are not set up to focus on a particular grade or numerical evaluation of student work. Our single-point rubrics are about assessing students' work, giving them clear feedback, suggesting areas of growth, and identifying areas of strength. We view assessment as "a form of feedback to students regarding their progress" with a goal of "enhanc[ing] learning" (Marzano 5). Robert J. Marzano's research indicates that the most meaningful feedback students can receive "should be frequent, give students a clear picture of their progress and how they might improve, and provide encouragement" (11). Our single-point rubrics are designed to meet these requirements, and our personal classroom experience with these rubrics has been extremely positive. Additionally, Jarene Fluckiger's work with single-point rubrics points out that "descriptive feedback is more helpful than a number, a grade, a score, a ranking, or a single descriptive label" (20). If you wish to adapt these rubrics to assign a grade, you're welcome to do so, but we find that emphasizing assessment over grading aligns with our goals of viewing learning as a process rather than an end goal.

As an added benefit, single-point rubrics can be used as excellent tools for "responsible student self-assessment" as we prioritize giving students autonomy and ownership over their literacy skills (Fluckiger 18).

Activity 1: Crafting Persona

Writing Activity 1 Materials

For this activity, we ask students to write and record an NPR *Moth Radio Hour*-style audio memoir in which they tell a true personal story between four to eight minutes in length. The goal of this assignment, as reflected in our process documents, instructions, and assessment rubric, is to prompt students to practice the skill of demonstrating their authorial persona, how they position themselves in their role as the author of the text, when composing. We strongly recommend this activity be completed individually, allowing each student to work on their narrative to develop and strengthen their own individual **voice** and persona.

Common Core ELA Standard(s)	Description of Standard(s)
W.3	Write narratives to develop real or imagined experiences or events using effective technique, well-chosen details, and well-structured event sequences. *Note: Within W.3, this activity specifically works on W.3.C and W.3.D*
Objectives: SWBAT write an audio memoir about a real event or experience in which they clearly develop an authorial persona through the use of narrative techniques, precise diction, and the sound strategies.	

We have a variety of prewriting options for this activity available to students in the linked materials; however, we feel that the most relevant prewriting tool to discuss in this section is **"Creating Author's Persona Prewrite—Step 4, Part 2 Handout,"** the portion of the process in which we ask students to consider their tentative outline for their chosen personal story and consider where their persona as authors may appear. We've included this graphic organizer filled out with the kinds of answers we look for from students. For context, at this point in the activity, students should have brainstormed personal stories, considered their authorial persona, and then begun the process of considering how they will craft and communicate that persona throughout the telling of their personal story.

Crafting Author's Persona Prewrite—Step 4, Part 2—Student Sample Responses

Looking at your responses in part 1, how will you tell these parts of the story in order to emphasize your persona? Consider details you should add as well as descriptions of how you will say things. If you plan to include sound effects, music, silence, or layering, also describe that here.

	How do you establish your persona?
Setting the Scene/ Establishing Characters	My story takes place in a mosque with my mother. This detail will communicate that I was raised as a practicing Muslim in a Muslim family. You can tell from my tone of voice that, as a younger me, I didn't want to be there for worship. I'm considering including a recording of an adhan, or call to prayer, near the beginning of the memoir. It's an important part of my faith, and it's been a constant in my life since very young.
Anticipation	When I tell about how my mother and I argue about my attendance at the prayer service, the voice I use as my younger self will show the listener how difficult and stubborn I was. The listener will also get a sense of how important Islam is to my family tradition.
Moment of Highest Excitement or Significance	When my mother tells me I no longer have to attend prayer services, I plan to pause and include silence after that statement to show how difficult it was for her to say that and to emphasize how much guilt I felt at pushing her to stop asking me. At this point, I plan to adjust my voice slightly to sound gentler, older, and more mature. This was the point at which, for me, I shifted to becoming responsible for my own faith.
Conclusion	I hope my voice sounds adult, more like my current-day self, at the end of the memoir. And I want to use my tone of voice to communicate that I attend mosque regularly and that it brings me and my family joy. I'll probably say some of that explicitly, but I will also try to sound settled and happy with my choices.

This prewriting tool will push students to consider their authorial persona explicitly along with how they can use the mode of sound to establish that persona.

After completing this step in the prewriting materials is the point in the writing process when, if we were going to require alphabetic scripts before recording, we assign them. For an audio memoir, we always ask for outlines, but we do not usually require alphabetic scripts; we allow students to script out as much as they feel they need before beginning to record. For some students, the prewriting documents we've provided are sufficient. Other students may create more detailed outlines using bullet points or listing out primary talking points with notes for vocal inflection or volume. Other students may complete a full alphabetic telling of the memoir from which they read as they record.

There are pros and cons to all of these options, and we find that giving students the choice between them allows students to reflect on which composition strategies and writing process steps work best for them as individuals. Students who prefer a more fluid, spontaneous vocal delivery may find they work best with talking points and cues that allow them to ad-lib and infuse candid statements into their audio work. Students who feel most comfortable with linear reasoning and logic may find they work best with a clear, numerically organized outline of their content. However, students who prefer to labor over the precise diction, phrasing, or sentence structure may find a more traditional script best assists their writing process. Because students have such an array of prewriting choices, a valuable optional element to add to your reflection steps for this activity could be to prompt students to consider how and where they used alphabetic materials in their process.

Writing Activity 2 Materials

Activity 2: Addressing an Audience

This activity will ask students to take on the role of the owners of a company that manufactures, markets, and sells a new energy drink called Electric. Taking on the persona of the owners of the company, students will work to compose a radio advertisement trying to get people to buy the new product. The catch is that students have to choose a target audience at which to aim their advertisement. Our assignment statement offers them a list to choose from, including working moms listening to pop radio, teens on Spotify, college students listening to their college radio station, etc.; however, we encourage students to think of their own target audience and, with teacher approval, write an advertisement that caters to them.

The advertisement should be around thirty-five to forty-five seconds long, use at least one **voice**, and bring in some of the other sound strategies. This activity is a great opportunity for collaborative writing; students love working together to create a dynamic advertisement, and there are plenty of roles in this work for everyone.

Common Core ELA Standard(s)	Description of Standard(s)
W.1	Write arguments to support claims in an analysis of substantive topics or texts, using valid reasoning and relevant and sufficient evidence. *Note: Within W.1, this activity specifically works on W.1.B*
Objectives: SWBAT write an argument-based audio advertisement using reasoning and support that is best suited to their audience. SWBAT use information they have gathered and deduced about their audience to employ the sound strategies in effectively bolstering their advertisement's reasoning and support.	

In the prewriting process materials for this activity, we include a step that asks students to choose a target audience and to brainstorm information about that audience; we encourage teachers to monitor students as they complete this section to ensure that no one is making problematic assumptions or stereotyping peoples or groups. If teachers do encounter any questionable assumptions that students make about their audience, teachers may pose questions like "what specifically about your audience made you think that?" or "would multiple people from your audience agree that this is true for them?" In Figure 6.1, you'll find a model of a student's work that demonstrates some assumptions about motherhood based on societal norms and expectations; while these assumptions are based on some stereotyping of gender roles, students could easily use the reflective component of this assignment to explain how they utilize these assumptions in order to conform to the expectations and norms of marketing companies.

Next, students will consider their target audience's priorities in an energy drink and how all this information will impact the sounds they use to compose their advertisements, including **voice**, **music**, **sound effects**, **silence**, and **layering**. We've included an example of part of **"Addressing an Audience Prewrite—Step 5"** to demonstrate what a student's work may look like when outlining this radio advertisement using our timeline template.

This outline template is an example of a student strategizing on how the different **layers** of this radio advertisement will fit together. Short radio advertisements are a great genre to use when encouraging students to experiment with **layered**, dense sound texts, but it can sometimes be difficult to visualize how those elements will all work together. We've designed this template to help with that.

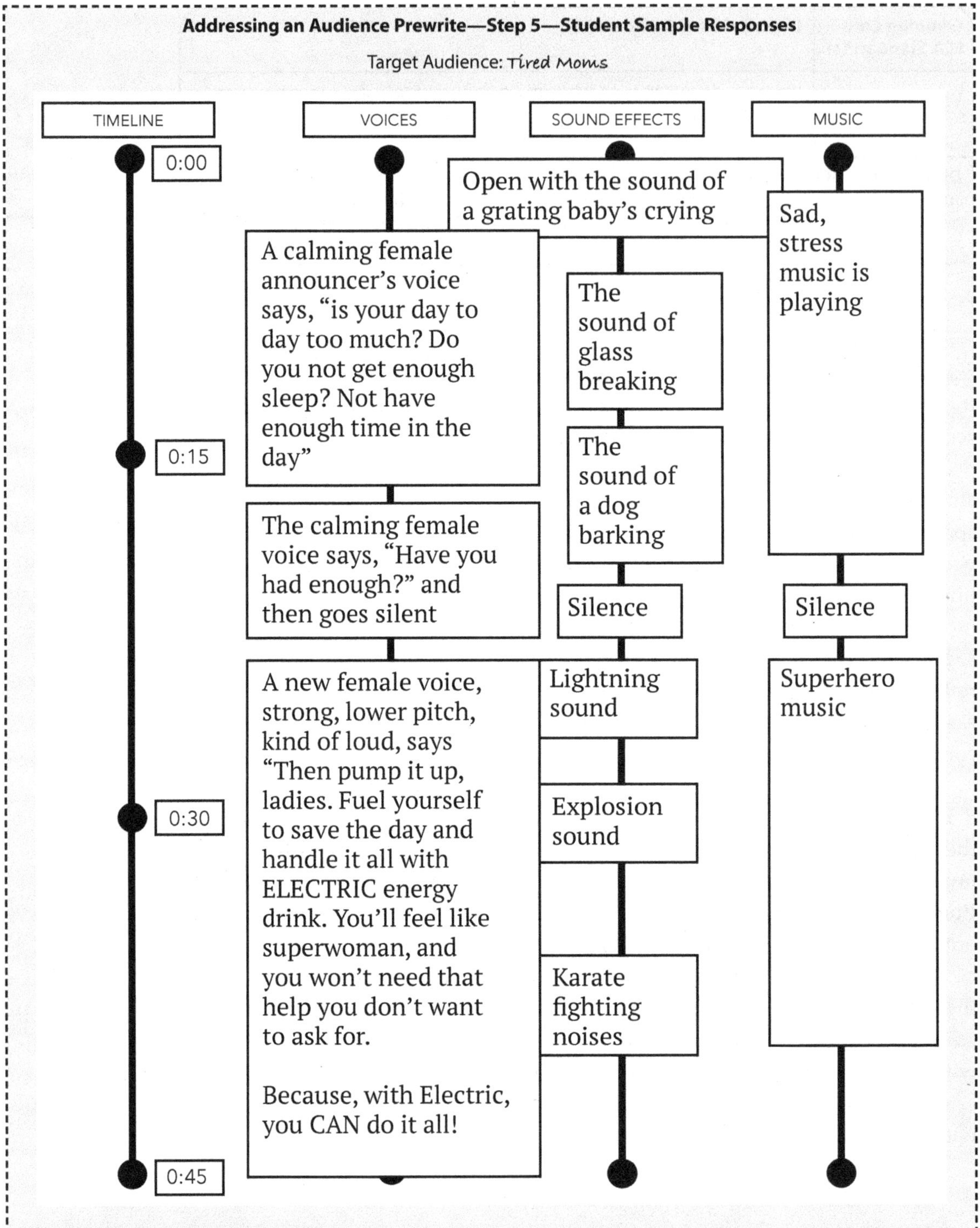

FIGURE 6.1: Student Outline

You'll notice that this template has three lines representing three of the five sound strategies: **voices**, **sound effects**, and **music**. **Silence** and **layering** do not have their own lines in this template. We want to stress that this is not intended to communicate that these three sound strategies are more significant. **Layering** and **silence** should and will appear on this template in their own respective ways.

- **Layering** will appear across the three lines as students consider how **voices**, **sound effects**, and **music** work together, interact with one another, and overlap.
- **Silence** may appear on a single line (speaking **voices** may go silent while **music** continues), or it may appear across all three lines, indicating that, for a moment, the advertisement cuts to total **silence**. We think it helps students to envision how **silence** will appear in each individual line as opposed to having them consider it separately on its own line.

After completing some form of outlining, assign the writing of alphabetic scripts, if you were planning to do so. In our experience, whereas the genre of radio advertisements usually feature short, quick statements or interactions, students tend to inadvertently script out a fair amount of the dialogue when they complete their outlining and general brainstorming. An official alphabetic script is not usually something they need; however, this is entirely up to you and your students.

Activity 3: Crafting an Argument

Writing Activity 3 Materials

We find that students, and humans in general, adore giving their opinions on matters, and so, to practice the skill of crafting an argument, we have designed this activity to ask students to draft and record a podcast episode in which they give a review of something of their choosing. The genre of a review in general, even a review podcast, is something many students will have a familiarity with, and this can be valuable preknowledge for this assignment. The argument students craft will assess the quality, or lack thereof, of something they have personal firsthand experience with. Our assignment statement offers a few ideas for things to review: a summer reading book, a movie they watched recently, a restaurant they visited, etc., or we invite students to pitch their own ideas for teacher approval.

This episode should range from five to ten minutes, include at least one clear, arguable claim about the thing being reviewed, evidence to support the claim(s), and, of course, sound strategies. This activity can foster incredible opportunities for collaboration, particularly if a group of students shares strong feelings on the same thing that they can review together. However, it works just as well when assigned and completed individually with each student reviewing the thing of their choosing. In scenarios like this one in our own classrooms, we often give students the choice to collaborate or to work independently.

Common Core ELA Standard(s)	Description of Standard(s)
W.1	Write arguments to support claims in an analysis of substantive topics or texts, using valid reasoning and relevant and sufficient evidence. *Note: Within W.1, this activity specifically works on W.1.A and W.1.B*
Objectives: SWBAT write a clear claim, which they support with evidence, in the form of a review podcast. SWBAT employ the sound strategies to construct, support, and enrich their argument.	

The prewriting materials we have created for this assignment will prompt students to choose the thing they are reviewing, brainstorm their rating and supporting rationale, consider how different sound strategies can work together to craft their argument, and then begin outlining and making lists of sounds they will need. Below is an example of what it can look like when a student uses our outlining organizer in **"Crafting an Argument—Step 5 Handout"** to arrange and build their argument.

Crafting an Argument—Step 5—Student Sample Responses

1. What will you title your podcast episode? "What Max Thinks Is Good: Mom's Cinnamon Bread"
2. How will you transition between each part of your podcast episode? Will you use sound effects? Music? Vocal cues? "What Max Thinks Is Good" will have a theme song that plays at the beginning and end of each episode, and then, for this episode, I will use the sounds of happy people eating cinnamon bread to transition between parts.

Next, complete one of the following options.

Option 1: *Complete the following graphic organizer*

	Will there be dialogue here? If so, who will be saying what?	What sound strategies will appear in this section?
Introduction	It will be me, Max, telling you that I am Max and that this is my podcast about things I say are good. I'll explain that today's episode is about my mom's cinnamon bread because it is superior to all other cinnamon breads, and your life is incomplete without it.	I'm going to have a short, silly, instrumental song to lead into the episode, and then I, Max, will be speaking authoritatively and confidently, as my mom's bread is the one in question. I'll move to my first point with the sound of someone happily munching on bread and going "mmmm, this bread is life changing."

Point 1	I will explain that my mom is a cinnamon bread expert.	Maybe the sounds of some kitchen utensils and noises in the background.
Evidence	I will interview my mom about her history perfecting her cinnamon bread and how she hunts for fresh organic ingredients.	As my mom is talking, I will be ooooing and ahhhhing to emphasize what a cinnamon bread expert she is. I will transition into the next point with the sound effects of applause.
Evidence	N/A	
Point 2	I will explain that everyone I know feels the same way about the cinnamon bread.	More sound effects of someone eating and enjoying cinnamon bread.
Evidence	I will interview a group of my friends who come over [to] my house a lot. Without naming them individually, I'm going to just record them enthusiastically talking over one another to explain how much they need more cinnamon bread.	I think the sounds of my friends talking (probably all at once) is going to be pretty busy, so I may not put anything else in this part.
Evidence	I will also interview my aunt because she grew up with my mom and can attest to the fact that my mom has been making this cinnamon bread since before I was even born, and it has always been legendary.	More sound effects of someone eating and enjoying cinnamon bread.
(Optional) Counterclaim/ Rebuttal	I will say that there are some haters. My grandfather does not like, nor has ever liked, the cinnamon bread.	When I mention the haters, I'm going to play foreboding, spooky music. Include the sound of someone gasping.
Evidence	I'm going to interview either my mom or my aunt telling me how he never liked it.	More sounds of disapproving whispers and hushed gasps.
Evidence	However, my mom and aunt can attest to the fact that my grandfather can't eat gluten, and so he is unreliable and biased.	Return to the sounds of applause.
Conclusion	I'll wrap things up by reviewing the facts quickly, sharing a personal story about how the cinnamon bread saved my life, and then dedicating the episode to my mom, the bringer of cinnamon bread. I will end with a farewell and an invitation to join me next time, as I review potholes: are they really as bad as people say?	I'll play the same instrumental music I played during the introduction.

Note: You may have more or fewer points or required pieces of evidence than this outline provides; you should add or subtract as necessary.

The above outline is something teachers should feel very free to adjust and alter based on what is best for your students and classrooms. Your template or outline could require more or fewer points, more or less evidence, specific kinds of evidence, a required counterclaim, or could leave these choices open to students, allowing them to choose the number of points, kinds of evidence, and whether or not to include a counterclaim.

Here again is the point in the activity at which you could prompt students to write a complete script; however, as was the case with the prior activities thus far, this podcast episode can reasonably be drafted and recorded without a complete verbatim script. Whereas the genre of podcasts in general is so often informal, spontaneous, and playful, requiring scripts may actually create too much structure for some students.

Activity 4: Making Choices around Genre

Writing Activity 4 Materials

In this activity, students will be creating and recording a voicemail message that they would leave on someone's phone if the person they were trying to reach didn't pick up their call. Before beginning to draft their voicemails, students have to choose from a list of options to construct a rhetorical situation to respond to. They will have a list of potential speaker roles to represent, audiences to address, and purposes to achieve; they will have to choose one of each. The voicemail they create has to make a variety of genre-related choices that respond effectively to their particular rhetorical situation, and it has to do it in under a minute and a half.

When developing the skill of making genre-related choices in their own writing, students can sometimes feel hesitant to play with more established, traditionally academic genres (like poetry, which the corresponding reading activity for this skill uses in Chapter 4). Because of this, for this writing activity, we've chosen a less firmly established, less quintessentially academic genre that we hope invites students to play and experiment with principles of genre. A voicemail message is something we expect students to at the very least have some experience with, and it is something we expect them to be able to explain the basics of while also recognizing the wide range of different characteristics and norms that help make up the vaguely defined genre.

This activity can be completed in groups, but we recommend individual work for this one. Practically, it's unusual for a group of speakers to leave a voicemail, and these voicemail sound texts should require minimal editing and **layering**, so there won't be a range of roles for different students to take on.

Common Core ELA Standard(s)	Description of Standard(s)
W.3	Write narratives to develop real or imagined experiences or events using effective technique, well-chosen details, and well-structured event sequences. *Note: Within W.3, this activity specifically works on W.3.A*
Objectives: SWBAT write a voicemail message in which they clearly establish a situation and develop that situation with specific details and sound strategies. SWBAT create a realistic speaker's voice and compose their dialogue for their specific audience and situation.	

Before you dive too deeply into this activity, our prewriting docs have materials to guide you and your students through a more general analysis and discussion of the genre of the voicemail message. Students can generate a broad genre analysis for the genre of a voicemail individually, in small groups, or as a whole class. We love when students have voicemails on their phones that they don't mind sharing with the class as samples or genre artifacts for everyone to consider in their analysis of the genre. The example of **"Making Choices Around Genre Prewrite—Step 1 Handout"** below offers some ideas for what kinds of genre norms your students may list as part of their brainstorming.

Making Choices Around Genre Prewrite—Step 1—Sample Student Responses

Before you begin creating your voicemail message, work in groups with your classmates to gather what you know about the genre of a voicemail message. Fill out the following table with at least three items in each column. You can listen to any voicemail messages you may have on your phone for guidance.

Genre Norms in Almost Every Voicemail Message	Genre Norms in Some Voicemail Message
• Introduce who is speaking • Brief greeting • Only one speaker • Clear and straight to the point • Gives a clear explanation of the purpose close to the beginning • A farewell or signoff	• Noise in the background • A cameo or brief hello from a related person • A call back number or way to get in touch • Includes some narrative

Once your class has demonstrated an understanding of what the genre norms are for a voicemail, the subsequent prewriting steps ask them how their rhetorical situation will impact their voicemail and how the sound strategies can be used to accomplish their chosen purpose. Then students can begin outlining and drafting their voicemail. The list students created above can be a reference point as they consider how they want to compose their voicemails.

While reflection is an essential part of the writing process for all activities, for this activity in particular, we strongly emphasize the reflection questions. The most important element for students learning to make appropriate choices around genres in particular rhetorical situations is having to explain those choices. As part of their writing process, whether they do this consciously or unconsciously, students will decide the ways in which their voicemail will conform to the genre norms and how it will deviate from or subvert genre expectations. Students should be ready to discuss these choices in light of their chosen rhetorical situation. For example, while it is unusual for a voicemail to include multiple central speakers, if a student is speaking as a teenager at a party calling their parents to let them know that they will be missing curfew, it might be effective to have the reassuring **voice** of a parent from the house where the party is taking place speak briefly on the voicemail to assure the speaker's parents that they are safe and headed home soon. It is the discussion and reflection on these choices that builds the awareness of genre students need to make savvy and effective choices as readers and writers in any mode.

Activity 5: Integrating Literary Devices

Writing Activity 5 Materials

Students working on this activity will be asked to compose audio poetry around the topic of love, intentionally working at least three literary devices into their poem. The audio recording of the poem they compose should be between a minute and a half to three minutes in length, and instructions encourage students to consider how they can use both their **voices** as well as the strategy of **silence** in their poetry to communicate content, transitions, stanzas, and other poetic elements. Although audio poems don't typically include all five sound strategies, this assignment welcomes students to integrate **sound effects**, **music**, and **layering** into their poems, if they choose.

While we anticipate this activity being completed individually, we see no reason why students can't collaboratively compose an audio poem on the topic of love. This may be a good opportunity to offer your students some choices!

Common Core ELA Standard(s)	Description of Standard(s)
W.3	Write narratives to develop real or imagined experiences or events using effective technique, well-chosen details, and well-structured event sequences. *Note: Within W.3, this activity specifically works on W.3.C and W.3.D*
Objectives: SWBAT write literary devices that integrate into their poem, share something specific about love, and rely at least partially on sound strategies to communicate their meaning.	

The assignment statement we have provided for this activity offers a word bank of potential literary devices for students to choose from, but teachers can remove this word bank, edit it, or make one of their own. We also recommend that if reading poetry in any mode has played a role in your classroom already, you direct students to write the same kinds of poetry they have been studying or reading so they have models. If sonnets, villanelles, or odes have featured in your curriculum recently, students will be able to explore those genres more deeply as well as have prior knowledge to draw from as they work through this activity.

The prewriting materials for this activity first ask students to narrow down a topic under the larger category of love, deciding what kind of love they want to depict and how they feel about it. For example, student poetry can center on familial love, friendship, or romance; their poem can go on to depict their chosen category of love as dangerous, beautiful, mysterious, etc. Next, students brainstorm some of the images and ideas they associate with the kind of love they've chosen, considering figurative and abstract associations in order to prepare them to represent their message about this kind of love through literary devices.

In **"Integrating Literary Devices Prewrite—Step 3 Handout,"** we've included some examples of what we expect students to include as they synthesize the brainstorming work of the prior prewriting steps into some ideas for literary devices that could help present their message about and understanding of the love they've chosen to feature in their audio poem. The table we've created for **"Integrating Literary Devices Prewrite—Step 3 Handout"** asks for three literary devices, but teachers using these materials can and should feel free to require a different number of literary devices or make the number more open-ended, inviting students to include whatever number of devices resonates with them.

Integrating Literary Devices Prewrite—Step 3—Sample Student Responses

Given what you responded in steps 1 and 2, what literary devices might help you convey your message about love to your audience? You may refer to the word bank provided if you need some suggestions.

Message about Love: The Challenges of Loving Your Mother

Literary Device	How it will convey my overall message
Simile	Loving my mom is like a funhouse mirror. I see myself in the reflection, but it's all messed up and hard to recognize. And it's kind of fun and cool but also unsettling and a little scary, and I want to keep looking at her and moving around her to see what I look like from different angles.
Personification	The relationship between my mom and me has a mind of its own, and sometimes it's kind to us, and other times it makes us feel bad about ourselves, but the relationship is its own member of our family, and it's not really going anywhere, so we have to be kind to it and try to get it to cooperate with us.
Polysyndeton	My mother and I love each other and can't stand each other and protect each other and support each other and battle each other and hurt each other and worry about each other and hold each other and fear each other.

We like using poetry to explore this skill because it's a genre of writing that invites figurative and nonliteral expression, which is a large element of effective use of literary devices. This step of prewriting creates space for students to explore some of the nonliteral and abstract elements of the kind of love on which their poem centers in order to prompt them to consider which literary devices might help them communicate their message. Students may or may not end up using the literary devices they brainstorm in this step; the goal is to get them thinking about abstract content and how to creatively leverage literary devices to communicate the parts of their message that are nuanced, complicated, or difficult to articulate.

Once students have some ideas about the content in their poems, it's time to begin the process of choosing how to express that in the mode of sound. The next prewriting steps prompt students to consider their vocal qualities like pitch, tempo, volume, etc., how and where **silence** will appear in their recording, and whether or not they plan to integrate any of the other sound strategies. Specifically, we ask students to consider ahead of time what their **voices** will sound like as they speak the literary devices they brainstormed in the prior steps, with the main goal being to encourage students to compose by using what they say as well as how they say it.

Generally, the genre of poetry most often uses fewer words than other genres and also relies very heavily on each individual word to construct a poem's overall meaning, so we ask that students entirely script verbatim their audio poems before recording them, giving student authors ample time to reflect on each literary device, its location, its purpose, and its exact diction. In these scripts, we prompt students to make notes alongside or in the margins of the scripted words to direct themselves on *how* to read the poem, giving cues for volume, pauses of **silence**, punctuated repetition, etc. While this is not necessary to the assignment, our experiences with requiring an alphabetic script for this assignment have been positive.

Activity 6: Making Choices around Organization and Structure

Writing Activity 6 Materials

We return to the genre of a podcast for this activity. Students create a podcast episode in which they make a clear argument about a particular subject or topic of their choosing, which they support with reliable sources they have researched. As we've mentioned before, our personal view and belief is that all genres of writing in any mode make arguments, taking positions and making cases regarding different elements of their composition and subject; however, this assignment could certainly be adapted to be a more informational or explanatory episode. For teachers who adapt the assignment in this way, the activity will then address a writing standard (W.2) that we, due to our own bias toward argument, haven't covered in our activity list.

As with other podcast episode writing assignments in this chapter, we believe this genre of writing lends itself well to collaborative group composition, and we heartily encourage teachers to take advantage of that.

Common Core ELA Standard(s)	Description of Standard(s)
W.1	Write arguments to support claims in an analysis of substantive topics or texts, using valid reasoning and relevant and sufficient evidence.
W.8	Gather relevant information from multiple authoritative print and digital sources, using advanced searches effectively; assess the usefulness of each source in answering the research question; integrate information into the text selectively to maintain the flow of ideas, avoiding plagiarism and following a standard format for citation.
W.9	Draw evidence from literary or informational texts to support analysis, reflection, and research. *Note: Within W.1, this activity specifically works on W.1.A, W.1.B, W.1.C, and W.1.E*
Objectives: SWBAT research a particular topic using reliable databases and determine the most relevant information. SWBAT integrate evidence from multiple sources to support their writing. SWBAT write a podcast in which their organization and structure demonstrate a clear progression and sequencing of information around a topic they wish to teach, relying at least partially on sound strategies to introduce, transition between, conclude, and overall communicate the organizational structure of their text.	

Our prewriting documents begin by asking students to consider the rhetorical situation surrounding the topic they've chosen, settling on some central goals and messages they intend to accomplish and communicate through their episode. Next, students gather research materials relating to their chosen topic, considering how these materials fit together with one another; **"Making Choices Around Organization and Structure Prewrite—Step 2"** uses a table for recording information about each source, which should visually demonstrate the connections between sources. We often encourage students during their research to consider a range of materials in a variety of modes, potentially ones that contradict or disagree with some of the points their podcast episode makes. If you are presenting this podcast as an argumentative podcast, you can articulate this to your students as a counterpoint and rebuttal; however, regardless of framing, it is always important to encourage students to gather a range of perspectives on a given issue.

Next, students begin the process of considering how to construct, order, and arrange the materials for their podcast episode; the questions in **"Making Choices Around Organization and Structure Prewrite—Step 3"** below represent some of the responses we expect from students as they navigate this part of the prewriting process. We have not given sample responses for all questions, only the ones we feel are most relevant to the skill of structuring and organizing a text.

Making Choices Around Organization and Structure Prewrite—Step 3—Student Sample Responses

Answer the following questions to start crafting your podcast's organization and structure

1. Podcast Topic: The Mental Health Benefits of Being Outdoors

2. How will you introduce your podcast episode and subject? What will be most effective in appealing to the audience you've chosen, grabbing their attention, and preparing them to understand your episode?

I want to open my episode with the sounds of birds chirping, a stream, and the faint sound of children laughing. I will ask my audience how those sounds made them feel and, through this, introduce the idea that the outdoors have great mental health benefits. Since my audience is parents and educators, I think they will find a moment of soft outdoor sounds really relaxing, and maybe this will remind them of either their childhood or their own kids' childhood.

3. What are the main points that you will share with your audience in order to teach them about your subject? In what order do you think your audience will want to experience them, and why?

I think I want to start with my own experience of joining the adventure club at my high school and how having more time outside to play really helped me feel happier and less anxious. I think this personal story will help the audience see why this matters and why it might help their kids/ students.

Next, I will include data/studies that support my argument. These will include statistics about the mental health differences in children who spend a significant amount of time outside versus those who don't. It will also briefly include studies about technology and the negative impact it can have on children, making the connection that more time outside means less time on tech.

4. What primary counterpoint do you think your audience would make to your argument about your chosen topic or person's significance? How will you address and refute this counterpoint? Where in the episode does the audience need to see this counterpoint addressed and why?

My counterpoint will focus on how difficult it can for some people be to spend time outside (either due to weather, finances, or guardian time constraints). I will spend most of the counterclaim going over how some people struggle to spend time outside due to weather constraints; this is something that is even more of a concern as the climate keeps changing.

In order to refute the counterclaim, I will include potential solutions for each concern. I will also use data that suggests the mental health benefits are cumulative, meaning if someone can't get outside one day, that won't undo all of the benefits they've gotten every other time they've been outside.

5. How will you conclude your episode? What information and/or sound strategies will help your audience remember the most important element(s) of your episode?

I want to finish my episode by interviewing different youth involved in the adventure and outdoor clubs at schools around me. This will leave the audience with personal anecdotes that show just how valuable this is. I think a lot of people think kids would rather be inside on their phones or computers, but I hope by ending with stories from kids, my audience will see that narrative just isn't true.

6. What is your main message or main idea about your chosen topic in this podcast episode? Will you state this explicitly, or will you leave it to your listener to conclude as they listen to your episode? Why?

My main idea is that children should be encouraged to spend more time outside in order to help improve their mental health. I'm arguing that the adults in our lives need to work to make changes and try to get more programming that will make it easier and more accessible for all youth to spend more time outside.

From this point, students will need to outline their planned episode. Teachers may choose to require complete scripts or variations on them. Then students can begin recording, revising, editing, and working toward their finalized sound text!

Activity 7: Conveying Tone

Writing Activity 7 Materials

In order to promote the skill of conveying tone in student writing, this activity requires students to deliver a speech in which they construct an argument supported with researched evidence and directed toward their school's principal, superintendent, and/or school committee. This speech can be delivered live to the class, but we strongly prefer requiring students to hand in audio recordings; this prompts students to focus exclusively on the mode of sound and their audio delivery of the speech as opposed to considering gestures, dress, facial expressions, and other visual elements of in-person speeches.

Student speeches can address any school-related topic; the assignment statement offers a few ideas to get students started, including subjects like cell phones in classrooms or standardized testing prep during the school day. The recording of the speech should fall between five and eight minutes long, rely on at least three sources, and integrate a counterclaim and rebuttal. Most important of all, a listener should be able to clearly identify how the student feels about the topic of their own speech; in short, a listener should be able to identify a targeted, intentional tone.

While we're sure there are ways to compose a collaborative speech, we think the genre norms in policy or issue-related argumentative speeches lean toward assigning this activity as individual work.

Common Core ELA Standard(s)	**Description of Standard(s)**
W.1	Write arguments to support claims in an analysis of substantive topics or texts, using valid reasoning and relevant and sufficient evidence.
W.8	Gather relevant information from multiple authoritative print and digital sources, using advanced searches effectively; assess the usefulness of each source in answering the research question; integrate information into the text selectively to maintain the flow of ideas, avoiding plagiarism and following a standard format for citation.
W.9	Draw evidence from literary or informational texts to support analysis, reflection, and research. *Note: Within W.1, this activity specifically works on W.1.A, W.1.B, W.1.C, and W.1.E*
Objectives: SWBAT research and gather relevant and reliable information from databases in order to support their argument. SWBAT write a clear argument that is supported with evidence from their researched sources. SWBAT make use of voice, vocal cues, and silence to convey a clear tone and opinion within their speech that is appropriate both for their argument and their audience.	

The materials for the assignment walk students through the process of brainstorming for their speech by considering the rhetorical situation, gathering sources and reliable evidence, identifying a target tone and how that tone will impact sound choices, and then outlining the content and structure of the speech. **"Conveying Tone Prewrite—Step 4 Handout (Option 2)"** below shows examples of work we expect to see from students working through how conveying a particular tone might impact their compositional choices in the mode of sound, specifically with their own **voice**.

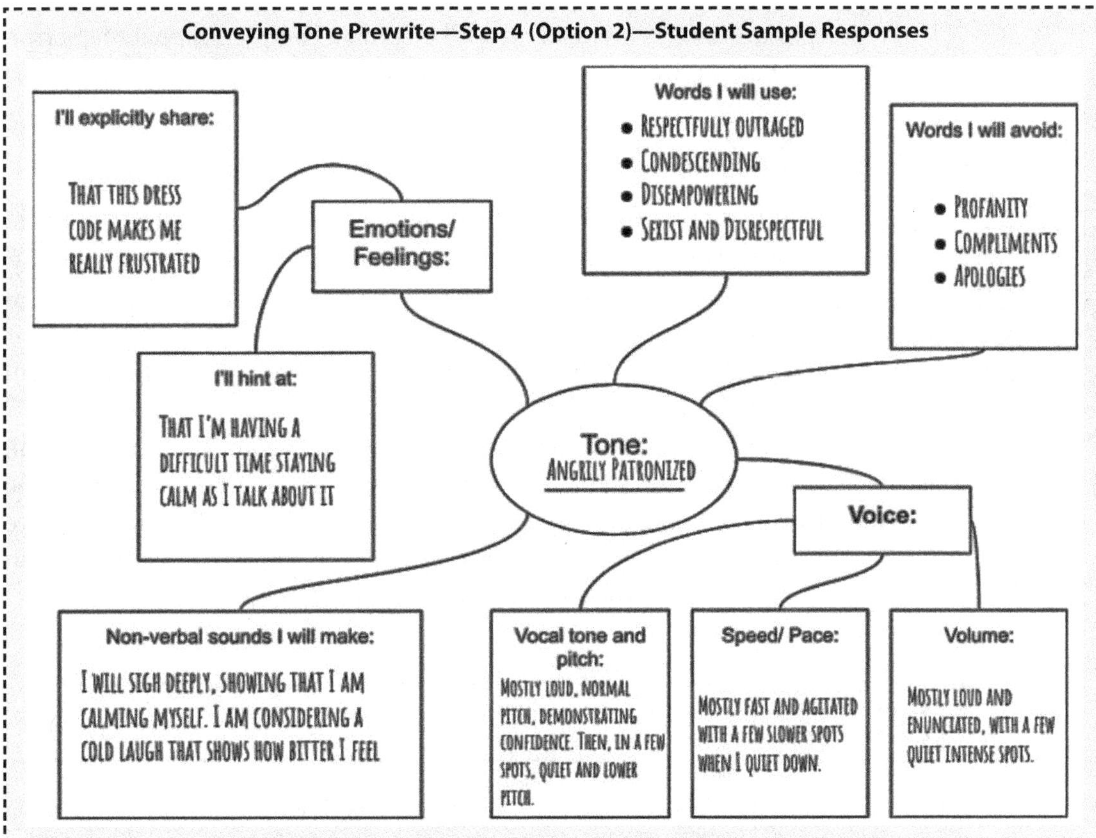

FIGURE 6.2: Conveying Tone Student Sample

We find the above step of the prewriting process to be one of the most valuable in this activity, and we recommend emphasizing it with students to get them to consider the varied strategies and tools they have at their disposal for conveying tone both explicitly and implicitly. Once students have completed this, the following materials ask them to outline and arrange their arguments. This is a great opportunity to exercise the skill of crafting an argument (skill 3) and making choices around organization and structure (skill 6). Making Choices Around Organization and Structure"; you may choose to call students' attention to their use of these supporting skills or adjust classroom materials to emphasize them.

At this point, students are ready to either script a complete alphabetic script, create a set of talking points, or launch into recording—teacher's choice!

Activity 8: Crafting Mood

Writing Activity 8 Materials

This activity asks students to have a little fun by meeting an imaginary need to give incoming students into your ELA class a taste of what is headed their way. Your students will create an audio trailer giving future students a preview of what to expect from this English class. Students will work in groups on their separate trailers, all of which share the same purpose; however, each group will be assigned a different mood.

Teachers can choose from moods for the audio trailers such as cheerful, ominous, spooky, humorous, intense, etc., and each group will need to generate that mood in their audience—your class's future students—as that audience listens. The audio trailer should fall between one and a half to three minutes in length, and students need to use **layering** to accomplish the task.

Common Core ELA Standard(s)	Description of Standard(s)
W.3	Write narratives to develop real or imagined experiences or events using effective technique, well-chosen details, and well-structured event sequences. *Note: Within W.3, this activity specifically works on W.3.A and W.3.D*
Objectives: SWBAT write a compelling trailer for their class in which they use precise diction, literary techniques, and layered sound strategies to create a specific mood for their audience.	

The prewriting materials for this activity support students in generating ideas for content for the trailer as well as considering how the sound strategies can generate the intended mood. The answers to the freewrite questions from **"Crafting Mood Prewrite—Step 2 Handout (Option 1)"** below suggest how some students may approach planning to generate a particular mood in their audience. The materials in this section also offer a graphic organizer version of these questions, depending on what teachers think their students would prefer.

Crafting Mood Prewrite—Step 2 (Option 1)—Student Sample Responses

Answer the following questions:

1. How will this assigned mood impact the way I speak? Are there any particular words I will or won't use? How will my voice sound as I deliver the content in the trailer? Will I make any nonverbal vocal sounds like sighs or grunts or laughs?

   We will have two speakers, one low-pitched, grumbly male voice and a second high-pitched, cackly female voice. We will use words like "beware, gruesome, brutal, and horrific." The speakers' voices will sound spooky and scary. We want the female voice to have a wicked witch-sounding cackle, and the grumbly male voice will grunt like the Frankenstein monster.

2. Will I be using music to generate mood in this trailer? If so, what kinds of music will I use and why? What will my audience respond to most strongly, and why?

   We're going to have slow, quiet, instrumental music that is maybe in a minor key.

3. Will I be using sound effects to generate mood in this trailer? If so, what kinds of sound effects will I use and why? What will my audience respond to most strongly, and why?

   We are going to include spooky sounds like a wolf's howl, creaking steps, gusting wind, flocks of crows cawing, etc. We also want to use our school's class change bell throughout the trailer because our audience will recognize it.

4. How can I use silence to prompt my audience to respond in the way I am intending?

   Silence can be spooky. We may leave more silence in the trailer than there normally would be. A longer pause at the beginning, a strength of silence layered over the sound of howling wind at the end. This might create a sense for the audience of waiting for something bad to happen.

5. Where will I intentionally layer sound strategies to craft my intended mood in my audience?

   There will always be some kind of layering because we want the sound effect of howling wind or wolf howls or the class bell to always be running underneath the voices, and we think the music will also be playing at the same time. We don't expect total silence at any point.

From this point, students are ready to outline their plans for the trailer; our prewriting materials offer a few different options for outlining this activity, and, because the genre of an audio trailer offers a lot of flexibility, we recommend allowing students to choose an outlining tool or strategy, as some approaches to the trailer will be more linear and/or literal than others. Students next brainstorm what sounds they need to collect in order to accomplish their outlined plans, and then teachers can decide whether or not a full alphabetic script is needed before proceeding to the drafting and recording phase.

Activity 9: Crafting Theme

Writing Activity 9 Materials

Because this is one of the later skills on our list, this activity is larger and would serve well as a summative or unit-closing assessment. Students working on this activity brainstorm, draft, script, and record an audio drama that explores and develops a clear theme.

The audio drama must fall between six and twelve minutes in length, feature at least two characters in a particular setting, and must clearly establish and develop a theme through the use of genre, literary devices, mood, and tone. Undoubtedly, students will use other tools at their disposal to construct their theme; however, the elements listed in the assignment statement are going to be central to the prewriting process in this assignment. Students must use **sound effects** in their composition, and then they should choose at least one other sound strategy (**music**, **silence**, **layering**) to work into the drama.

Given the assignment requirement to have at least two characters in the audio drama, this is an assignment that works best when completed collaboratively in groups. This not only allows for multiple speaking characters voiced by different students, but it also allows students to share the work of prewriting, gathering sounds, scripting, recording, and editing.

Common Core ELA Standard(s)	Description of Standard(s)
W.3	Write narratives to develop real or imagined experiences or events using effective technique, well-chosen details, and well-structured event sequences. *Note: This activity works on all parts of W.3*

Objectives: SWBAT create a specific and clear theme in their audio drama, which they develop through their use of literary devices, tone, mood, and sound strategies.

Working through the prewriting materials for this activity will guide students through the following steps: brainstorming a theme, considering the basic elements of their drama's narrative (title, characters, plot, setting, mood, tone, etc.), making connections between theme and the basic story elements, and deciding how and where the theme of the drama should appear and develop.

Once students have done the prewriting work of assembling their ideas on theme, story elements, and how the story elements will develop their chosen theme, we recommend using our storyboarding tool from **"Crafting Theme Prewrite—Step 4 Handout"** to help with the drafting process. Our storyboarding tool guides students on how to organize their audio dramas by scene, so teachers may choose to require a certain number of scenes and/or review with students what exactly constitutes a scene. Some students' audio drama ideas may technically involve a single prolonged scene; in this case, we'd recommend that student authors consider how to break that single scene into a certain number of subsections in order to plan the details of their story and its exploration of the chosen theme. Below, we've included what we would consider a successful use of **"Crafting Theme Prewrite—Step 4 Handout"** to plan the first few scenes of an audio drama developing the theme of the costs of ambition.

Crafting Theme Prewrite—Step 4—Student Sample Responses

Now that you have considered the above aspects of your audio drama, create either a draft of a script or a storyboard (see the template below). Be sure to include not only dialogue but also all sounds. Also, for each scene, consider where your chosen theme will appear.

Chosen Theme: The Cost of Ambition

Audio Drama Title: The Cost of Living

You can modify this template to include as many or as few scenes as needed.

Storyboard Template for Audio Drama

Scene 1: Introduction to Characters, Early Marriage

- Setting: A bright sunny kitchen. We'll set the scene by having the sounds of dishes clanking, a faucet running, birds singing. This is in the house of the two main characters. The dialogue will make it clear that this scene takes place in their first year of marriage.
- Characters present: The two main characters, a married couple, Julie and Karen, are making breakfast together. Their beloved dog Barley is scuffling in the background.
- Summary of any dialogue, action, or events: Julie and Karen are chatting happily as they make breakfast. Their flow of conversation is intermittently interrupted by one asking the other to hand them something or to look out for something. The main conversation will include reflecting on how amazing their first year of marriage has been and mentioning a fun camping trip they took together over the weekend. Barley loved it.

  Karen will mention her upcoming interview at a new law firm where she might be a temp. Julie will reassure Karen that the firm would be lucky to have her and stupid not to take her. The scene will end with them kissing goodbye, and Julie wishing Karen good luck at her interview.
- List of sound effects, music, or silences to plan for: We will need lots of breakfast-making sound effects: water boiling, bacon sizzling, dishes clanking, etc. We also want a dog barking or sniffing in the background that Julie responds to. (They have a dog, Barley, that they love and dote on.) There will be very little silence in this scene; instead, there will be lots of joyful, fun, chaotic, loving sounds.
- Estimated length of scene in minutes and/or sections: We think this scene can take place in around two minutes.
- Where will your theme appear in this scene? This scene will take place before Karen's ambition to climb ranks in the law firm, so the theme will appear in the love and interaction between Karen and Julie that exists before Karen's ambition costs them. We will see them living simply, with little tangible ambition, and they will be very happy. The title "The Cost of Living" will foreshadow that this happiness may be at risk.

Scene 2: Jump Ahead to Five Years Later

- Setting: A different kitchen several years later in a different house.
- Characters present: Karen and Julie are both in the kitchen, and there is a housekeeper, Max. We don't hear Barley anymore.
- Summary of any dialogue, action, or events: Julie is sitting at the table quietly reading a book. She thanks Max for breakfast, and Max says "You're very welcome, Ms. Roller." We hear Karen enter in a rush, speaking quickly and angrily on a phone call. She shouts something and hangs up, and then says, "Hey, Julie. Sorry I missed dinner last night, and I'm sorry, but I'm going to have to hop in the car now. Don't have time for breakfast. Maybe dinner tonight?" Karen will then say angrily, "Max! I told you the coffee had to be ready for me on my way out the door!"

  Julie sighs deeply as Max apologizes. There is a long silence. Karen breaks it by saying, "What? What now? I can tell you're pissed." Julie will pause before saying softly, "I'm fine." And Karen will launch into a tirade about how hard she works to make this nice life and how much pressure she is under and how Julie can live this way because of everything Karen does for her, etc. When she finally stops, we will hear her breathing heavily, and we will hear Julie start to sniffle and cry quietly. There will be a pause of silence where we just hear those two sounds.

  Julie will quietly say, "I just want things to be the way they were." Karen will angrily ask if Julie means when they couldn't pay their student loans, when they couldn't ever travel or take vacations, when they couldn't even afford a trip to the dentist? And Julie will again pause and quietly respond, "At least we had each other then. But it seems like you have everything you want now." And we will hear her footsteps leave the room.

  Karen will yell something at Max and exit the kitchen, slamming the door.
- List of sound effects, music, or silences to plan for: This scene is going to make more use of silence to emphasize the emptiness of their new lives. There will be longer pauses and a lack of laughter. We will use sound effects to make it clear that Max is working in the background when Karen enters and leaves the room and when Julie leaves the room. There will be door slams and sighs.
- Estimated length of scene in minutes and/or sections: We think this scene will be around two or three minutes.
- Where will your theme appear in this scene? The contrast between this scene and the prior scene will emphasize the theme. Clearly, Karen's ambition has caused her to be successful, but it has cost her several things. Julie is unhappy. The way that Karen and Julie speak to one another will emphasize this. The absence of the dog Barley will stand as a kind of symbol for the soft, caretaking love that no longer exists. Now they have Max, who Karen treats poorly. We hope this contrast in scenes creates a mood of sadness and grief at the lost safety and connection in Julie and Karen's marriage.

The depth and complexity with which students complete their storyboards may vary. If students have several, brief scenes in their audio drama, they may have minimal write-ups for each block in their storyboarding tool.

Depending on how thorough students' dialogue planning is on the storyboard, teachers may decide to require scripted dialogue. As we mentioned earlier, if teachers are going to require an alphabetic script before students record an audio text, the audio drama is the perfect assignment for which to do so. Given an audio drama's proximity to and roots in theater and stage productions, there are a lot of valuable elements for students to consider when scripting dialogue, **sound effects**, and stage directions.

Activity 10: Employing Rhetorical Appeals

Writing Activity 10 Materials

As the final activity on our list, this activity is a fairly complex one, making it a good fit for a cumulative assessment or a unit-closing task. The central task in this activity asks students to compose a text in a genre that we expect them to find unfamiliar: an audio tribute.

The activity asks them to choose an individual in their lives who has impacted them powerfully and compose an audio profile that captures and honors that individual's identity and the ways in which that individual has impacted them. The final sound text should be between four and eight minutes in length, and it should weave together a variety of sounds and types of content, including interviews, **sound effects**, **music**, biographical information, and various other elements to honor and represent the chosen individual. As they do this, students will be constructing an argument about how this person has been important in their lives; this activity specifically asks students to consider which rhetorical appeals—ethos, pathos, and/or logos—will best serve their goals.

Because an audio tribute is not a firmly established genre, student authors will have a lot of flexibility in the compositional choices they make. They can experiment and play with a variety of sounds, styles, strategies, and approaches to the assignment. This lack of genre guidance may initially feel daunting to students; however, it will also prompt them to return to their understanding of the rhetorical situation as a way to guide their choices. Without knowing exactly what an audio tribute usually looks like, it can be difficult to know how and where to start; that sensation is an extremely valuable experience for a developing writer. We teach all our developing writers that, when in doubt, they should return to the rhetorical situation. Who are they as authors? Who are they addressing this composition to? What are their goals? What writerly choices will fit that rhetorical situation? Our hope is that this activity is a fun, personalized way to explore the process of using rhetorical appeals to respond to an unfamiliar task and situation.

Common Core ELA Standard(s)	Description of Standard(s)
W.1	Write arguments to support claims in an analysis of substantive topics or texts, using valid reasoning and relevant and sufficient evidence. *Note: Within W.1, this activity specifically works on W.1.B and W.1.C*
Objectives: SWBAT write an argument that is supported with reasoning that clearly and carefully considers the best ways to persuade their audience. SWBAT make use of sound strategies to promote and construct their argument and accomplish their goals in the text.	

There is a lot of prewriting and planning required to compose a text in response to this prompt, and so we have designed a range of prewriting materials for teachers and students to choose from. Students will brainstorm ideas for choosing which individual to honor in their texts, sounds that reflect and capture their chosen individual's identity and roles, and elements of their unique rhetorical situations as student authors.

Below are some sample questions from **"Employing Rhetorical Appeals Prewrite—Step 4 Handout,"** which ask students to consider the way their foundational skills can help them in this activity. Questions in this prewriting step prompt students to consider genre norms, organization and structure, literary devices, tone, mood, and theme. Teachers may choose to emphasize or omit some of these questions based on which of the skills from our skill lists students have been focusing on. In the selected questions from **"Employing Rhetorical Appeals Prewrite—Step 4 Handout"** below, we've offered sample student answers to demonstrate how a student might use their foundational skills to support their work in this activity.

Employing Rhetorical Appeals—Step 4—Student Sample Responses

Chosen Individual: My tete (grandmother in Arabic)

Consider the following questions before proceeding with your drafting:

1. How will you organize your audio tribute? Will you explain your subject's life chronologically? Will you feature different areas of their life, like work, home, and a religious center? Will you list the most significant things they've done? Will you structure it around a series of interviews with people about your subject? Explain your idea for how to set this tribute up to best meet the needs of your rhetorical situation.

My idea is to divide the tribute into the groups of people that my tete has impacted in her life. She does so much for the different people in her life, and she's taught me everything about making the lives of others better, so I think I'll have sections: one for her family, one for her former students, and one for the people she works with at our mosque.

2. What literary devices will you use to capture and represent the subject of your tribute?

I'd like to use the sound of laughter as a symbol for my tete's influence in life. She brings laughter wherever she goes. I can use her laughter, but I'd like to include the laughter of other people as well to capture how she shares her laughter with others and makes sure everyone is laughing together. I also think we will be using the device of repetition to emphasize how much joy and love she's brought to the people in her life. I expect we will have repeated concepts and ideas shared as I interview different people about her influence on them.

3. What mood will your tribute generate and how? How would you like your audience to feel in response to your tribute? What sounds and choices can you use to evoke that response throughout?

I'm aiming to create a mood of joyful respect and honor. I want my audience to feel inspired but also joyful. My tete's goal is to bring joy to people, and I think she would be honored if I used her story to bring even more joy to the people who listened to this tribute. I think including lots of recorded laughter will generate that mood. I also want to include my tete's favorite song in the transitions between scenes—the song is "Sallimleh Alay" by Fairuz. It's a love song, which makes sense for my tete. I think the song is beautiful and will also help people understand her goals to promote joy and love for everyone.

4. Is there a particular theme that will guide your tribute or develop over the course of your audio tribute? How will that theme appear?

I want to create a theme of the legacy of love, exploring the ways that people can leave a trail of love and care behind them that has a life of its own. My tete's legacy is all about how bringing others joy and making others feel loved and special is its own presence in the world. She's loved me in that way, but she's also taught me the importance of love. I think that theme will appear in what people say, how people say it, the repetition of her acts of service, the repetition in the accounts of how she loves and helps people, and the sounds of laughter from her and others.

Based on the questions from **"Employing Rhetorical Appeals Prewrite—Step 4 Handout,"** we don't expect all students will use all foundational skills equally. It is more likely that a student will capitalize on one or two of them in order to promote their goals for their audio tribute, but it is still important for students to consider as many foundational skills as possible as they plan.

"Employing Rhetorical Appeals Prewrite—Step 5 Handout" is where we begin asking students to intentionally consider their use of rhetorical appeals. At this point, students will have considered their rhetorical situation, goals, and a variety of other factors, so they should feel ready to organize those into thoughts on which rhetorical appeals best fit their goals and where and how those appeals should appear. Below, we have included the table from **"Employing Rhetorical Appeals Prewrite—Step 5 Handout"** with some sample student responses to what this brainstorming may look like.

Employing Rhetorical Appeals—Step 5—Student Sample Responses

Appeal	Will you make use of this appeal? Why or why not?	If you plan to use this appeal, what sound strategies do you think would be most useful in employing this appeal (music, voice, sound effects, silence, layering)?	If you plan to use this appeal, where do you expect it to appear in the tribute and why? You can say the beginning, middle, or end, or you can give me a sense of where it would fall relative to other content.
Pathos	Yes because my tete's legacy has a lot to do with making people feel things. I want my listeners to feel some of the joy that she brings so they can understand how amazing she is.	I think the sound effect of recorded laughter is going to be the biggest tool. I don't expect a lot of silence in this tribute because there is very little silence around my tete. There are always jokes and laughter and fun. I do expect layering to occur regularly so people understand her as a kind of bundle of energy and joy that sort of overflows in all situations.	I expect pathos to be the most common and consistent rhetorical appeal in my tribute. Each of the sections I have planned will rely on this appeal in different ways, and the overall argument and mood I am crafting are both pathos-based, working to have the audience feel respect, joy, and love for and with my tete. I definitely want to open and close with a very strong pathos appeal.

Ethos	I think there may be implicit or secondary ethos appeals, but I won't be emphasizing this in my tribute. My tete is someone who has overcome a lot of suffering in her life. She had to flee violence in Syria, where she grew up, and she has lost a lot, and this gives her a lot of credibility, but she never brings that up or shares that with people. I'm not sure she would even want her credibility to be a large part of a tribute honoring her.	I mostly expect any information along these lines to appear in peoples' voices in interviews and maybe in the music I choose.	If anything, as people tell stories about her, the listeners will learn bits and pieces about her story and the things she has overcome. I think the Fairuz love song I chose will emphasize her ethos as a loving, joyful person, and that will appear throughout the tribute.
Logos	I think this appeal will appear just the by sheer fact of all the practical good and kind things she has done for people. I'll very practically be giving lots of examples of the ways in which she has helped and loved people with her actions and words.	My examples here will mostly be stories that I or others tell about things she has done, so I expect voices to share most of this.	I don't think this will be as relevant in the beginning and end, but I think some logos will appear in each of the sections I've created for my tribute.

It's very likely, even probable, that students will not use all three kinds of rhetorical appeals. While our activity requires students to use at least two different kinds of appeals, teachers should feel free to change that requirement based on their students and goals. The table from **"Employing Rhetorical Appeals Prewrite—Step 5 Handout"** prompts students to consider what appeals they may use and reflect on why they may not use one. This reflective act of discussing why a particular rhetorical appeal isn't a good fit for a student's audio tribute can prompt them to articulate and understand quite a bit of valuable information about their goals, their process, and their style as writers; it also demonstrates respect for their authority and choices as writers, encouraging them to take ownership of those compositional elements. It's for this reason that we highly encourage using the reflection questions for this activity—the metacognitive act of explaining their choices is incredibly valuable for students in demonstrating their understanding of the rhetorical appeals and their function in their work.

From this point, students can outline and script out their audio tributes in the ways that you and they feel are most helpful. We find the timeline templates to be the most useful for this activity, as this sound text will most likely involve all five sound strategies along with a degree of **layering**. Once students have completed this, they are ready to record and move forward with their audio tributes!

Conclusion

Chapter 6 Conclusion Audio

Chapter 6 Conclusion Transcript

Conclusion

Conclusion Audio

Conclusion Transcript

WORKS CITED

Anderson, Erin. "Toward a Resonant Material Vocality for Digital Composition." *Enculturation: A Journal of Rhetoric, Writing, and Culture*, vol. 18, 18 Aug. 2014, http://enculturation.net/materialvocality. Accessed 9 July 2020.

Artz, Kate, et al. "Teaching Composition Using Transcripts." National Council of Teachers of English, 16 Oct. 2017, https://ncte.org/blog/2017/10/teaching-composition-using-transcripts/. Accessed 29 May 2024.

Baker-Bell, April. *Linguistic Justice: Black Language, Literacy, Identity, and Pedagogy*. Routledge and NCTE, 2020.

Bamo, Qubumo, et al. "Documenting Living Oral Traditions: China's Institute of Ethnic Literature as Case Study." *The Journal of American Folklore*, vol. 129, no. 513, 2016, pp. 270–87.

Beaufort, Anne. *College Writing and Beyond: A New Framework for University Writing Instruction*. UP of Colorado, 2007.

Bogaerds-Hazenberg, Suzanne T.M., et al. "A Meta-Analysis on the Effects of Text Structure Instruction on Reading Comprehension in the Upper Elementary Grades." *Reading Research Quarterly*, vol. 56, no. 3, 2021, pp. 435–62.

Bunn, Mike. "How to Read Like a Writer." *Writing Spaces: Readings on Writing*, edited by Charles Lowe and Pavel Zemliansky, vol. 2, Parlor Press, 2011, pp. 71–86.

Coles, Justin A., et al. "Wading through Coloniality: Critical Processes for Re/Thinking Body, Place, Space, Speech, and Tongue." *Equity & Excellence in Education*, vol. 55, no. 3, 2022, pp. 165–68.

Danforth, Courtney S., et al., editors. *Soundwriting Pedagogies*. Computers and Composition Digital Press; Utah State UP, 2018, http://ccdigitalpress.org/soundwriting. Accessed 16 Aug. 2019.

Definition of Literacy in a Digital Age. National Council of Teachers of English, 7 Nov. 2019, https://ncte.org/statement/nctes-definition-literacy-digital-age/. Accessed 10 Oct. 2023.

de los Ríos, Cati V., et al. "Upending Colonial Practices: Toward Repairing Harm in English Education." *Theory Into Practice*, vol. 58, no. 4, 2019, pp. 359–67.

Deniz, Fatma, et al. "The Representation of Semantic Information across Human Cerebral Cortex during Listening versus Reading Is Invariant to Stimulus Modality." *Journal of Neuroscience*, vol. 39, no. 39, 2019, pp. 7722–36.

Devitt, Amy J. "Generalizing about Genre: New Conceptions of an Old Concept." *College Composition & Communication*, vol. 44, no. 4, 1993, pp. 573–86.

Dirk, Kerry. "Navigating Genres." *Writing Spaces: Readings on Writing*, edited by Charles Lowe and Pavel Zemliansky, vol. 1, Parlor Press, 2010, pp 249–62.

Dobbs, Christina L., and Christine M. Leider. "A Framework for Writing Rubrics to Support Linguistically Diverse Students." *English Journal*, vol. 110, no. 6, 2021, pp. 60–68.

Echevarría, Jana, and Anne Graves. *Sheltered Content Instruction: Teaching English Learnings with Diverse Abilities*. 5th ed., Pearson, 2015.

Echevarría, Jana, et al. *Making Content Comprehensible for English Learners: The SIOP Model*. 4th ed., Pearson, 2013.

Emanuel, Gabrielle. "Unlocking Dyslexia: Millions Have Dyslexia, Few Understand It." *National Public Radio*, 28 Nov. 2016, www.npr.org/sections/ed/2016/11/28/502601662/millions-have-dyslexia-few-understand-it. Accessed 2 Nov. 2019.

España, Carla, and Luz Yadira Herrera. *En Comunidad: Lessons for Centering the Voices and Experiences of Bilingual Latinx Students*. Heinemann, 2020.

Fluckiger, Jarene. "Single-Point Rubric: A Tool for Responsible Student Self-Assessment." *The Delta Kappa Gamma Bulletin*, vol. 76, no. 4, 2010, pp. 18–25.

Forman-Katz, Naomi. "For National Radio Day, Key Facts about Radio Listeners and the Radio Industry in the U.S." *Pew Research Center*, 17 Aug. 2023, www.pewresearch.org/short-reads/2023/08/17/for-national-radio-day-key-facts-about-radio-listeners-and-the-radio-industry-in-the-us/#:~:text=In%202022%2C%2082%25%20of%20Americans,of%20the%20U.S.%20coronavirus%20outbreak. Accessed 18 Oct. 2023.

Framework for Success in Postsecondary Writing. Council of Writing Program Administrators; National Council of Teachers of English; National Writing Project, 2011, http://wpacouncil.org/aws/CWPA/asset_manager/get_file/350201?ver=7548. Accessed 10 Jan. 2021.

Greenfield, Laura. "The 'Standard English' Fairy Tale: A Rhetorical Analysis of Racist Pedagogies and Commonplace Assumptions about Language Diversity." *Writing Centers and the New Racism: A Call for Sustainable Dialogue and Change*, edited by Laura Greenfield and Karen Rowan, Utah State UP, 2011, pp. 33–60.

Grosjean, François. "What Is Translanguaging? (Interview with Ofelia García)." *Life as a Bilingual*, Cambridge UP, 2021, pp. 171–74.

Herrera, Luz Yadira, and Carla España. "Se Hace Camino al Andar: Translanguaging Pedagogy for Justice." *English Journal*, vol. 111, no. 5, 2022, pp. 27–34.

Hess, Mickey. "Metal Faces, Rap Masks: Identity and Resistance in Hip Hop's Persona Artist." *Popular Music and Society*, vol. 28, no. 3, 2005, pp. 297–311.

Illich, Lindsay, and Melissa Alter Smith. *Teach Living Poets*. National Council of Teachers of English, 2021.

Jao, Cheng-Yueh, et al. "Exploring the Effects of Robot-Assisted Multimodal Composition on Students' Audience Awareness for English Writing." *Computer Assisted Language Learning*, 2024. Taylor & Francis Online, https://doi.org/10.1080/09588221.2023.2300972.

Landrieu, Yana, et al. "Argumentation in Collaboration: The Impact of Explicit Instruction and Collaborative Writing on Secondary School Students' Argumentative Writing." *Reading and Writing*, vol. 37, no. 6, 2024, pp. 1407–34.

Lee, Eunjeong. "Writing toward a Decolonial Option: A Bilingual Student's Multimodal Composing as a Site of Translingual Activism and Justice." *Written Communication*, vol. 40, no. 1, 2023, pp. 59–89.

Lunsford, Andrea, and John J. Ruszkiewicz. *Everything's an Argument*. 8th ed., Bedford/St. Martin's, 2019.

Lunsford, Andrea, et al. *Everything's an Argument with Readings*. 7th ed., Bedford/St. Martin's, 2016.

Lyiscott, Jamila. "3 Ways To Speak English." *TED*, Feb. 2014, www.ted.com/talks/jamila_lyiscott_3_ways_to_speak_english?language=en#t-127735. Accessed 20 June 2020.

Maringe, Felix, and Nevensha Sing. "Teaching Large Classes in an Increasingly Internationalising Higher Education Environment: Pedagogical, Quality and Equity Issues." *Higher Education*, vol. 67, no. 6, 2014, pp. 761–82.

Marzano, Robert J. *Classroom Assessment & Grading That Work*. ASCD, 2006.

McKee, Heidi. "Sound Matters: Notes toward the Analysis and Design of Sound in Multimodal Webtexts." *Computers and Composition*, vol. 23, no. 3, 2006, pp. 335–54.

Mirra, Nicole. *Educating for Empathy: Literacy Learning and Civic Engagement*. Teachers College Press, 2018.

Multimodal Literacies. National Council of Teachers of English, 17 Nov. 2005, https://www2.ncte.org/statement/multimodalliteracies/. Accessed 9 July 2019.

Murray, Donald M. *Read to Write: A Writing Process Reader*. Holt, Rinehart & Winston, 1986.

National Writing Project, et al. *Because Digital Writing Matters: Improving Student Writing in Online and Multimedia Environments*. Jossey-Bass, 2010.

Öhman, Emily, and Riikka Rossi. "Affect as a Proxy for Literary Mood." *Journal of Data Mining & Digital Humanities*, vol. NLP4DH, 2023, https://doi.org/10.46298/jdmdh.11164.

Player, Grace D. "'People Get Mistaken': Asian American Girls Using Multiple Literacies to Defy Dominant Imaginings of Asian American Girlhood." *Reading Research Quarterly*, vol. 57, no. 2, 2021. pp. 431–48.

Position Statement on Writing Instruction in School. National Council of Teachers of English, 29 Aug. 2022, https://ncte.org/statement/statement-on-writing-instruction-in-school/. Accessed 10 Oct. 2023.

"Reading." *Merriam-Webster.com*, Merriam-Webster, 2020, www.merriam-webster.com/dictionary/reading. Accessed 18 Nov. 2020.

Rodrigue, Tanya K., and Kyle Stedman. *Soundwriting: A Guide to Making Audio Projects*. Broadview Press, 2023.

Rodrigue, Tanya K., et al. "Navigating the Soundscape, Composing with Audio." *Kairos: A Journal of Rhetoric, Technology, and Pedagogy*, vol. 21, no. 1, 2016, http://kairos.technorhetoric.net/21.1/praxis/rodrigue/index.html. Accessed 13 Aug. 2019.

Sale, Maggie. "Call and Response as Critical Method: African-American Oral Traditions and *Beloved*." *African American Review*, vol. 26, no. 1, 1992. pp. 41–50.

Selfe, Cynthia L., editor. *Multimodal Composition: Resources for Teachers*. Hampton Press, 2007.

———. "The Movement of Air, the Breath of Meaning: Aurality and Multimodal Composing." *College Composition & Communication*, vol. 60, no. 4, 2009, pp. 616–63.

Strunk, William, Jr., and E. B. White. *The Elements of Style*. 4th ed., Allyn & Bacon, 2000.

Sukirno, Sukirmo, and Bayu Suta Wardianto. "The Religious Oral Tradition of 'Maca Syekh' and the Concept of Preserving Oral Literature in Schools." *IBDA': Jurnal Kajian Islam dan Budaya*, vol. 20, no. 2, 2022, pp. 289–307.

Sweeney, Meghan A. "Audience Awareness as a Threshold Concept of Reading: An Examination of Student Learning in Biochemistry." *Research in the Teaching of English*, vol. 53, no. 1, 2018, pp. 58–79.

Trehub, Sandra E., et al. "Cross-Cultural Perspectives on Music and Musicality." *Philosophical Transactions: Biological Sciences*, vol. 370, no. 1664, 2015, pp. 1-9.

Vété-Congolo, Hanétha, editor. *The Caribbean Oral Tradition: Literature, Performance, and Practice*. Palgrave Macmillan, 2016.

Wargo, Jon. "Rhythmic Rituals and Emergent Listening: Intra-Activity, Sonic Sounds and Digital Composing with Young Children." *Journal of Early Childhood Literacy*, vol. 17, no. 3, 2017, pp. 392–408.

———. "#SoundingOutMySilence: Reading a LGBTQ Youth's Sonic Cartography as Multimodal (Counter)Storytelling." *Journal of Adolescent & Adult Literacy*, vol. 62, no. 1, 2018, pp. 13–23.

"What is Podcasting?" *Pew Research Center*, 19 July 2006, www.pewresearch.org/journalism/2006/07/19/what-is-podcasting/.

Wilkinson, Bethaney. "Building Equity from the Ground Up with Dr. Darnisa Amante-Jackson." *The Diversity Gap Podcast*, The Diversity Gap, 10 June 2020, www.thediversitygap.com/podcast/building-equity-from-the-ground-up-with-dr-darnisa-amante-jackson. Accessed 10 Oct. 2023.

Wright, Zach. "A Handy Strategy for Teaching Theme." *Edutopia*, 25 Feb. 2020, www.edutopia.org/article/handy-strategy-teaching-theme/. Accessed 29 May 2024.

Yancey, Kathleen Blake. "Learning to Write Effectively Requires Different Kinds of Practice, Time, and Effort." *Naming What We Know, Classroom Edition: Threshold Concepts of Writing Studies*, edited by Linda Adler-Kassner and Elizabeth Wardle, UP of Colorado, 2016, pp. 64–65.

Young, Vershawn Ashanti. "Should Writers Use They Own English?" *Iowa Journal of Childhood Studies*, vol. 12, no. 1, 2010, pp. 110–17.

Zhang, Qiang. "The Impact of Collaborative Writing on English Continuation Tasks of Senior High School Students." *International Journal of TESOL Studies*, vol. 2, no. 4, 2020, pp. 64–79.

SOUND ASSETS

Blackbox. "[Intro Music] BLACK BOX — Simple Guitar + Drum Fill." *Pixabay*, 28 Dec. 2021, https://pixabay.com/sound-effects/intro-music-black-box-simple-guitar-drum-fill-13021/. Accessed 16 Oct. 2023.

dobroide. "20061223.why.wav." *Freesound*, 23 Dec. 2006, https://freesound.org/people/dobroide/sounds/27559/. Accessed 16 Oct. 2023.

locrpg. "deep breath sigh." *Pixabay*, 27 Mar. 2022, https://pixabay.com/sound-effects/deep-breath-sigh-104109/. Accessed 23 Sep. 2023.

Modestas123123. "Cash Register (Kaching) — Sound Effect." *Pixabay*, 4 Nov. 2022, https://pixabay.com/sound-effects/cash-register-kaching-sound-effect-125042/. Accessed 23 Sep. 2023.

Pixabay. "AE0092 Volvo 740 GLE handbrake turn 03." *Pixabay*, 4 Aug. 2021, https://pixabay.com/sound-effects/ae0092-volvo-740-gle-handbrake-turn-03-6362/. Accessed 23 Sep. 2023.

———. "awww why?" *Pixabay*, 29 Aug. 2022, https://pixabay.com/sound-effects/awww-why-97694/. Accessed 23 Sep. 2023.

———. "Bass loop 009 dry 120 bpm lipstick both pickups pick." *Pixabay*, 24 Aug. 2022, https://pixabay.com/sound-effects/bass-loop-009-dry-120-bpm-lipstick-both-pickups-pick-94832/. Accessed 15 Sep. 2023.

———. "cheering and clapping crowd 1." *Pixabay*, 4 Aug. 2021, https://pixabay.com/sound-effects/cheering-and-clapping-crowd-1-5995/. Accessed 23 Sep. 2023.

———. "Driving by Noisy Car." *Pixabay*, 31 May 2022, https://pixabay.com/sound-effects/driving-by-noisy-car-33855/. Accessed 23 Sep. 2023.

———. "Epic Logo." *Pixabay*, 9 Aug. 2021, https://pixabay.com/sound-effects/epic-logo-6906/. Accessed 23 Sep. 2023.

———. "How could you." *Pixabay*, 6 Sep. 2022, https://pixabay.com/sound-effects/how-could-you-106121/. Accessed 23 Sep. 2023.

———. "Man grunt, struggling 2." *Pixabay*, 19 July 2022, https://pixabay.com/sound-effects/man-grunt-struggling-2-68927/. Accessed 23 Sep. 2023.

———. "Room Full of Talking People." *Pixabay*, 24 May 2022, https://pixabay.com/sound-effects/room-full-of-talking-people-30342/. Accessed 23 Sep. 2023.

———. "Success Fanfare Trumpets." *Pixabay*, 4 Aug. 2021, https://pixabay.com/sound-effects/success-fanfare-trumpets-6185/. Accessed 16 Oct. 2023.

———. "Thriller Score Horror Scene." *Pixabay*, 9 Aug. 2021, https://pixabay.com/sound-effects/thriller-score-horror-scene-6730/. Accessed 23 Sep. 2023.

———. "yes." *Pixabay*, 28 Aug. 2022, https://pixabay.com/sound-effects/yes-96786/. Accessed 23 Sep. 2023.

INDEX

Note: Page numbers followed by letters denote specific content:
"b" = box
"c" = Common Core State Curriculum Standards
"f" = figure
"q" = QR code links to activity worksheets, process documents, and rubrics
"t" = table

AUTHORS

Danah Hashem is a former chemical engineer turned reading and writing teacher-scholar currently teaching composition courses at the University of Massachusetts Boston to both undergrad and Early College students from various high school settings. Hashem also works as the assistant director with the UMass Boston Writing Center. Prior to working at UMass, she taught at the high school level for the better part of a decade, and she has a particular interest in bridging the gap for student readers and writers transitioning out of high school and into successful college experiences. Her areas of scholarship include audio rhetoric, writing pedagogy, and digital and multimodal composition, and she is passionate about flexible, student-centered learning that encourages intellectual play and exploration.

Anne Mooney is a high school English teacher at Malden High School in Malden, Massachusetts. In her nearly a decade of teaching, she has taught students in grades 9 through 12. Teaching at the most diverse urban public school in Massachusetts, Mooney has worked with multilingual students, students of various socioeconomic backgrounds, and students with a multitude of disabilities; her teaching and pedagogical practices have been both informed and improved through her experiences with each and every one of them. Her areas of scholarship include audio rhetoric, multimodal composition, and trauma theory, which have worked to establish her trauma-informed and student-centered classroom.

This book was typeset in Myriad Pro and Palatino by Barbara Frazier.

The typefaces used on the cover include Cera Pro, Kapra, and Neue Pro.

The book was printed on 50 lb., white offset paper.